D1171556

DATE			

Labor's Capital

Labor's Capital

The Economics and Politics of Private Pensions

Teresa Ghilarducci

The MIT Press
Cambridge, Massachusetts
London, England

This book was set in Palatino by APS, Salisbury, England, and printed and bound in the United States of America.

Library of Congress Cataloging-in-Publication Data

Ghilarducci, Teresa.
  Labor's capital : the economics and politics of private pensions /
Teresa Ghilarducci.
      p.   cm.
  Includes bibliographical references and index.
  ISBN 0-262-07139-8
  1. Old age pensions—United States. 2. Pensions—United States.
I. Title.
HD7105.35.U6G45   1992
331.25′2′0973—dc20   91-38544
                                                                                              CIP

For William

Contents

Preface

The 120-year-old private pension system involves five distinct groups, or actors, and shapes American society in five different ways: 1) employer pensions are useful collective bargaining points for both unions and management; 2) workplace pension coverage relieves the federal government of pressure to expand the Social Security system; 3) employers use pensions as personnel devices that alter quit and hiring decisions; 4) firms incorporate pension funds in their corporate finance decisions; and 5) employer-provided pensions constitute the largest single source of funds for America's financial sector.

No research on pensions, nor pension policy reform, has focused simultaneously on all five aspects of the system. This lack of research and policy synchronicity divides constituencies and dilutes responsibility for the system's performance. Since the early 1980s, Senator Howard Metzenbaum (D, Ohio) has introduced legislation to prevent firms from terminating pension funds and using pension fund assets for corporate purposes. Corporate lobbyists successfully fought off passage by claiming that such legislation would chill and shrink pension plan formation, which implicitly would harm workers. In this particular case, advocates for pension finance reform were stymied by the argument that, above all, private pensions are essential retirement income security. Unions bargain for pensions, even though most union members would be better served by an expanded Social Security program. Firms, too, are conflicted in their use of pensions. Firms eager to use excess pension funds for cash in the short term may lose the loyalty of valuable workers in the long term.

Naïveté and defensiveness during the last forty years have characterized both public and union policy toward pensions. Similarly, employers offer pensions for personnel management reasons, but then find themselves caught in a complex system in which financial institutions, government agencies, and unions have particular interests. Complaints over unmet retirement income needs were partly responsible for the rapid union, employer, and government development of private pensions after World War II. Abuses prompted the Internal Revenue Service to promulgate antidiscrimination rules and regulations in the 1950s, but the possibility that employers would misrepresent pension promises and abuse pension funds was overlooked.

Fund abuses prompted other rounds of defensive regulation: the Landrum Griffen Act of 1959 and the Employment Retirement Income Security Act of 1974. The Retirement Equity Act (REACT), passed in 1984 amid a growing realization that coverage in private plans was stagnating, required firms to cover workers immediately upon hiring. This provision, and the requirement that spouses must provide approval in writing before a participant can elect to forgo survivor pensions for a larger pension, caused REACT to be celebrated as a victory for women's rights. Unjustifiable pension plan terminations—so-called healthy terminations—provoked Congress to consider, but ultimately to defeat, termination legislation throughout the 1980s. Congress increased premiums to the federal pension insurance system, the Pension Benefit Guaranty Corporation, in 1988, fearing that bankruptcies in manufacturing and transportation industries would lead to a collapse of the insurance system.

Only by viewing the system as a product of evolution can one understand who benefits from the system and how legislation designed to cajole the system into helping the average worker is defensive at best and too weak at worst. Pensions emerged as personnel devices before the turn of the century; modern unions embraced them as rallying points for bargaining and organizing in the post–World War II period. Unions and management cultivated pensions in the evolving capital-labor accord in the 1950s and 1960s. Private pensions have staved off a major expansion of the Social Security System. In the late 1970s and 1980s, pensions mutated into a form of finance capital for firms. The private pension system's evolution explains its contradictory structure and how pensions became labor's capital.

Recent research on pensions from the Brookings Institution and the National Bureau of Economic Research has not adequately addressed whom the system benefits, what the system's direct and social costs are, and the possibilities of reform—leading to consideration of the related problems of capital formation and retirement income security. Merton Bernstein's *The Future of Private Pensions* (1964) and Paul Harbrecht's *Pension Funds and Economic Power* (1959) are now out of date.

I am grateful for the following people's time: Randy Barber, Director, Campaign for Economic Organizing; Daniel Beller, Research Analyst, Department of Labor; Merton Bernstein, Professor, Washington University; Greg Buchholtz, graduate student, University of Notre Dame; John Carroll, Executive Vice President, Communications Workers of America; Theodore Bernstein, Director, International Ladies Garment Workers of America Pension Trust; Roy Dickenson, Executive Vice President, International Brotherhood of Electrical Workers; Karen Ferguson, Director, Pension Rights Center; John Fleming, Executive Vice President, Bakery, Confectionary, and Tobacco Workers; Floyd Hyde, Chief Executive Officer, and Mike Arnold, Director, Building Investment Trust; John Joyce, President, International Union of Bricklayers and Allied Craftsman; Meredith Miller, Assistant Director, Department of Employee Benefits, AFL-CIO; Richard Prosten, Director, Industrial Union Department, AFL-CIO; Bert Seidman, Former Director of the Department of Social Security, AFL-CIO; Harvey C. Sigelbaum, President and Chief Executive, Amalgamated Life Insurance Company; Richard Trumka, President, United Mine Workers of America; Joseph Uehelein, Coordinator, Industrial Union Department, AFL-CIO; Howard Young, Actuary and Professor of Mathematics, University of Michigan; and Edward Zuckerman, author of *Small Fortunes*.

I am indebted to Lloyd Ulman and George Strauss at the University of California at Berkeley for their advice at the beginning stages of the project. Clair Brown, also at Berkeley, has been a consistent source of encouragement. James Medoff and Larry Katz, both at Harvard University, gave special attention to parts of this manuscript. I benefited from the comments at the labor economics seminars at Cornell University, the University of California at Berkeley and Riverside, the University of Massachusetts, Amherst, Harvard University, and the University of Notre Dame. Portions of chapters 4 and 6 were published in different form in the *Journal of Labor Research*, Spring 1990 and in *The Review of Radical Political Economics*, Winter 1988.

I am grateful for the support of the Mary Ingraham Bunting Institute at Radcliffe College, the Institute for Scholarship in the Liberal Arts and a Jesse H. Jones Research Grant at the University of Notre Dame.

Labor's Capital

1   Introduction: Actors, Paradigms, and Pensions

Pensions are an economic Rorschach test. The five principal actors in the private pension system—workers, unions, firms, finance markets, and government—perceive five different entities. Workers view pensions as deserved and deferred compensation desperately needed for retirement income security. Employers see pensions as personnel tools for encouraging retirement and loyalty. Unions celebrate their pension victories and the advantage union workers have over their relatively nonpensioned non-union counterparts. Those in financial markets consider pensions the nation's bright hope for accumulating finance capital, especially when savings rates languish. Government views employer pensions as a $50 billion tax expenditure that helps soften the clamor for a better Social Security system.

In addition to these five major actors, additional groups are involved with and concerned about pensions. Governors and mayors look at public sector pension plans and see a financial base for economic development in their communities. Women's advocacy groups decry the unequal coverage and small benefits for women. Progressive organizations hope pensions can help democratize financial markets. Chief executive officers fold pension funds into their corporate financial strategies. Pensions take many forms, helping widows and corporate raiders alike. No wonder public policy toward pensions is reactive, disjointed, and seemingly schizophrenic.

Pension funds own most of the value of U.S. corporate bonds and a major portion of corporate equity. Tax breaks afforded the private pension system take a large bite out of federal revenues: over $50 billion, or about one-third of the 1990 budget deficit, is lost each year because pension savings are tax deferred. But less than half of the nation's private sector labor force—and only 25 percent of women workers—are covered by employer pensions. Only 9 percent of income to the elderly comes from private pensions; six times that amount comes from Social Security.

Why are pension funds so large and benefits so small? Part of the reason is that pensions are funded on a group basis but distributed individually. They are a major component in the peculiar American system of a private-public mix of social insurance. The system affects the lives of most Americans, but not only in the most obvious way, through the benefits side. In the end, the system fails to provide adequate retirement income security, its most prominent goal, whereas its more obscure roles—as a bargaining issue, a personnel tool, finance capital, and private social insurance—exert enormous influence over the quality of life in old age.

So far, economists—the most significant group of intellectuals influencing pension policy—have generally interpreted employers goals in sponsoring pensions from a neoclassical economic paradigm. They see pensions as a convenient financial intermediary allowing individuals to make choices between consumption now and consumption later. Marxists have added their own interpretations of pensions as control devices, but they have had little say in pension policy. Institutionalists understand pensions as compromises. Each paradigm predicts a particular set of pension characteristics in specific time periods—for each perspective determines vision, and vision constructs policy—but each alone is insufficient for creating sound public policy.

Pensions as Efficient Contracts: The Neoclassical Perspective

Neoclassical theories place individuals at center stage. Workers naturally want security and welcome schemes that provide them with income protection, even if those schemes are designed to control their behavior. In the neoclassical view, workers are not tricked into working more loyally or harder for pensions; they agree to the swap. Neoclassical economists would not disagree with Marxists that employers seek to reduce labor costs; in fact, they would contend that pensions would not be adopted if they did not lower labor costs in some way. But neoclassicists would look to individual workers and their desires as the initiators of pension contracts. The explosion of pension growth coincident with growing tax breaks made pensions a preferential way for workers to save and lends support to the argument that worker preferences (abetted by tax incentives) have driven pension formation (Ippolito 1986b).

If, however, employers simply wanted to maintain productivity and profits, would it not be cheaper to fire the superannuated employee? Neoclassical economists offer several answers to this question. The first is reputation. Companies that fire aging workers would lose the favorable reputation required to attract good workers and retain the best. The reputation effect is more important in tight labor markets, so we would expect pension growth to increase during periods of low unemployment and fall when labor markets are soft. Figure 1.1 shows no discernible relationship between plan growth (measured in terms of the percentage of the work force covered each year) and the male unemployment rate. Events of the 1980s especially disprove the reputation effect. Pension coverage stagnated while unemployment remained high, fluctuating between 5.2 percent and over 9.5 percent.

In the neoclassical view, firms also provide pensions for technical reasons. Workers learn on the job: they gather skills specific to the firm and become more valuable over time. Because slavery is not legal, workers cannot sign ironclad contracts promising that if they are trained, they will remain on the job. Firms therefore provide pensions (and other forms of compensation) that increase with a worker's length of service. (This argument appears in the literature on specific skills and on-the-job training: (see Abraham and Farber 1987; Doeringer and Piore 1971; Oi 1965).

Finally, the "shirking effect" says that employers know that workers can alter their effort on the job and that employer detection of this shirking is quite costly. The possibility of losing one's pension as well as one's job increases the disincentive to shirk (Lazear 1980). This argument makes clear

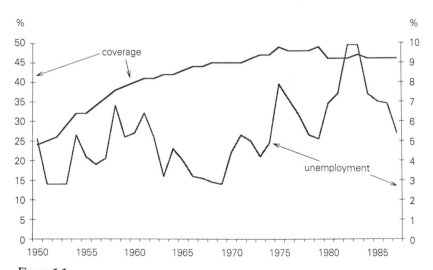

Figure 1.1
Relationship between unemployment and pension coverage

Sources: Council of Economic Advisors, *Economic Report of the President*, various years; and Turner and Beller 1989.

that the neoclassical and marxist paradigms cannot be surgically separated. The neoclassical shirking argument sounds much like the Marxist-radical control argument. When Marxists talk about shirking, they see the motivation as alienation, whereas for neoclassical economists it is malfeasance (for a quick glance into the extensive literature on worker shirking, see Alchian and Demsetz 1972 and Bowles 1985).

Pensions as Worker Control Devices: The Marxist Perspective

The Marxist interpretation emphasizes the fact that pensions emerged at the same time that manufacturers (especially) were developing scientific management techniques to increase productivity and wrest control of the labor process from skilled workers. In the radical analysis, employers objectives in industrial relations are to lower labor costs and maintain control over production. Employers can lower labor costs by increasing the intensity of work, by lowering real wages and dividing workers to inhibit collective action (Edwards et al. 1982), or by maintaining a reserve of nonworkers who can and will work (Edwards 1979). In the radical model, pensions would have to buttress at least one of these motives.

Pensions can intensify work by fostering paternalism, one element of which is the belief that employers owe employees more than a day's wage, while employees owe employers more than the minimum effort required to keep from getting fired. This is especially true when pensions are voluntary and regarded as gifts—the beneficence of a caring firm.

Pensions can divide the work force by pitting older workers against younger workers or against workers without the tenure required to become eligible for a pension. These shorter-term workers may resent their contributions to another group. Pensions may also provide a pool of retirees who, because they are not receiving full earnings, would be available for part-time, low-paying, or strikebreaking work.

Olson (1982) argues that the mixed public-private retirement income security system helps sustain class divisions. Social Security redistributes money within the working class, whereas private pensions are for the elite. The existence of private pensions, as Stevens (1988), and Orloff (1988) point out, blunts support for expanding Social Security. The mixed public-private system creates a habitual way of separating the two classes—even though the private pension system is not truly private but is created and maintained by collective and government action.

The Marxist literature on corporate finance and control is also relevant. The Marxist paradigm looks at pensions from aspects of the labor relations and capital accumulation. Pensions are seen as a means to dilute corporate equity ownership, further separating ownership from control. In the "managerialist" debates, the development of pensions is used to argue that managers have become more powerful, checking the influence of capitalists and making capitalism less effective in accumulating capital and maintaining sufficient levels of investment (Pitelis 1987).

Although each paradigm can explain some part of the system, each is self-contradictory. Another framework is needed to explain corporate pension goals.

Pensions as Social Institutions: The Institutionalist Perspective

The institutionalist framework is sometimes viewed as a synthesis of neoclassical and Marxist views, but that is a mistake: Institutional economics does not merely combine or integrate these two paradigms. An institutionalist framework situates pensions within an evolutionary process and identifies pension structures that have outlived their function. Just who the gainers and losers from the pension system are may change over time.

In 1958, Berkeley economist Arthur Ross used an analogy to describe pensions. In asking "Do We Have a New Industrial Feudalism?" Ross wondered if pensions limited mobility to such an extent that they fostered a form of "industrial feudalism." The conceit is evocative even though Ross found that pensions in fact inhibited worker mobility less than age, unemployment, and unions. The institutionalist framework takes the feudalism metaphor seriously, but goes beyond the neoclassical-inspired focus on worker mobility, allowing for a broader view of pensions. The concept of industrial feudalism draws on the neoclassical and Marxist notions of what pensions do. A feudalistic or paternalistic employer and system describe a combination of relationships and motives among employers, workers, unions, and the community.

The metaphysical condition of alienated labor, according to Marx, might dispose workers toward pensions and other industrial social insurance schemes. According to Marx, industrial society and wage work cut workers' connections to the products of their labor and diminish their control over their labor process. Families cease to be points of production, and communities become based on a corporate culture. Alienation is a reaction to loss of control over the pace of work, the product of work, and the social relations surrounding work—a reaction engendered by the shift from feudalistic home-based work to factory wage work. These losses create a yearning for recovery. Simultaneously, the cause of these losses takes on power and influence. Workers respond to their deprivations either by calling for the transformation of capitalism or by accepting compensation when it is offered. Thus workers may welcome the paternalistic tendencies of large corporations.

One analysis for the greater incidence of employer-based social insurance in the United States than within European corporations is that U.S. employers have succeeded in controlling the labor force through welfare-capitalist measures (employer-based social insurance such as health care and pensions). An alternative analysis is that U.S. workers and unions have not formed an independent political movement and have adapted to the feudalistic tendencies in U.S. industrial capitalism and simply were victorious in some major battles, such as the right to bargain over employe pensions.

The segmentation of the work force, in terms of coverage by fringe benefit plans and access to pension income, also can be analyzed within an institutionalist framework of industrial feudalism. The fact that employer pension plans are skewed toward managerial and higher-paid employees implies a more feudalistic relationship with these workers than with wage laborers. Present-day pension fund activism by unions (discussed in chapter 6), when seen from this view, is a refinement of the unions' reactions to workers' dependence on the firm and the role of the firm in the community. Without understanding the feudalistic framework, important aspects of "social investment" activities would have been difficult to foresee and explain. Interviews with labor officials responsible for pensions endorse the view that employers provide pensions out of concern for the reputation of their companies and feelings of obligation toward their older workers.

The industrial feudalism view embodies both radical and neoclassical analyses. In a feudalistic system, the employer is a virtual monopsonist —serfs cannot leave the lord's employment. The lord/firm has many responsibilities, one of which is to maintain productivity and profitability over a long period of time—a longer period than one would expect from a pure capitalist. A feudalistic employer has an entrenched relationship with the community and is concerned with controlling workers, but this relationship takes on a different cast (of nonbenign paternalism) from the viewpoint of the Marxist paradigm, in which a bureaucracy would institutionalize and blunt conflict.

The industrial feudalism model incorporates the neoclassical model's recognition that employers need cost flexibility and the ability to alter work-force composition as technology and the labor market change. But in the industrial feudalism model, the flexibility is slightly different. Unlike the employer envisioned by the Marxist model, a feudalist employer would "care" about "firing the old guy" and regret sending him to a poor farm. Unlike a neoclassical-type employer, this kind of employer's concern is not just about affecting recruitment and retention but about moral authority in the community.

Pension Policy Issues

Government policies that head in the direction of mandating employer pensions must consider all of the employers' interests in having pension plans. Beliefs about what pensions do will influence the direction and scope of pension policy. If pensions are a means by which workers can conveniently save, then tax breaks and tolerant regulations are called for, and mandating pensions would create an undesirable limitation of choice. If, however, pensions are seen as personnel control devices, then taxation and regulation are warranted; a mandated pension may even help blunt the ability of firms to engage in pension manipulations and the incentives to compete by eroding the pension promise. If pensions are a source of flexibility in costs of bargaining, then mandated pensions reduce this source of flexibility. If pensions are important sources of funds for the sponsor firm or industry, then who controls the funds will be a major issue in any mandated pension policy.

The U.S. government started to regulate pensions early in this century. Legislation affecting pensions was passed almost every year in the 1980s. Yet, the United States has no coherent private pension policy. President Carter's Commission on Pension Policy, which revived some of Bernstein's 1964 proposals and recommended a mandatory universal pension system (MUPS) in 1981, was a weak attempt at reform. Under MUPS, a mandatory defined contribution plan, every employer would contribute 3 percent of earnings into a worker's account for retirement. Because the system would be mandatory, MUPS can be viewed as a type of advance-funded Social Security system without the social insurance aspect (a worker's contribution would not pay for other retirees, and the pension would be based on the size of the account, not on need). The idea of the plan ended with the Carter administration.

This book describes the development of the private pension system and its political and economic bases. Only by viewing the system as a product of evolution can one understand who benefits from the system and how legislation designed to cajole the system into helping the average worker is at best defensive and at worst, impotent. The private pension system's evolution explains its contradictory structure and how pensions became labor's capital. Because the private pension system exists, workers add to both the production and accumulation sides of the economy; under pension plans, workers create wealth not only from the sweat of their brows but as deductions from their paychecks.

2   The Pension Idea

Employer pension schemes have existed in the United States for over 100 years. This long history provokes a number of questions: Have pensions allayed worker insecurity about income during retirement? Has income equity among the aged changed because of employer pension schemes? Who benefited in the past and who benefits today? Have private pensions hindered the development of a broad-based social insurance program in the United States? Finally, what explains U.S. exceptionalism? That is, why is social insurance in the United States, unlike that of other industrial countries, in that it is derived from one's status as an employee and not as a citizen (or resident)?

By the late 1800s, U.S. industrialization finally produced old workers with ties to their companies. Because there were more workers with company histories, "firing the old guys" became troublesome tasks for employers. At the same time, feeding workers who were, in the words of Joe Glazer's song, "too old to work and too young to die," became more difficult for society. When the Social Security Act of 1935 was passed, more than half of all workers died before reaching retirement age (Latimer 1932: 171). Those who survived, if they were poor, lived with their children, on private charity, or, worst of all, in a county poorhouse. The retired elite lived on savings, public sector pensions for teachers, judges, and veterans, or private occupational pensions.

The United States lagged behind Europe in developing uniform and federalized pension, unemployment, and health insurance programs, and today we still stand apart from all other developed economies (Sckopel, et al. 1988). U.S. exceptionalism—using the private sector to provide social insurance—is explained by the peculiar emphasis on individualism in U.S. political and social life (Lubove 1986) and public distrust with the resulting underdevelopment of federal bureaucracy in the 1910s and 1920s (Orloff 1988). A review of the debates over government's role in providing retirement income reveals an early reverence for private initiative and a concern that the best of the private models be left alone. The private, company-based pension was given special ideological status precisely because it did not come from charity-based government programs but presumably from economic production, though the notion that the worker owned the company pension was not kindled until the 1970s.

Who Should Provide Retirement Income: Government or Business?

The development of the European welfare state in the late 1800s and the increasing need for worker income security in the industrializing United States engendered controversy about what role government should have in providing pensions. One theme in the debate reflected a concern, born of the Progressive era, about how much professionalism and efficiency could be expected from the federal government (Orloff 1988). The other theme is still significant today: How will government pensions affect private efforts to provide retirement income security?

Before the Social Security Act of 1935 and the Railroad Retirement Act of 1937, government took on some responsibility for superannuated workers. It was indirectly responsible for retirees through county- and state-supported poorhouses, where the impoverished elderly lived with the mentally impaired, the disabled, and all others unable to work.

The first dimension of the controversy over the government role in providing social insurance was "scientific": It offered efficiency as a criteria for deciding which sector should care for the poor. What form of relief—public stipends or poorhouses—was the most efficient way to care for old folks (Beman 1927: 239–247)? Some argued, incredibly, that the indigent, who obviously had not withstood the rigors of free society, needed the protection of poorhouses and poor farms and would not benefit from stipends of their own.

The federal government was also responsible for some aged workers in its role as former employer. Public discord over the size of military pensions for veterans (and their dependents) of the War of 1812, the Mexican War, the Civil War, the Indian wars, and the Spanish American War, stymied progress toward establishing a broad-based federal pension program (Orloff 1988; Epstein 1972: 173–175). Indeed, the cost of pensions for the Civil War seemed preposterous; they were double the cost of the war. The pensions were distributed, presumably on need as derived from war injuries; however, almost all beneficiaries were white Northern veterans and their wives and children, and complaints about false claims were common (Beman 1927; Keller 1977). In a similar vein, pensions for government workers were regarded as patronage and not as relief or rightful compensation. Even without the existence of a competing ideology that extolled private initiative over government relief, government pensions were suspect and sullied.

Another argument used by opponents of federal pensions ninety years ago—that a Social Security scheme would erode incentives for workers to live prudently and save for their own retirement—remains popular today. There was also concern that a federal scheme would inhibit the growth of industrial plans as well as the tiny but noble ventures in voluntarism undertaken by some trade unions.

Proponents of government pensions—members of the inchoate field of social workers, academics, and reformers—appealed to efficiency, arguing that federal pensions would be less expensive than chronically mismanaged poorhouses. Proponents also argued that the wages of most workers were too low to enable them to save for retirement (Epstein 1926), and that the localized, charity-based system was often arbitrary and inequitable. By 1915 only a select group of people—judges, teachers, veterans, and some industrial workers—and citizens in an even more select number of states and territories (Alaska, Arizona, Pennsylvania, Montana, Wisconsin, and Kentucky) had access to pension schemes. Most members of the industrial and lower-paid working classes had no claim to income after retirement or disability.

Before the Social Security system was established, social reformers also argued that industry had a responsibility to superannuated workers. They compared the superannuated worker to industrial waste, a by-product whose cleanup was the responsibility of the firm or industry. This argument harkened back to feudal societies in which lords were the employers who, through custom and rule maintained workers throughout their lives (Latimer 1932: 896).

Who Got to Retire?

The controversy over the desirability of federal pensions was focused on an elite group—those who worked for pay. For all practical purposes, this excluded women and African-Americans. Also excluded were those who did not live past sixty-five—the retirement age as decided in Bismarck's Germany. In the United States seventy was a common company target in

1920, despite the fact that white males at birth had a life expectancy of fifty-four. In contrast, white males born in 1986 are expected to live until seventy-two. Although life expectancy has increased by one-third, the target retirement age has remained essentially the same. The magnitude of the difference in the relationship between mortality and the retirement age in the 1920s and in 1986 can be seen in another way. If pensions today covered the same percentage of the population that they covered in 1920, retirement age would be over ninety.

In addition to benefiting only the few hardy souls who survived to age sixty-five in 1920, a national pension policy as envisioned at that time would have been limited by another reason. Only 40 percent of the adult population worked in 1920 and many of these were foreign-born eastern and southern Europeans. The fact that a broad-based, national scheme would cover select groups, and that those groups included workers for whom English was a second language, who lived in ethnic ghettos, and who joined radical labor unions, affected the national debate and dampened momentum for a federal system. Ethnicity in the industrial history of the United States can once again help explain why the country lagged behind Europe in developing labor standards and income-security programs.

Types of Government Schemes

At the turn of the century, Europe offered two models of national pension plans. The first was a needs-based welfare plan. The second and more popular was a forced-savings plan financed by contributions (taxes) and employer contributions, combined with state subsidies. The major advantage of this plan was that, regardless of the extent to which workers contributed to their final benefits, the mere existence of employee "contributions" took away the stigma of charity. In 1889, Germany became the first country to adopt a national plan financed by a progressive income tax. The United Kingdom replaced its voluntary scheme (a savings plan) in 1908 with combination plans that were partly needs-based and partly contributory. In France in 1910, mothers and veterans received credit toward their pensions for child-rearing time and military service. The link between paid work and contribution to the benefit was preserved in all those cases. Reformers in the United States in the 1910s and 1920s drew inspiration from these European examples, which influenced the structure of the Railroad Retirement Act of 1937 and the Social Security Act of 1935.

The question of whether schemes should be contributory or noncontributory resonates through the political and philosophical debates about pensions—public or private. The U.S. Social Security program is based on contributions, although the benefits are skewed toward low-wage earners. After World War II, making employer plans noncontributory was a major bargaining demand of unions, one that employers conceded to without much objection. The role of insurance companies and tax law changes that exempted employer contributions from taxation help to explain the relative lack of resistance to that demand. The contributory debate illustrates why the argument for citizen rights to old-age income security has never been separated, in this country, from the notion of individual initiative. The legislative history of the Social Security system reveals that the Roosevelt administration rejected its own economic advisors' arguments that deductions from workers' pay would be regressive and that funding from general revenues would be more progressive. Political advisors argued that the program would have more support if private insurance metaphors guided the new federal system and taxes would be referred to as "contributions" or "premiums." Today many U.S. workers believe that they have a Social Security "account" from which their benefits are drawn.

The heated debate over the necessity of a government pension scheme took place in a context in which many former "workers"—fortunate industrial workers, civil servants, and veterans—were already receiving employer pensions, and many more were promised pensions in the period between 1875 and 1929. The labor force was entering a process of segmentation (one that economists Richard Edwards, Michael Reich, and David Gordon [1982] deemed to be in full force after World War II), dividing those who had some income security in case of superannuation, disability, or unemployment from those who did not.

The debate eventually found common ground. Neither side decried the work-force cleavage; both sides saw company pensions as desirable. The fact that some workers were covered and some were not was not viewed as worrisome; it is a characteristic of private social insurance. Both sides of the government pension debate shared the impossible-to-attain vision that all employers should and would provide some pension benefits. All agreed that some pension support should come from one's occupation or industry. The employer's responsibility was never in doubt; the extent of the government's help and whether employer pensions should be mandated was the subject of debate. The debate also focused on how a government program would affect employer pensions. This mattered quite a bit to social reformers. Indeed, the extent of a government's influence on employer pensions depends on why employers want pensions at all.

What Employers Want from Pensions

The American Express Company, originally a large shipping firm connected to the railway industry, is credited with sponsoring the first industrial pension plan in 1875. During the next ten years, scattered plans were established by the largest companies in railroads, public utilities, manufacturing, banking, insurance, and other industries such as department stores and mail-order houses.

The Montgomery Ward Company is credited with establishing the first comprehensive insurance plan in July 1921; it included group life, disability, and pensions. The Equitable Life Insurance Company pioneered group life insurance through its policy with Montgomery Ward. The London Guaranty and Accident Company took on the disability portion and Montgomery Ward sponsored the pension plan itself, which provided a pension equal to 25 percent of final earnings and 1 percent for each year of service over twenty years to those workers retiring at age seventy. The group life insurance policy took into account the status of the family and salary, which according to Louise Wolters Ilse constituted "the first practical applications of the ideas that eventually were crystallized in the Social Security program" (Ilse 1954: 44). In fact, the plan had better features for women than today's Social Security, because a widow did not suffer the Social Security "widow's gap," the period after care of a dependent child stops and retirement age begins, during which a widow does not receive Social Security benefits. Under the 1912 Montgomery Ward plan she received her annuity without interruption for the rest of her life. A great burst of pension formation activity among large employers occurred between 1911 and 1915, and an even greater number of plans were established by smaller companies between 1916 and 1920 (Latimer 1932: 17–61).

The rate of pension formation fell considerably during the 1920s, however, and of the little growth found, most was attributed to the prowess of insurance companies in selling annuity plans to small companies. This trend calls into question the popular notion that pensions were a key ingredient of the anti-union motives of the "welfare capitalism" movement in the 1920s, in which employers provided social-based insurance and personnel functions to forestall unionization and excessive turnover (Brandes 1976; Jacoby 1985). Their maintenance during this period may be explained partially by that movement, but the existence of pensions is rooted in other employer motivations as well as in the marketing skills of the insurance companies.

By 1929 between 14 and 16 percent of workers were covered by a pension scheme, compared to approximately 46 percent in 1990. And the coverage rate then, as now, differs considerably from industry to industry, and occupation to occupation. Ninety percent of railroad workers and 80 percent of public utility workers were covered, but there was almost no coverage in service industries. Workers in the largest companies, as is the case in 1990, were more likely to be covered. Eighty-seven of the largest 200 companies had a pension plan in place. Yet only 2 percent of all the large employers (those with 250 or more workers) and .02 percent of small employers had pensions (Latimer 1932).

Initial Employer Pension Goals

Murray Latimer, economist and pension analyst for the Industrial Relations Counselors, Inc., a private research council created by John D. Rockefeller, Jr., identified five theoretical reasons why an employer would implement a pension scheme and examined each reason for its force in practice. Technological developments and professionalized personnel management encouraged a new class of managers to explore ways to replace older workers with younger workers. A pension scheme could facilitate such substitution by making mandatory retirement seem more humane.

Firing a loyal and long-service employee and banning him or her to a county poorhouse would cause embarrassment and real economic loss to a firm connected to and dependent on a community and local work force. The militant railroad unions and the threat of a burgeoning trade union movement made pensions attractive as an industrial relations tool. Pensions could be used to inhibit strikes and union organization.

A pension plan would have the same salubrious effect on productivity as any welfare capitalist program by easing worker fear of superannuation and loss of income. This comfort would foster goodwill, loyalty, and efficiency. And pensions would help firms compete for skilled employees, who were in chronic short supply and grew more valuable the longer they stayed with the firm.

In short, pensions had many contradictory purposes. Pensions were to encourage long tenure and loyalty, while simultaneously affecting timely separation. Pensions were designed to promote goodwill and attract workers, and at the same time they were intended to repel worker organizations. Pensions were meant to prevent former workers from living in poverty and to lower business costs.

Employers were to gain by having pensions in the compensation package because, especially before the 1970s, plans were voluntary and funded at the discretion of the employer. Pension promises are a flexible labor cost that can help business weather loss of profits and fluctuations in demand. Wages might be sticky, but pension plans make labor costs more flexible. In the modern period, pension plans fulfill a collective or macroeconomic function by serving as a major means of accumulating capital. The evolution of employer pension plans comes about through the interaction of these objectives.

Government policies that head in the direction of mandating that employers provide some minimal pension must consider employers' interests in having pension plans for the obvious reason of wanting to intelligently anticipate support or criticism of a mandatory, universal pension plan.

Characteristics of Early Employer Pensions

What is striking about private pension plans of the early twentieth century is that their basic structure and character survived the Depression, the ascent of Social Security, World War II, industrial unions, and the dramatic increase in the life span of Americans'.

Early pension plans had three general characteristics: pensions existed at the total discretion of the firm; very few companies advance-funded their plans (the corporations that did put their own stock into the trust); and white- and blue-collar employees were covered by the same plan (Latimer 1932:713). Most contributory plans did not pay interest on employee contributions, and the noncontributory plans made the rights to pension benefits contingent on both length of service with the firm and particular kinds of workplace behavior, for example, "loyalty."

According to the neoclassical paradigm, employers first implemented pensions to reduce costs and improve labor productivity. Therefore, we would expect pensions to have reduced the turnover of select workers and to have aided in introducing technological improvements by encouraging older, less flexible workers to retire. There is some evidence that fringe benefits do inhibit turnover (Mitchell 1982). I have uncovered no literature on the relationship between the growth of pensions and technological innovation.

A Marxist analysis would emphasize the use of pensions to control workers and inhibit unions, both to reduce costs and to ease the introduction of new technology, but also to retain control over the workplace. If this view is correct, we would expect pensions to have inhibited union organization.

An institutionalist model would view pensions as influencing labor market structures and the evolution of the balance of power between employers and workers. The desirability of pensions is rooted in their flexibility. If pensions help create noncompeting groups or labor market segments, then we would expect that they would be maintained on that basis, instead of on the basis of an efficient contract, or for employer control.

Samuel Gompers, first president of the American Federation of Labor in 1886, was strongly opposed to government pension schemes and employer pensions. He saw both as a means of reducing worker and union autonomy. While firms were establishing pension plans, unions formed their own mutual aid societies—a course of individualism and self-help approved of by the president of the largest and most powerful U.S. union.

The development of union and employer plans did not intersect, except in railroads, and indeed, anti-union sentiments did affect the development of employer-based pensions in the railroads and utilities (streetcars) (Epstein 1972). But a significant number of plans were established in the insurance, banking, and retail industries where unions did not and still do not have much of a presence. The industrial and union pension movements were almost entirely separate during this period of early pension formation.

In theory, there was the potential for pensions to be used as a tool for union avoidance and union busting. In the first half of this century, however, Latimer concluded that employers were not providing company pensions to inhibit union activity. Latimer (1932: 756) quotes a railroad president, who wrote,

We look for certain beneficial results from the pension system ... but freedom from strikes or favorable settlement of labor trouble is not one of them. Our experience leads me to say that when men act collectively in accordance with the orders of their organizations, the individual interest is completely in the background for reasons best known to the individual.

Latimer (1932: 759) summarized his views, based on interviews with railroad presidents and observations of the steel and railroad strikes—the major strikes in the first two decades of this century—in this way:

Pension systems, therefore, seem to have played little part in either the beginning or ending of two major strikes in recent years. ... Trade Union executives appear to also concur in the opinion that pension systems have little effect on strikes. ...

Another brotherhood official expressed the opinion that no pension plan would prevent or seriously interfere with a strike.

Latimer also stated that he knew of cases in which railroad officers had attempted to induce pensioners to return to active service as strikebreakers, but had learned of no case in which such efforts were successful. In one instance, however, pensioners who refused to help break a strike on the Western Maryland Railroad in 1926 were thrown off the pension rolls but later were reinstated. After Latimer inspected the effect of reemployment provisions of pension plans in 1929, he rejected the notion that pensioners acted as potential reserve armies of labor. A notable feature of most early, noncontributory, guaranteed plans was that the employer could revoke the pension if pensioners engaged in work detrimental to the well-being of the firm. Although the possibility existed of reemploying pensioners as a reserve army, Latimer (1932) found only one strike, in the railroad industry, during which pensioners were strikebreakers. In ten railroads, pensioners were, however, required to reenter service when called.

The small effect pensions have on strikes is partly determined by the nature of a strike. Striking, after all, means potential job loss. Once someone has taken that risk, the possible loss of a pension would not matter. Thus the pension plan was only a minimal control device.

Latimer (1932: 756) did admit that "The inauguration of a pension system has rarely if ever been brought about in response to the demands of workers, certainly not of those in the organized trades." Yet this is not proof that company plans inhibited union organization. Latimer ultimately rests his case on two developments. First, those industries with pensions —oil refining, explosives, rubber, electrical equipment, metals—experienced insignificant attempts at organizing workers. Second, railroads were the locus of successful union organization, widespread company pension plans, and some union-sponsored social insurance funds. He found no instance in which union activity was followed by the implementation of company pensions that in turn led to union declines.

Pensions might have functioned as a device to lower labor costs directly. By encouraging workers to accept lower wages in exchange for a pension promise that was not financed by contributions to a pension trust or fund, labor costs were reduced. Indeed, Latimer was most concerned about the fact that most funds were not secured by a trust. Pensions were not advance-funded, which lowered immediate costs, but there is no evidence that firms lowered wages when they offered a pension. In fact, high-wage firms were more likely to provide pensions than low-wage firms. This suggests that pensions were not substitutes for wages in a certain segment of the market, but complements. Wherever the cost-reducing component of a pension fits in, it does not dramatically lower wages for all workers.

In the neoclassical view, a second and important reason employers want pensions is to facilitate the replacement of older workers with more productive younger workers. This function is consistent with neoclassical models of employers and workers making optimal contracts. Older workers would agree to leave the firm based on a prearranged pension at a time when younger workers could provide relatively cheaper and sufficiently productive labor. But the terms of these contracts were not automatically protected. Both workers and employers could renege, but an employer's violation—firing the worker or not paying the pension—was more plausible than a fifty-five-year old threatening to quit before the optimal (from the firm's point of view) departure point. Much union bargaining around pensions since World War II has been to secure the promises and protect the senior worker from being replaced by the cheaper younger worker.

Another notable feature of plans, which adds to their attractiveness to firms, is their regressivity. Corporations could provide a promise with no guarantees and provide blue-collar workers with a plan that mainly benefited white-collar workers. Tax law changes in 1928 placed restrictions on how much a pension plan could be skewed toward high-income workers, but most early pension plans covered all workers and were still able to legally favor the highest earners and remain tax exempt. This inequality was striking to Latimer, but he saw no evidence in 1932 that it caused worker militancy. Indeed, he suggested that people were largely unaware of the redistributive effect of pensions. Pension plans are still regressive. In chapter 4, I develop an argument that shows how this may explain employers' (and to some degree, unions') motives for supporting company pension plans.

Control over pension funds was not an issue in this period because, much to the dismay of experts, firms did not generally advance-fund the pensions. There was a great deal of concern about the negative effect of pensions on savings, but there is little evidence that anyone foresaw that pensions could be an institutional way to accumulate capital.

In summary, restrictive conditions had to be met before a worker could receive a meaningful pension. These restrictions meant that a large group of workers was covered by a plan, but only a few would receive benefits. For a worker to receive a pension (these provisions still apply unless otherwise noted), she or he

1. must remain with the company for a specified number of years (the vesting period),

2. must not die before retirement,

3. must not be discharged or laid off before retirement or vesting,

4. must not cause the employer to refuse the pension payment because of some disciplinary reason (outlawed in 1974),

5. must be in a company that continues,

6. must be be in a plan the firm does not abandon,

7. must experience no inflation in retirement, or be in a plan that guarantees inflation adjustments, and

8. must be a member of an elite group—the type to which the firm wants to provide a pension.

What emerges from an examination of early and, by extension, current plans is that their main attractiveness to companies was their flexibility. And the fact that workers were not assigned property rights to the pensions meant pensions were provided at the discretion of management. They served as a control mechanism sometimes and as efficient contracts that helped determine the timing of retirement at other times. Not one function dominated. Pensions help segment the labor market in an interesting way. Pension coverage before the Depression, as now, extended to a far larger group than those who eventually received benefits. But because mortality and other factors seemingly out of the control of the employer, or not class based, determined who received pensions, the skewing of benefits to high-income workers did not cause worker mobilization against the plans.

Pensions and Social Security

Did company pensions affect the establishment of Social Security? Employers opposed the passage of a government plan and spoke out against it. The passage of the Social Security Act however, certainly did not mark the demise of company pensions. To the contrary, the passage of the Social Security Act of 1935 helped spawn a remarkable growth of pension funds from 1932 to 1935. The Social Security system is skewed toward low-income workers. On the benefit side, the cap on benefits and the proportionality of the income tax ensure that low-paid workers receive a higher replacement rate (the ratio of pensions to preretirement income) than higher-paid workers. But on the revenue side—the payroll tax—the system is regressive. On the whole, the Social Security system is mildly progressive.

Firms maintained that the progressivity of Social Security benefits obliged them to supplement higher-income earners. Employer pension plans were adopted in this period, not because workers and their organizations demanded supplements to Social Security, but because the plans could be truly dedicated to the higher-income groups as Social Security had eliminated the need, as corporations saw it, to be terribly concerned with the lower-paid groups. The Railroad Retirement Act of 1937, in contrast to the effect of the establishment of Social Security, caused the demise of hundreds of railroad plans for railroad workers, with the exception of those for railroad executives.

Between 1932 and 1938, the number of pension plans established grew dramatically to forty-two per year, due primarily to the activity of small employers. The plans were mostly contributory. The number of new employees covered did not offset the number who lost coverage, however, because of revisions and terminations between 1929 and 1932. The fact that small firms were establishing plans during the Depression is remarkable. What is even more surprising is that during the Depression, despite the fact that the payment of noncontributory pensions was at the discretion of the employer, very few pensioners lost their benefits (Latimer and Tufel 1940: 17).

Moreover, during the 1930s most pension plans were revised along the lines Latimer had advocated in the 1920s. Almost all funds, contributory and noncontributory, were advance-funded, interest was guaranteed on contributions, and survivor benefits were adopted. Inflation protections were not considered important during this period when prices were falling faster than wages.

Pensions and Moral Authority

Pensions are not merely labor control devices or efficient contracts devised by management to enhance productivity. They were part of a particular environment in which government competed with, and cooperated with, corporations over who would manage the vagaries of capitalism, vagaries that denied people access to income through no fault of their own. Employer pension plans helped corporations to maintain their superior moral standing relative to government and to manage what seemed always to be an unpredictable supply of labor (Jacoby 1985). Indeed government officials gladly conferred the responsibility and moral authority to business with regard to who should insure workers. Ilse (1954: 52) quotes the Insurance Commissioner for the State of Colorado, who in 1914 made the employer's case for paternalism when referring to the developments of group insurance in particular.

Group Insurance is a valuable contribution to the solution of modern industrial problems. The employee is encouraged to become a permanent and efficient member of the community, his mind relieved of the fear that his family will be destitute should he die. ... The corporation gains through an improved esprit de corps. Society gains because there are fewer destitute families dependent on the community, fewer wasteful strikes, a smaller amount of floating labor, and generally, through the improved social and industrial conditions.

As with any institution in U.S. society, rights were, and are, important issues in pension policy. Whether pensions were a deferred wage or a gift preoccupied the economics profession in the 1940s and 1950s. A deferred wage concept implied a right to pensions; a gift certainly did not have the same connotation. In the 1980s, the use of the concept of a deferred wage was used by unions and labor-aligned advocates to argue that workers whose defined benefit plan was terminated should have access to the entire fund; that is, no monies in the pension fund belonged to the firm.

This debate was especially important because most manufacturing employers offered noncontributory plans, whereas other industries offered contributory plans. The rights to the pension promise seemed more concrete in contributory plans because the promise was quantified by the money in a trust fund. Liberal reformers argued for contributory plans on this basis, but unions, in the period following World War II, pushed for noncontributory plans. Tax law later made it a moot point; contributions made by the employer could be made before taxes, and employees contributions could be made after taxes.

Insurance companies were major players in the development of the employer pension system. Insurance companies provided annuities to workers for a fixed sum, which took from the employer the risk of workers living too long. Insurance companies also tended to provide contributory plans for their own employees; much of the pension growth during the pre–World War II period occurred in finance-related industries. The insurance companies' monopoly in this area partly explained why unions and employers abandoned contributory plans. The rate of return offered by insurance companies was low after the war, and the possibility of handling their own pension funds was attractive to firms.

Outcomes and Contradictions: The New Private Pension System

After World War I a combination of factors—social pressure from poverty activists and social reformers, the aging work force and productivity problems, the "welfare capitalism" movement, and the tendency of companies to mimic one another—prompted employers to adopt company pensions. From that point on, social insurance in the United States swerved off the European road leading to universal social insurance. Government, unions, and employers have stayed on the new U.S. path, so that now pensions, vacations, and health insurance in the United States are linked to one's status as employee, not as resident. Employers were very much the progenitors of company pensions, but other institutions nourished their growth.

When corporations first developed pension plans between 1885 and the 1930s, inadequacies and trends became apparent. Workers with pensions were elite members of the work forces of large and paternalistic firms. The plans were managed entirely at the discretion of management. Regardless of the form, contributory or noncontributory, the promises were not backed by an advance-funded pension trust nor mandated by government. Interest generally was not paid on employee contributions before 1932, survivor benefits were not common, and because the employer did not have a legal responsibility to pay the pension, there was no sense of responsibility to maintain the spending power of the pension (although, until the 1970s, large employers occasionally granted cost-of-living increases).

Employers cited their need for loyalty and better employee relations as reasons for having pensions, and indeed, the pension plan was always seen as a management tool, instrumental in solving particular labor problems that could change at any time. Employer discretion seems to have been one of the most important elements of an employer pension plan, and it is the one element that firms have not relinquished. The terminations and reversion moves of the late 1970s and 1980s attest to the advantages firms derive from a voluntary pension system.

One of the arguments circulating about the United States's belated and anemic formation of social insurance is that the growth of private plans limited the formation of the necessary coalitions to push for expansion of government plans. Ironically, workers' demands for retirement income were less legitimate and politically acceptable before the Social Security Act was passed than after. After the passage of the Social Security Act, industrial pension plans immediately began to complement the new national plan, because Social Security elevated retirement income to a commonplace expectation.

Social Security covered the foreign-born, lower-paid, ethnic working class, whereas company pensions developed as supplements for management and favored workers (disproportionately native-born and white). That firms retained their prerogative to change the terms of a worker's eligibility to collect a pension and to decide how to fund the plan points to another enduring source of employer's attraction to the pension idea. Pensions provide firms with labor-cost flexibility.

Unions and firms developed plans separately and simultaneously. Both sides were chary and conscious of political trends that led to the eventual establishment of Social Security in 1935. After World War II unions were stronger and expanded their new clout to influence the development of private pension plans.

3 Social Insurance with a Union Label

How the U.S. labor movement represented worker interest in company pension plans and how unions nourished their own survival by acceding to and helping to shape employer-based pensions is the subject of this chapter.

Since 1926, the year pension plans appeared in the tax codes, the U.S. government has both sanctioned and regulated employer-based social insurance programs. Moreover, the explosive growth of pension plans in the 1940s was often attributed to government actions. Though there were some acts deliberately designed to expand the private pension system, the growth of fringe benefit programs was only a side effect of the government's attempts to cure inflation and limit excess profits during the two world wars. These wartime policies, coupled with the existence of unions that were in their most vibrant and militant phase, significantly altered the future structure of workers' income security programs, although such policies were not examples of deliberate planning for secure retirement income.

Unions, Pensions, and Segmented Labor Markets

During much of the postwar period unions commonly were viewed as reactive agents. An aphorism depicting U.S. industrial relations, "management moves, the union grieves," describes the role of unions in employer-based pension plans for nonexecutive and managerial employees. The employer would establish the pension plan and the union would attempt to modify it. Beatrice and Sidney Webb's (1894: 1) definition of unions as a "continuous association of wage earners for the purposes of maintaining or improving the condition of their working lives" generally has been understood to mean that unions are agencies that workers use to improve their lives by altering employer behavior. Economic theory reflects this view and advises pension policy to rely on union actions to monitor, grieve, and protect workers' pension interests. This advice assumes not only that unions have sufficient information and strength to react but that unions also can be narrowly focused advocates for pension interests specifically, with no other competing and contradictory goals.

The multifaceted interests of unions are revealed by the history of their pension plans. Unions are communities that seek to improve the condition of their members' lives, regardless of employers actions, through mutual assistance programs, consumer advocacy, and political action. The earliest unions were self-help agencies—semifraternal societies that often were based on ethnicity, culture, or occupation—that provided insurance plans for death and disability and maintained old-age homes. These activities transcended the unions' advocacy and representational roles in capitalist production relations. Unions also were close-knit communities with familial elements. The history of union-sponsored social insurance in the late nineteenth and early twentieth centuries, when the only legal union activity was mutual aid, and union strategy in the developing industrial relations of the 1940s help explain the growth of union and non-union employer-based industrial plans.

The basic structure of company pensions has remained constant—skewed toward long-tenured workers and based on pay and service—but union activity in the 1940s and 1950s did affect the coverage and the type of plans established. For example, the auto workers negotiated to stop the integration of the benefit with Social Security. One of the enduring features of private pensions is their ability to polarize, to create divisions in the work force. Unions are factors in defining the poles, but as by-products, not as causal agents. The structure of industry is seen as key in defining the poles or divisions.

The polarization in the U.S. labor market is best described as segmentation; there are barriers and boundaries among sectors that prevent workers from competing for all the jobs for which they are qualified. Jobs in the primary sector—the large firms—are protected from outside competition and are safer, better-paid, and relatively more secure. Jobs in the secondary sector—smaller firms—pay less, are more dangerous, and encourage high turnover. An additional characteristic that divides good jobs from bad is fringe benefit coverage, or privatized social insurance programs. Workers in large firms, unionized or not, will likely be covered by some type of pension plan and other forms of social insurance—vacations, disability insurance, and formal personnel rules. But workers in the secondary labor force will probably not be covered, unless they are organized. Whether privatized social insurance causes segmentation, or segmentation prompts the expansion of privatized social insurance, is unlikely to be established. What is clear is that employer-based programs do not threaten the persistence and maintenance of labor market segmentation.

A less-emphasized union effect is the union's ability to transform secondary industries into primary sectors by rationalizing competitive practices in such industries as trucking, construction, longshoring, mining, and, in some cities, hotels and restaurants, by taking wages out of competition when negotiating industrywide contracts and by creating administrative units for welfare and pension plans (Ulman 1961; Cobble 1991).

For example, one mining company competing against others on the basis of price would not be able to pay a living wage, health insurance, and pension contributions. But by organizing virtually all coal mines, the United Mine Workers of America (UMWA) helped stabilize the industry. Coal companies were able to invest in capital once the cycle of destructive price competition was broken. In addition, the UMWA and the employer organization, the Bituminous Coal Operators Association (BCOA), serve together as a central agent that coordinates the collection of premiums on behalf of each miner from every mine worked in. The pension credit is based on time worked in the industry and not for a particular mine owner. In the economics literature, the problem of coordination is known as an agency problem that the union corrects.

Multi-employer contracts were the hallmark of national union development in the first half of the century, and the centralizing and rationalizing effects of the union continue to the present day. For example, the Service Employees International Union (SEIU) has begun negotiating defined-contribution, portable plans for its unskilled, low-paid, largely female membership. The benefits are likely to be small, but the union may be able to gain a foothold in organizing other workers in the industry by demonstrating success in obtaining even a small percentage of coverage. The SEIU has not succeeded, however, in organizing employers such as those in the nursing home industry into an employers' association; so it has not obtained the leverage and pension benefits of the construction and mine workers.[1] The SEIU is an example of a union attempting to reconfigure the labor contract in the secondary sector through fringe benefits.

For workers in competitive and oligopolistic industries, unionizing has meant a larger probability of being covered by a pension plan. In 1928, over 40 percent of union members were in pension plans (Freeman 1978; Dearing 1954; Latimer 1932), but only about 20 percent had access to a significant pension. The rest were eligible for residence in an old-age home or some nominal life or disability pension (Sass 1989). By 1979, over 83 percent of union members were covered, compared with only 39 percent of nonunion workers (Freeman 1985). The coverage-rate gap between union and nonunion workers has remained steady since then. Unionization (after accounting for firm size and industry) increases the probability that an employer will provide a pension plan, although plenty of nonunion workers participate in employer-sponsored plans. Unions also have influenced the structure of the plans, the direction of improvements, and the philosophy governing coverage and benefits. But the transformation of the U.S. industrial relations system and finance capital in the 1980s has increasingly made unions unable to protect their members against the financial abuses, inflationary erosion of benefits, and systemic weakness of any voluntary programs. Although unions have enfranchised many low-paid workers into the society of old-age insurance, it is unlikely that collective bargaining can succeed in expanding significant coverage to most of the nonprofessional or nonmanagerial class.

Recognizing that companies and unions have their own pension agendas can help policymakers distinguish and evaluate the policy advice served up by economists. Since World War II, government pension policy has been biased toward the neoclassical economic paradigm. The government supports employer pensions primarily through the tax code; the theory guiding policy is that individuals are induced by tax savings to prefer pensions to higher wages or higher current consumption, and that those same individuals encourage or in some other way demonstrate their preferences to their employer (or union) to substitute wages for tax-deferred pensions. Employees can reach higher levels of satisfaction, so the theory goes, if they forfeit wages for pensions, although employer costs remain constant. Pension plans are presumed in the neoclassical view to be efficient market mechanisms through which employers and workers achieve mutually beneficial contracts, thereby justifying little government interference.

Policies guided by neoclassical theories, which emphasize the individual, view the motivations of employers, unions, and the pension industry as secondary in analyzing the impacts of pensions. Moreover, policies based on the presumption that pensions are paternalistic schemes, at best, and manipulators of workers against their best interests, at worst, also are misguided. Policymakers should take into account an institutionalist framework that presumes that pensions are an element of a labor management relationship, which in turn is a product of an evolutionary process in which power relations among institutions and mutual cooperation are important forces in determining the structure and extent of pension coverage.

Union Influence on Pension Coverage

By the 1950s, unions and management settled into a relatively harmonious bargaining relationship in regard to pensions. This peace came after strikes, litigation, and sophisticated bargaining on both sides of the table. Unions and employers developed many common pension goals; however, who should administer the plan and manage the large, single-employer funds was, and is, a sharp point of philosophical disagreement. Unions pushed for and employers agreed, in principle, to advance-fund the defined-benefit promise to take advantage of the tax exemption. And, because employer contributions were tax deferred although employee contributions were not, the labor movement's demand to have employers pay all the contributions met with little resistance.

Unions now and then take credit for early retirement provisions, which coincide with employers' original intentions to use pensions to encourage superannuated workers to retire. The conflict over who decides who is superannuated, the employer or the worker, may seem to have been won by workers, especially for unionized workers and for all workers since the abolishment of mandatory retirement. And, when technology is changing and older workers who may have difficulty adapting earn substantially more than younger workers, employer interests in enabling persons to retire before age sixty-five, or after thirty years of service, may not conflict with union goals.

Investments

Although the issue of who would control pension fund investments was a source of conflict, notably in the auto industry, investment principles generally were not contested. In 1989, employers controlled over 70 percent of the pension investments covering workers, although in 1954 the UAW and the AFL-CIO advisory council recommended that unions negotiate for participation in pension investments. Many other unions supported that demand only in principle. On a practical basis, the industrial unions accepted employer management of the details of pension accounting and benefit distribution. Moreover, if unions such as the UAW did have control of their members' pension investments, the trust portfolios might not have been different, except that they would have been better funded. Despite accusations from officials in the Reagan administration that unions cause firms to underfund their pensions, unions have generally pushed for stiffer funding standards (Ippolito 1986b). For example, in 1952, the UAW struck Chrysler for 104 days over the issue of full funding. And the AFL-CIO included advance funding in their 1952 and 1954 pension bargaining guide (Kirkland 1961).

Although employer-controlled and union-involved trusts share the same goal—to maximize investment earnings to safeguard pensions as well as the financial institutions—some unions have carved out distinctive investment philosophies. The Amalgamated Clothing and Textile Workers (ACTWU), the International Ladies Garment Workers Union (ILWGU), the United Mine Workers of America (UMWA), and the International Brotherhood of Teamsters (IBT) use both ideology and market principles to guide their jointly trusteed pension investments. These unions are sources of investment innovations, but they also have deeply entrenched differences that help set the stage for understanding the current labor strategies toward pensions.

Early Union Plans, 1900–1935

Alongside the corporate pension movement, from the 1890s to 1932, there existed a smaller but significant trade union income security movement. That movement developed a connection between income security plans and union membership. By 1930 union pension plans covered 20 percent of all trade union members, whereas corporate plans covered only about 15 percent of the private sector work force (Latimer 1932). Union and company pension plans did not compete with each other. The railroad industry was the only one where a worker could choose to be covered by a union, a company plan, or both, and only 20 percent of railroad workers chose to participate in union plans. This may not reflect lack of union support as much as decisions not to supplement their railroad company retirement. This small group of trade union plans was significant because it formed the pattern for multi-employer plans that developed in the 1940s and 1950s. Union plans grew out of American individualistic sentiments and union experiments with mutual aid and self-help that were motivated in part by the anti-union judicial environment (Lubove 1986). The mutual aid plans occurred mainly in the railroad, construction, and printing trades. The first union pension plan (1900) is credited to the Pattern Makers of North America.

Bricklayers, carpenters, sheet metal and iron workers, electrical workers, locomotive engineers, railroad fire fighters, and unions in the printing trades had their own plans, which were financed by union dues between 1893–1929 (Dearing 1954). Later, the pension plans helped these unions rationalize their industries with multi-employer contracts and insurance plans.

The primary purpose of these plans was to unify union members and provide some life insurance and disability income. The goal of providing pension income came later. The mutual aid plans did have some provenance in religious and ethnic associations, mostly because of the ethnic-based segmentation of the occupations.

Mutual aid pacts and programs help groups form cohesive bonds by eliciting worker loyalty. Unions maintained these self-help plans to enhance the attractiveness of belonging to a union, to reward loyal membership, and to hold the union together when job actions failed. Institutional self-interest coincided with the union's desire to fill a large need for old-age and disability support in their communities. The first priorities of these plans were payments for disability, burial benefits, and income to widows. Superannuated workers needed income, but pensions were hardly ever paid; the first forms of help were union old-age homes (Slichter et al. 1960). In some ways these goals were no different from management's, except in one important respect.

Unions generally are more democratic than the workplace, and they are voluntary institutions. The distribution of benefits was less arbitrary in union plans than in company plans. Also, unions were inherently more concerned with welfare issues, and their plans took on more charity aspects than company plans. Union plans paid more attention to disability and widows' pensions than retirement income, and pension income was often distributed according to need.

Obviously, this arrangement required a decentralized union structure and a rather small group to administer the plan and allocate funds according to need. Social insurance program funds affected the internal structure of the union. The most common structure had the international union administering the pensions, but because they were means-tested, the locals had to police the system. In the 1980s, however, international unions, mostly in the building trades, sought to centralize the investments of the union pension funds, rather than make benefits uniform.

The ACTWU and the ILGWU plans are notable exceptions to this general description of union pension plans. Their social insurance plans were part of a larger social vision derived from the European cooperative.[2] In the early part of this century, cooperative movements challenged the established systems of consumption and production. In the pension area these unions went beyond the notion of pooling funds in cases of desperate need—using pensions as mere insurance. The cooperative union seeks to minimize the occurrence of these desperate needs by substituting cooperative housing for landlords, consumer-oriented banks and credit unions for traditional banks (the Amalgamated Bank, for instance, survives to this day), and nonprofit insurance companies for profit-making ones. The union-insurance money and the members of the union served as the basis for the capital and the customers.

The American Federation of Labor (AFL), at its forty-third annual convention in 1923, also took an offensive stand against the group-insurance/welfare capitalist movement of the period and authorized the AFL executive council to find ways in which the "beneficial features of the trade union movement in America may be strengthened . . . so that a unified policy of defense . . . may be directed at the misuse of group insurance by those who would . . . destroy . . . the trade union movement."[3] In response, two years later, the federation entered the insurance underwriting business and formed the Union Labor Life Company one year after one AFL affiliate, the International Brotherhood of Electrical Workers, had established its own insurance company. The ACTWU established the Amalgamated Life Insurance Company in 1944.

The Depression, Union Pensions, and Government Intervention

The Depression had a much more devastating effect on union pension plans than on company plans, and it transformed the labor movement's wary encouragement of proposals for Social Security to urgent support. In 1928, the United Mine Workers and the International Association of Machinists began pressing for federal action on pensions. The AFL joined the call in 1929 (Latimer 1932: 11). But when worker incomes fell and union membership plummeted, union demands for a federal system of retirement income became solid. The 1980s was the only other time since the 1930s that pension coverage fell and that the finances of remaining plans became more insecure. Only during the 1930s, however, the persistent issue was what happens to private, voluntary plans when the voluntary spirit withers during widespread industrial decline. The issue of retirement income was met by an affirmative move toward governmental income support plans, through the establishment of Social Security.

In the 1930s, old-age groups, social reformers, and successful programs in Wisconsin and other states formed the political base for the passage of

Social Security. The labor movement's support contained moral weight but offered politicians small political payoffs. Not only was the labor movement shrinking, but its backing was hesitant and late in coming. Also, the labor movement's eventual support for Social Security did not stem from a cultural base inspired by European roots, which favored citizen-based social insurance as opposed to firm-based social insurance, except for the support from the needle trades unions. Nor did it stem from what could have been a reasonable strategy to bolster union strength in relationship to management by supporting an alternative to company-based plans. The bulk of union support for Social Security came from the overwhelming collapse of the economy in the 1930s.

Employer pension policies also affected union concerns about company pensions. The 1935 Social Security Act, which became effective in January 1937, prompted many employers to develop and exaggerate the inequities in their pension plans between high-paid and low-paid workers. An analyst writing in 1953 concluded, "It was ordinarily believed that the Social Security benefits would relieve employers of the necessity of providing a retirement income to workers earning less than $3,000 per year." (Ilse 1954: 296).

The proposed Clark Amendment sought to exempt employers who had a "proper" retirement program from the Social Security system. In the last hour of negotiations the amendment was withdrawn on the promise by the Social Security agency's general counsel that a workable plan for exempting employers would be established. The catalyst behind the Clark Amendment was not employers but an ambitious group-insurance salesman who sold pension plans to companies. The salesman was concerned that Social Security would be bad for the insurance business. Months after the amendment was dropped, staffers initiated the amendment along the lines the insurance salesman and Senator Clark had wanted, but no politician or lobbying group wanted to pursue it. Insurance companies had all the business they wanted; it seemed that the new Social Security system had unleashed a demand for all kinds of insurance, and the industry boomed (Longman 1987).

Not only did the Social Security system not take business away from private insurance, it also served employer interests. The Social Security Act let employers indulge in their reluctance to provide pensions for lower-income workers, and they continued to skew their plans toward higher-paid workers and management after Social Security passed. So-called "integrated" or step rate formulas in pension plans were initiated, skewing pension plan benefits so that the percentage of income replaced by a pension plan would increase with earnings. In some cases, integrated plans completely eliminated coverage for lower paid workers.

Ten years later, the intensifying pension disparity between white- and blue-collar workers and the 1935 Wagner Act, which gave workers the right to form unions and employers the duty to negotiate with them, laid the foundation for the labor movement's own schemes for industrial pensions. But these schemes were not uniform and reflected the schisms within the labor movement.

In the 1930s, the AFL and the Congress of Industrial Organizations (CIO) differed in their vision for activist politics and the role for government in providing old-age pensions. The growing CIO advocated support for the New Deal program with a definite socialist flourish. The AFL was more reluctant to support state intervention and to encourage its members to become politically involved. The possibility of legally pro-tected collective bargaining and state intervention into procedures for union recognition lured the AFL to support the Social Security Act and the National Labor Relations Act of 1935, which protects union members from retaliation by employers and requires employers to negotiate in good faith with duly elected representatives (Greenstone 1969).

The CIO incorporated the well-established and accepted obligation of the firm to pay for capital depreciation to describe the obligation employers had to pay for the depreciation of its labor, either with employer-based pensions or Social Security, the mix did not matter. In putting forth this argument, the CIO had help from President Truman's Steel Industry Board (SIB), formed in response to a strike threat after negotiations broke down between the United Steel Workers of America (USWA) and the steel companies and a strike was threatened in 1949. The SIB rejected union demands for wage increases as too inflationary but defined pension and health benefits as, according to Sass (1989: 105), "a social obligation [that] rests upon industry to provide insurance against the economic hazards of modern industrial life." The SIB "reasoned that 'human machines, like inanimate machines, have a definite rate of depreciation,' and blamed industrial work for this gradual loss in human productive power. The concept allowed the SIB to argue that ... insurance and pensions should be considered part of normal business costs ... not a fringe benefit offered only by profitable firms" (Sass 1989: 103).

The AFL, mostly representing craft workers, sought multi-employer plans and viewed pensions as deferred income that granted workers property rights to the fund and to a pension promise. The AFL was indifferent as to whether the plan was funded by employer or employee contributions. The CIO eventually used the deferred wage concept in its arguments for inclusion of pension plans in the scope of bargaining under the National Labor Relations Act (NLRA). The tax code changes that exempted employer contributions from taxation encouraged the employer to be the sole contributor to the fund, which obliterated any need for a principled stand for or against contributions. When the CIO demanded that pensions be a mandatory subject of bargaining—to make pensions part of working conditions defined by the Wagner Act—it abandoned its emphasis on the employers' obligation to pay full price for pensions and accepted the AFL notion that pensions are deferred wages and, therefore, a substitute for current wages. The CIO dropped its argument that the Social Security system and employer pensions were similar programs, programs that paid for the depreciation of the worker. And the federation, the AFL-CIO, has all but separated its political agenda for Social Security from its initiatives on private pensions.

The reason the labor movement goes in two directions in its agenda for retirement income security may lie in the movement's dual identity. Organized labor has political and business roles. It is the only lobbying group for the working class, and it must negotiate and service its members at the workplace. The labor federation must support Social Security and push forward collective bargaining for pensions although success in one pursuit may hinder success in the other.

Pensions during World War II

The federal government made its first significant mark on the development of private pension plans during World War II, with the passage of the Revenue Act of 1942 and a 1943 War Labor Board decision. Although scholars give the Revenue Act credit for the explosion in pension plans during World War II (Harbrecht 1959), it would be misleading to view the act, which exempted profits from profit tax if they were channeled into pension funds or health plans, as a thoughtful retirement income security policy. The purposes of both decisions were not directed at the private provision of pensions but toward wartime profits and inflation. The federal government did not deliberately set out to create a mix of private and public sector old-age income security (Stevens 1988). The 1942 act limited corporate profits to their prewar levels; excess profits were virtually taxed away. Corporations could legally lower prices, raise wages to attract scarce workers, or direct the excess to pension trusts. Firms did raise wages and direct monies to pension trusts, but only rarely did they lower prices.

The positive effect of the excess profit tax provision on the growth of plans was enhanced by the 1943 War Labor Board decision to check wartime inflation by curbing wage increases. The War Labor Board ruled, however, that contributions to health and pension funds would not be counted when determining whether a firm had heeded the board's 15 percent cap on wage increases. Firms could pay the excess profit tax, or divert their earnings into pension funds. Their choice was predictable. In 1941, corporate contributions to pension trusts were $171 million, and by 1945 pension fund contributions had soared to $857 million (Stevens 1988: 7–12). The number of plans increased dramatically from 659 in 1939 to 1,947 in 1942, and to 9,370 by 1946. The financial foundation for worker pension funds today stemmed from the profits made by supplying the Allies in the fight against Germany and Japan in World War II.

The 1942 Revenue Act also strengthened the 1926 IRS code, which prohibited discrimination against low-paid workers in tax-qualified plans. These antidiscrimination rules were designed to ensure that tax exemptions for pensions would not solely benefit the highly paid managers and executives most likely to be covered by a plan. But the antidiscrimination rules were weak; they merely put a limit on contributions and allowed for full integration of Social Security benefits. The act required that at least 70 percent of a work group must be covered by a firm's pension plan. Coverage rules were not, however, the main reason benefits were skewed toward highly paid workers. The final distribution of benefits is where the extent of discrimination should be evaluated. Benefit formulas and final eligibility rules, as well as coverage rules, enabled the firm to select the eventual recipients of pension income. Not surprisingly, employers did not lobby strenuously against either the 1926 or 1942 antidiscrimination rules.

Postwar Pension Strikes

The 1935 National Labor Relations Act (NLRA) was passed only six years before the United States entered World War II, and when the country declared war, wages, prices, and profits became regulated by the federal government. The accord between labor and management became something quite different after the war ended.

One of the looming issues was to define the scope of bargaining under the NLRA. Shop-floor issues, work rules, and job classifications were of paramount importance to locals, especially after the war years of labor intensification, or speedup (Lichtenstein 1982: 110–135). The militancy around shop-floor issues and local control gave unions strength and leverage when negotiating for pensions. Ironically, pension negotiation complemented the centralization of the bargaining process and a weakening of local union influence.

The emergence of pensions in collective bargaining is part of a process Richard Lester (1958) has called the maturation of unions. A key element of maturation is centralization, the subordination of the union local to the national organization. The pension plan was an item a national staff could negotiate over, something about which a local union would have little expertise (Ulman 1961: 440). Employer-based pensions therefore can serve the political interests of a centralizing union structure.

Three other factors contributed to the inclusion of pensions in the collective bargaining agreement. First, employers had adopted more pension plans and made them more generous in response to World War II's excess profits tax and the anti-inflationary policies of the War Labor Board. Second, the Labor-Management Relations Act of 1946, known as Taft-Hartley, revised the NLRA by limiting government protection of union organizing and strike activity. Unions fought back and won their efforts to make pensions a mandatory subject of bargaining when the Supreme Court decided that Inland Steel had to negotiate over pensions in 1949. Third, Social Security benefits had not increased, despite increases in consumer prices.

Unions broadly defined "conditions of work"—those aspects of the labor relationship that employers must or are permitted to bargain over. Unions claimed they included all employer actions and programs that concerned the welfare of the worker. For instance, the UAW sought to expand the scope by bargaining over the price of an automobile and the investment strategies of the pension plan. Employers responded and won "management rights clauses" that deemed everything not in the contract "management prerogatives." They thereby resisted bargaining over many work rules, job intensification, technological changes, marketing and production decisions, and pensions and health plans. Some of these issues eventually were included in the mandatory subject category; control of pension investments is still only a permissible subject of bargaining.

Pensions became the perfect issue with which unions could challenge and expand the legally defined scope of bargaining, in part because of the blatantly favorable pension privileges accorded to managers. Political support for pensions also grew from the fear of high unemployment after the war ended. More generous and more widespread pensions were needed to make retirement more attractive, because life spans were lengthening while real Social Security benefits stagnated, and jobs were expected to be scarce. The reasons for encouraging older male workers to retire were the same as those used to fire or demote women when the soldiers came home: young adult male unemployment was intolerable and a peacetime economy threatened to shrink the supply of existing jobs.

Most employers resisted including their employee benefit plans in the scope of collective bargaining, although they approved of the idea of pensions. Some unions were successful in negotiating pension contributions from their employers. The Amalgamated Clothing and Textile Workers Union (ACTWU) and the United Mine Workers obtained negotiated retirement plans funded by employer contributions in 1947. The ACTWU won an agreement with men's and boy's clothing manufacturers to provide benefits equal to those of Social Security. But it was the tripartite agreement worked out on July 1, 1947 among the coal companies, John L. Lewis (president of the UMWA), and the government—after President Truman intervened in the 1946 bituminous coal strike involving 400,000 soft-coal miners who struck principally over the pension issue—that established a new standard for union expectations concerning benefit levels and administration.

The UMWA pension plan provided $100 per month in addition to Social Security for workers with twenty or more years of service. The generous benefits were made possible by the pay-as-you-go method of financing, which later put the fund in financial jeopardy. Lewis won his demand that the pension fund be financed according to output (ten cents a ton), not hours, so that the tremendous mechanization that occurred in this industry did not impair the fund. The miners also were able to obtain joint trusteeship of the fund, although their initial demand was to be sole administrator of the fund. In the automotive industry, UAW president Walter Reuther tried but failed to obtain joint administration and contributions based on productivity. In 1949, pensions and other insurance issues accounted for 26 percent of all strikes (Wistert 1959).

Government actions and policies made during the next four years were crucial to the development of union pensions. The Taft-Hartley Act encouraged unions to focus on ways to expand the scope of bargaining. Developments in the steel industry helped advance this goal.

Since 1930, the Inland Steel Company of Chicago had a pension plan covering employees earning more than $3,000 per year. It expanded coverage to all employees in 1943. The original plan mandated retirement at age sixty-five, a rule that was dropped during World War II. In 1946, Inland reinstated the compulsory retirement age, and the steel workers objected, demanding that this move be the subject of collective bargaining.

Inland refused to bargain, but the National Labor Relations Board ruled against the company. The Supreme Court upheld the NLRB decision in April 1949.

Three months later, the Steel Industry Board (SIB) recommended against wage increases and instead encouraged what then were viewed as noninflationary payments into health, welfare, and pension funds. The steel companies balked at the SIB's recommendation for noncontributory pensions, and the USWA struck. After several weeks the Bethlehem Steel Corporation was the first to agree to a $100 a month pension (integrated with Social Security) for workers with twenty-five or more years of service. The other steel companies fell in line by October 1949.

While steelworkers were striking over whether the employer should be the sole contributor to the pension fund, autoworkers were negotiating a noncontributory employer plan with the Ford Motor Company, two years after the company had proposed it to the UAW. The autoworkers had rejected pensions in favor of an 11.5-cent wage increase and six paid holidays. But in 1949 they responded favorably to Walter Reuther's campaign and ratified the UAW–Ford Motor Company plan (Wistert 1959). The Ford agreement represented a pattern plan in basic manufacturing that incorporated steelworker demands for employer-only contribution plans and a defined-benefit formula that guaranteed a $100 per month benefit for employees with thirty years of service. The formula was integrated with Social Security.

Ambitious and innovative, Reuther reasoned that the integrated plans would induce employers to support Social Security increases, because employers payments would decrease when Social Security payments expanded. Not only did the UAW overestimate the tendency of management to perceive its narrow and short-term self-interests and act as a class to support more taxes and expanded social insurance, but the union leadership also underestimated the reluctance of workers to watch Social Security benefits increase and pension income stagnate. When Social Security monthly benefits were increased from $46 in 1949 to $80 in 1950, $85 in 1952, and $108.50 in 1954 (Barnard 1983: 139–142), the UAW pension did not change. The UAW members "revolted," and the 1950 General Motors–UAW agreement included a nonintegrated benefit.

Thus, a pattern of pension plans began to form in the rubber, automobile, steel, and other manufacturing industries. The pattern looked as if it was formed by the CIO unions, the UAW, and steelworkers, but the bones of the pension plans in each industry were also drawn from skeletons of preexisting employer plans. The steel pattern was an expanded and improved version of the white-collar plans. Auto firms maintained control over investments, even though they had to negotiate funding schedules. Coverage in large, single-employer, noncontributory plans grew at a rate that exceeded 50 percent between 1950 and 1956 (Sass 1989: 104). This history explains the current differences between nonunion and union plans. Union plans are much less likely to be integrated, or to require employee contributions. On the other hand, the old AFL unions—the mine workers and textile and construction trades—were able to transform their doomed self-help efforts into negotiated employer obligations.

The other characteristic of the emerging CIO union pattern was a trend toward simplification. The UAW complained loudly about the potential of employers to be capricious in determining benefits because eligibility and benefit rules were complex and informal. The potential for obfuscation was one rationale behind the UAW's goals for a "flat dollar amount" benefit formula. This formula determines the monthly pension by multiplying the years of service by a negotiated flat rate. This type of formula does not vary with preretirement earnings, so one of the side effects is that it reduces income inequality between workers after they retire. It is also simple to calculate and it makes plans easier to fund, because unpredictable wage growth is not an explicit factor. Much of the union effort to modify employer pension plans was directed toward eliminating the arbitrariness and mystery of the company pension plan.

After becoming federated in 1955, the AFL-CIO's first action concerning a unified bargaining agenda was in the area of pensions. The federation published a ten-point pension bargaining guide in 1956, which reflected a merger of the AFL-CIO philosophies about the role of private social insurance and government programs. Most of the booklet contains instructional material for the union negotiator on basic elements of pension plan provisions and financing, and a pension bargaining agenda. The goals include negotiating for no Social Security integration (with the provision that the pension and Social Security replace a worker's preretirement living standards), a cost-of-living clause, employer contributions only, disability and spousal benefits, credit for all years worked, and full vesting after ten years. The agenda also incorporated both the AFL and CIO's interest in obtaining information and control of the pension fund investments. The federation did not endorse progressive flat benefit formulas. Both the AFL and CIO had, before then, demanded that their member plans be advance-funded, so that even though that provision is not stated, the last goal implies that the AFL-CIO included a trust fund backing benefits as a major goal.

To date, labor has not won all these demands. There is no widespread inclusion of cost-of-living clauses, little portability, and no equal role in the administration of single-employer defined benefit plans. Not only have pension fund investments not been directed to projects that explicitly benefit workers before they retire, as well as after, but pension funds sometimes are used to relocate capital or restructure firms to the detriment of the workers. There are two reasons for union failure to achieve a say in the administration and investment of their employer pension funds. Union demands for access to pension plan information and control were fiercely resisted by management. Second, by the mid-1950s pension investment control was less important to unions than improving benefits and lowering vesting standards.

Despite strikes and litigation over pensions in the immediate post–World War II period, pensions became a relatively minor source of conflict between management and labor for the nearly thirty-year period from around 1950 to 1980. There were exceptions. Pensions and health insurance contributions are key issues in coal mining labor relations, and a few large pension defaults led to the passage of the Employment Retirement Income Security Act in 1974. The fact that pensions generated a relatively small amount of tension between labor and management should not be a surprise, because companies initiated pensions, the federal government encouraged them, and the unions, after the fact, claimed them as part of the scope of bargaining. Unions merely wanted to gain partial influence, control, and credit for their existence and maintenance. Each labor relations institution had a stake in this form of privatized social insurance. But are worker interests satisfied by employer-based pensions?

Do Union and Worker Goals Conflict?

Legal protection for unions is based on the presumed ability of a union to operate as a quasi-governmental institution in the pseudo republic of the workplace. Does union performance with respect to pensions conform to this view? An alternative to the representational view is the possibility that unions are leaders in the pension area.

Harvard economist Richard Freeman (1981) describes the representative process with a "median voter" model, which assumes that union action represents the average worker and that unions accede to the wishes of the vocal majority when bargaining for pensions. Because older, more senior, employees tend to be more active union members, Freeman surmises that unions demand pensions because their older and more influential members want them. This conclusion is in accord with our national tradition to judge policies, programs, and markets on their faithfulness to individualistic, private preferences. It also reflects the neoclassical tendency to put individuals at center stage in the decision making process.

On one level the issue of whether workers want pensions is trivial. Of course workers want pensions and if they have a pension plan they want it improved. Worker choices in regard to wages, Social Security, employer pensions, and alternatives to employer pensions are more difficult to determine. Support for a government retirement system mounted when some employer and union pensions crumbled during the Depression, but is this proof that workers choose government support only when the private sector fails? There are numerous ways to glean worker preferences regarding the sources of their retirement income security: from interpretations of union demands, job turnover behavior, responses to savings incentives, studies that try to explain savings behavior, and surveys.

Some voluntary employer contribution plans have a lot of participants, and some do not (Slitcher et al. 1960: 373–374). The Ford Motor Company first proposed a noncontributory pension in 1945. As we have seen, the UAW leadership supported the proposal, but the membership voted for a wage increase instead, later reversing itself after an intensive campaign by Walter Reuther. On the other hand, when General Electric workers were striking and living on minimum income they still contributed to their retirement insurance (Ilse 1954).

Overall, most economists believe that when Americans do save they save for nonretirement purposes. Moreover, people with high earnings and job security are more likely to save than others. Recent experience with the tax-deferred individual retirement accounts (IRAs) indicates that people who are already saving are sensitive to tax incentives and will shift savings assets to get the highest net interest rate. But a marginal change in the rate of return on savings has little effect on a person's decision to save (Congressional Budget Office 1987b). Most people support the Social Security system because it is considered a forced savings program (Yankelovich, Skelly, and White, Inc. 1985).

How workers respond to the provision of pensions also reveals the rank-and-file's concern for retirement income and interest in a forced-savings scheme. There is evidence that pensions do increase a worker's attachment to the firm (Mitchell 1982; Schiller and Weiss 1979), a hoped-for consequence among some employers but not all employers at all times. When employees have some protection from forced retirement, employers must delicately balance the contradictory incentives pensions create. A pension program encourages some people to stay with the firm to earn more pension credits while it encourages others to retire. The problem for the firm is to combine the pension incentives with other circumstances to ensure that the desirable workers stay and the superannuated workers take their pensions early and leave.

Economists have mixed opinions about what effect pensions have on the employment contract. Arthur Ross (1958) is the person most identified with the view that pensions would jeopardize economic efficiency because labor mobility would be hampered. Indeed, the long-term trend has been for workers twenty-five years and older to establish long-term relationships with their employers (Carter 1988). When Ross examined this allegation, he looked at cyclical trends and found that the unemployment rate influenced labor mobility more than pension provisions did. Ross concluded that pensions did not hamper labor mobility; if times were good people would leave their employer despite the existence of the pension plan. In 1987, Robert Clark, Steven Allen, and Ann McDermed showed that a work force with pensions of high value may actually increase the likelihood of a plant closing or takeover; this is another matter involving the role pension assets play in corporate financing decisions. This is the reverse of Ross's argument, because it focuses on the employer's response to pensions and pension liabilities.

The fear of worker hyper-immobility because of pensions is unfounded. This is not because workers do not value the implicit security, or insurance aspect, of their pension; it is just that other insecurities affect worker turnover behavior more.

In fact, one would expect that security-conscious workers would be wary of employer plans because the security of these plans depends on the business cycle and employer. Instead, employer health insurance and pension plans have only increased in importance for the groups of workers who have them. In 1980, total compensation was 10 times larger than it was in 1950, but employer contributions to pension funds were 50 times larger and contributions to health insurance were 115 times larger (Munnell 1988). With increases of this magnitude it is not likely that worker preference alone drives the private pension system.

Perhaps the very impulse to protect ourselves against market insecurity is the motivation that welcomes paternalistic relationships with employers. Cambridge economist Jill Rubery (1978) describes worker (union) strategies in seeking security as one reason for industrial hierarchies; such needs are also met by social insurance programs.[4] Unions would then have support from employers and workers for incorporating fringe benefits in union bargaining demands. The union strategy for protection has complemented employers' motives to create "feudalistic or manorial" relationships, and for workers to be protected by these relationships. This identification of latent feudalistic tendencies in work relations has caused economists to reinterpret employer motives to sponsor a pension plan and to reconsider what would make workers desire more or less pension income.

The security aspect of fringe benefits cannot be overstated. Employers are able to influence turnover with a pension plan, but they also care about the welfare of their retirees. Workers may respond somewhat to tax incentives for pensions, especially high-income workers, but the demand for pensions is inelastic, not that sensitive to tax rates because security is a main goal (Ippolito 1986b).

Information gleaned from interviews with high-ranking union officials responsible for pensions in the Communications Workers of America, the Bakery and Confectionery Workers Union, UMWA, International Brotherhood of Electrical Workers, ACTWU, and ILWGU, did reveal a few central trends. Single-employer plans were almost entirely in existence before the unions started negotiating them—in utilities, in the telephone company, food processing—and pensions were hardly ever a source of conflict between labor and management, especially compared to demands for health insurance.

The unions that have so-called thirty and out type plans, which allow retirement at full benefits after thirty years of service, are the beneficiaries of a reform that the membership strongly supported and encouraged in the 1960s. The trend was also commensurate with softening labor markets. Workers considered early retirement provisions good substitutes for disability pay or unemployment insurance. These pension officials also confirmed the hypothesis that pensions were a convenient and valuable bargaining tool. A negotiated increase in pension benefits can affect a relatively small number of people, cost the employer relatively little, and still garner significant and widespread support among the membership. Therefore pensions are a type of status good. Wage increases and Social Security were not traded for increased pensions. In the 1950s, 1960s, and 1970s pensions, wages, and Social Security increased, while in the 1980s only Social Security contributions increased (see table 3.1).

Certainly unions did represent worker demand for pensions. However, the context in which unions affected pension structures made unions more effective representatives of primary sector, older, stable, male, white workers.

Table 3.1
Weekly earnings and pension costs as a percent of total compensation and FICA tax rate: 1951–1988

Year	Average real weekly earnings[1] (private nonfarm) 1982 base	Pensions[2]	Old-age and surviors insurance: OASDHI[3]
1951	215.09	3.6	1.50
1955	243.60	3.8	2.00
1961	265.59	4.2	3.00
1965	291.90	3.7	3.63
1971	303.12	4.9	5.20
1977	300.96	5.9	5.85
1981	270.63	2.5	6.65
1985	271.16	4.2	7.05
1986	271.94	2.1	7.15
1988	266.79	5.0	7.15

Sources: 1. *Council of Economic Advisors* 1991: 336. 2. Chambers of Commerce, *Employee Benefits*, selected years. 3. Munnell 1977: 86; U.S. Bureau of the Census 1990: 378.

Multiemployer Plans

By the end of World War II most pension benefit funds were advance-funded (Slichter et al. 1960: 382). They were managed principally in three ways: multiemployer industry plans, single-employer plans, and insurance companies.

Multiemployer plans are organized on a regional or national level and cover workers in an industry or occupation who are in one union, but who are employed by many, often small and competitive firms, such as food processing, construction, mining, printing, trucking, and textiles. The 1947 Taft-Hartley amendment to the NLRA barred the sole control of pension plans by unions and forced these plans to become administered by a board composed of employer and union trustees. Many of the current, jointly trusteed plans in the construction and needle trades are the offspring of the older, mutual aid plans. The ILWGU plan actually served as a model for the Taft-Hartley legislation.[5] These plans shared similar philosophies about the management of the assets, that they should be managed for the sole interest of workers. They usually agreed on an actuary to properly tie employer contributions to benefit levels and to construct a safe investment portfolio, which often was administered by a bank or insurance company. Important exceptions to the view that the composition of investments in the portfolio did not matter, except for yield and stability, were the ACTWU, the ILGWU, the Teamsters and the UMWA. These unions managed their funds, with the acquiescence of equal numbers of management trustees, to enhance social, political, and economic power.

The ILWGU and the ACTWU wanted their funds to aid and induce the construction of housing in New York City. The ILWGU had an agreement with the Chase Manhattan Bank to set up a special division of mortgage loans that gave preference to working class applicants. But Chase Manhattan also was instructed by the ILGWU not to reveal where the mortgage backing originated. The Amalgamated for many years would invest only in government securities in order to remain aloof from the capitalist system it criticized.

What has been described as criminal, or incompetent, behavior on the part of the Teamsters and the ILGWU actually reflected a deeply embedded political analysis of labor's role in the capitalist system.

Union Skimming of Pension Funds

In 1955, James Hoffa, then an international vice president of the International Brotherhood of Teamsters (IBT), negotiated the union's first pension plan, which covered workers in midwestern and southern freight companies. The employers' contributions amounted to almost $1 million per month. The Central and Southern States Pension Fund (CSPF) was invested mainly in bonds, cash, and real estate and, occasionally, in non-union companies that rival unions were trying to organize (James and James 1965: 216).

Senator John L. McClellan (R, Arkansas) held hearings on union corruption between 1957 and 1959. Robert Kennedy was chief counsel and the Teamsters' union was Kennedy's principal target. Most of Kennedy's accusations (bolstered by wiretapping and questionable investigation techniques) failed to gain indictments until Hoffa's conviction for jury tampering in 1964. The persistence of the Justice Department's investigation of Hoffa and Hoffa's own bluster and defiant methods of managing the pension fund made the public, and unions themselves, wary about union management of pension funds. Union corruption in other areas—hiring halls, welfare plans, sweetheart deals, and internal politics—were also the subject of the Congressional and media scrutiny (Hutchinson 1970).

The management trustees on the Central and Southern States Teamster Pension Fund Board wanted to have a mainstream insurance company or a bank manage the fund. But Hoffa succeeded in making Maxwell Kunis of the Union Casualty Company the actuary for the Central States Pension Fund (CSPF) (James and James 1965: 225). Allen Dorfman, an alleged member of the so-called Chicago Mafia (and an eventual victim of mob violence) was a general agent of the Union Casualty Company (La Botz 1990: 131).

In addition to choosing Kunis as the actuary, Hoffa implemented other unusual pension strategies. Biographers Estelle and Ralph James accuse Hoffa of charging loans below market rates for the risk involved because of the Teamsters' fund persistent overvaluation of "single-purpose" properties (e.g. casinos and hotels) and, more important, because of Hoffa's ideological avoidance of stocks and FHA mortgages. Hoffa thought an upcoming economic crisis would cause the government to default on its bonds, thinking that was inspired by the Socialist organizer Farrell Dobbs. Hoffa's philosophy was "We are in this business to make friends" (James and James 1965: 269).

The trustees of the CSPF distributed the funds to seventeen banks in the south and midwest. Many of these banks were in the small hometowns of the sixteen union and management trustees (James and James 1965: 229). The minutes of the trustees meetings show that the intention was to build public, political, and financial power.

The Teamsters' pension controversies continued into the 1970s. Labor Secretary Ray Marshall intensified investigations into the fund and pressured Teamsters' president Frank Fitzsimmons and other pension fund trustees to resign in 1977 over various scandals, one involving Richard G. Kleindienst (attorney general under President Nixon), who received $250,000 from the fund for five hours of consulting work. The Teamsters for a Democratic Union intensified the scrutiny of the pension and welfare funds and filed class-action suits against the Central States Health and Welfare Fund, fifty-one Teamsters locals' pension funds, and officials for fraud, malfeasance, and unfair treatment during a two-year period from 1976 to 1978 (La Botz 1990: 63–64).

Of course, the Central States Teamsters pension fund was not the only one under scrutiny (Hutchinson 1970). And prosecutions during the 1950s have had a desirable effect; they affected the very nature of union pension fund structure and management. Union pension funds are now more conservatively funded than the not-so-scrutinized single-employer funds and have a cleaner record on malfeasance and fraud. Health and welfare plans are frequently under investigation by the Office of Inspector General of the Department of Labor, but not union pension funds. A 1990 report by the Congressional Research Service compared the investment portfolios of multiemployer plans with the four-times larger single-employer plans and showed that multiemployer plans, which are essentially in the control of union trustees, are more conservatively invested. Multiemployer plans have less funding flexibility than single-employer plans, because contributions are negotiated only periodically and do not permit access to company treasuries when cash-flow needs arise. Multiemployer plans invest in financial vehicles that are more liquid and stable than equities; they hold comparatively more cash equivalents and real estate (CRS 1990: 20–39).

Single-Employer Plans

The second type of pension fund is the single-employer plan. Larger employers, as we have seen, are inclined to sponsor their own plans and to administer them without union representatives. Most of these single-employer plans were defined benefit plans that promised contingent pension benefits to workers; an actuary calculated the proper annual contribution to fund the expected benefits. In the late 1940s the UAW spearheaded what was eventually a failed effort to win joint union-management control of defined-benefit plans. As articulated by the UAW, unions were aware that the large amount of capital amassed in pension funds was a potential source of economic power, but in the end, unions dropped demands for joint control and focused on negotiating higher benefits and on employer contributions that were sufficient to keep the fund well-funded.

In 1990, a junior member of Congress, Peter Visclosky (D, Indiana), introduced legislation to require firms to allow equal numbers of elected worker trustees on pension investment boards. This effort to expand the Taft-Hartley provisions to single-employer plans to obtain union rights was not initiated by the unions. These issues are discussed in chapter 6, but the answer to the question of why control of pension investments is not of primary concern to the unions may be found in the fact that unions are constrained by imagination and financial markets not to invest any differently than corporate pension fund managers.

Pensions and Labor Markets

By the 1950s, the pension movement was well underway. Management, prodded and accommodated by the insurance industry, adopted health and welfare and pension plans as standard practice. The AFL-CIO pushed for tax-deferred and collectively bargained employer pensions, increased government regulation, and expanded Social Security. At the same time, anti-union legislation and the nation's anticommunist ideology constrained union activity and vision. Unions had to be content with their successes and gain social status and legitimacy through the narrow confines of collective bargaining, rather than make great encroachments on management prerogatives, such as production, investment, and marketing. Unions began to insist on bargaining over what were once employer tools in welfare capitalism strategies, strategies viewed by the CIO as impediments to the expansion of Social Security and by the AFL as tools of employer control.

Unions established their role in the emerging industrial relations framework at the same time technological and market changes altered the structure of labor markets. Primary work groups became differentiated from secondary work groups. Establishments that enjoyed stable demand for their products and engaged in ever-increasing capitalization needed a steady, well-trained work force. These establishments formed the core of the economy. Many firms, usually smaller and more competitive, served these core firms. Technology and markets were not the sole determinants of which firms were in the primary and secondary sector. In fact, just what determines the sectors is a cause for considerable debate in the economics profession.[6] Labor segmentation theorists do agree, however, that unions have an active role in maintaining and sometimes creating a primary work force.

Neoclassical economists, the majority at least, believe that labor markets cannot be permanently segmented and that labor mobility will let workers sort themselves out, according to their preferences for insurance and wages (Scott et al. 1989). This view of the labor market harkens back to Adam Smith's notion of equalizing differences, that all labor contracts have different elements—wages, safety, responsibility, risk, and status—and that wage differences account for the compensation of these non-wage aspects (Smith 1965). The theory holds that some people will demand compensation with high wages for no pension plan.

The problem with this theory is that workers must have proper information about the wage and non-wage aspects of all possible employment contracts and that they can move freely between jobs, and contracts, to find the one that best compensates them for working. The private provision of pensions and, for that matter, other forms of social insurance causes problems and may contribute to forming cleavages in the labor market. The distinction between jobs with pensions and those without may be the distinction of jobs with or without limited mobility. Moreover, pensions cause divisions within a firm. We have seen how companies purposely structured the plans so that they benefit higher-income workers at the expense of lower-income, blue- and pink-collar workers—something the antidiscrimination rules in the tax laws try to mitigate, but allow.

Pensions have always been more likely to be offered by large companies. Where that is not the case, unions have helped create the administrative unit so that workers in industries that have employers with small work forces can be covered by a pension plan. Instead of pensions being trade-offs for higher wages, they are coincident with high pay; pensions and wages are not substitutes, but complements. Moreover, pensions, like most fringe benefits that serve a social insurance function, have an insurance aspect. Fringe benefits are not wage substitutes, paid *for* services rendered, but programs offered *because* services are rendered (Allen 1964: 297). To the extent that pensions are insurance plans, then the pension trust can be viewed as an insurance fund in which every "premium payer" (i.e., worker) holds a share. Pensions may not be labor's wages, but labor's capital.

Outcomes and Contradictions: Pension Bargaining without Conflict

There are two kinds of union-negotiated pensions. The oldest, the craft- and union-based pension plans established in the nineteenth century and at the beginning of this century as mutual-aid programs, either disappeared or evolved into collectively bargained multiemployer plans after World War II. These plans provide pension portability for workers moving among employers in the same industry. In 1947, the Taft-Hartley Act required that the craft unions strong enough to have employer contributions and sole administration of the fund put equal numbers of employer trustees on the union pension board. The unions, together with multiemployer plans and industry agreements, helped rationalize competitive industries by stabiliz-ing labor costs and labor supply.

The second major type of union pension is the single-employer plan. Coverage under these single-employer, union-negotiated pension plans, especially in manufacturing, expanded because unionized or unionizing firms were prodded into establishing and expanding company pensions by the War Labor Board's cap on wages and the federal government's excess profit tax.

Union-negotiated pensions also expanded, because they served the interests of both employer and union. The pension plan in the collective bargaining agreement also served union's organizational interests and the needs of the workers in the primary work force, those employees with career ladders and longevity with the firm. Bargaining over pension plans, not the idea of pensions, was resisted by employers in the 1940s.

Labor and management both wanted some sort of retirement income support. What form that support took was a bargaining item and unions have had some effect on the structure of pension plans. Unions seek to reduce the arbitrariness of the company pension plan by negotiating simpler benefits and a greater access to information about the plan for workers. Unionized plans are also less likely to discriminate against lower-income workers. Collectively bargained pension plans complemented and expanded company pension plans. Although coverage stagnated at about 46 percent of the work force in the 1980s, the smoldering issue of pension fund investments should certainly flare as pension funds and investments grow in importance. Questions about the adequacy of coverage and benefit levels will always haunt the voluntary system.

4

The Employer Pension System: Distribution and Moral Hazard

The dominant body of ideas reflecting the needs of government and business views pensions as voluntary and efficient contracts between workers and employers. Advanced by neoclassical economists, this view holds that workers choose to defer wages into pension funds and firms choose a payment scheme that encourages retirement at the crucial point at which the marginal, or incremental, increase in worker productivity is equal to the marginal increase in labor costs.[1] Armed with the theory that private pensions serve a market need, policymakers furnish the employer-pension system with the carrot of tax subsidies and the stick of regulation. But in reality, the U.S. employer-pension system operates counter to current beliefs about how the system makes labor contracts more efficient and tailored to the needs of workers.

The demand for advance-funded pension plans was fueled by government policies to limit warmongering profits and wartime inflation during World War II and the Korean War. Employers' paternalistic attitudes toward some long-service employees also inspired company pension plans. In the 1940s, the United States' newly enfranchised unions, struggling to establish themselves within an inchoate industrial relations system, folded company pensions into their own strategies for survival and increased bargaining power. Pensions exist because government, business, and unions have certain needs. To describe pensions as efficient market mechanisms merely rationalizes, but does not describe, their chief functions.

Pensions, principally defined-benefit plans, are group-based. In 1985, 49 percent of private pension participants were in defined-benefit plans and 79 percent of persons in plans with 100 or more participants were in defined-benefit plans (Ippolito 1990). The scope of the institutions and factors that govern their terms are anything but individual. Pensions are better described as insurance contracts and schemes, rather than a simple deferred wage. The former speaks of a complex relationship among risk, perception of risk, and the distribution of premiums paid and benefits disbursed; the latter of the individual's optimal trade-off between consumption now and consumption later.

Pensions and Moral Hazard

Pensions are group insurance plans. Workers are the insured and employers are the insurers. As in any insurance contracts, pensions are plagued with moral hazard problems. Most of the time the motives of parties in an insurance contract minimize the moral hazard, because insurers sell policies for cataclysmic and expensive events. These events are so undesirable that both the insuree and insurer have the same motives to prevent them from happening; such is the case in worker compensation, life insurance, liability insurance, and home fire insurance.[2] Yet, in the case of pensions, the incentives of the insuree and insurer are at odds. The worker generally wants the event to occur, that is, to live until retirement and collect a pension, but this is not in the employers' financial interest. When conflicts of interest abound and both sides have different information and ability to affect the insured event, moral hazard exists. When moral hazard exists the insurance contracts are not necessarily fair; not all participants "pay" a premium (lost wages) that is equal to their expected pension and valuation of risk.

What kinds of workers would be most vulnerable to moral hazard and nonactuarially fair pension contracts? What kind of firms would take advantage of the moral hazard? Theory and evidence help answer these questions. Hypothetically, the insurer as employer is in a position to offer an unfair contract to workers with the least information and labor market power. When an individual employee's valuation of pension benefits differs from the valuations of other employees and the employer, moral hazard exists. Thus, workers who have less labor mobility or bargaining power could be subsidizing other workers' pensions and reducing costs for their employer.

When a firm's workers have different levels of bargaining power and information, the employer encounters an opportunity to lower labor costs below the level they otherwise would have been without the pension. An employer may also be able to skew the benefits toward a select group (this is somewhat limited by tax law) and avoid an employee revolt or a bad reputation. Firms may also change the value of the pension promise after the contract is made by changing funding levels and terminating the plans.

During the 1980s recession in the steel industry, the Continental Can Company (CCC) used a sophisticated computer program to identify persons just about to vest in their pensions and fired them. "The court held that the employer's goal was to lay off steel workers whose benefits had not yet vested and, indeed, attempt to rid itself of steel workers eventually" (U.S. Bureau of National Affairs 1989: 844). The Continental Can Company was later convicted of violating age discrimination law, but the practice of firings and layoffs right before vesting is not an uncommon complaint, according to the advocacy group, the Pension Rights Center.[3] The tumult caused by corporate mergers and acquisition also causes pension abuses. Just before the takeover by the LTV Steel Company, the Republic Steel Company offered top executives favorable interest rates on their lump-sum disbursements, so that the remaining salaried workers were left with an underfunded and precarious plan (Dolan 1986). Although several federal agencies and Congressional offices probed the action, it was not considered a violation of the officers' and actuaries' fiduciary duties.

These well-known cases involving large employers are examples of a large number of abuses that are watched anxiously by frustrated and aggrieved pension plan participants. Often employed in small firms, these participants must police and scrutinize, and hope their pension contract is sincere, funded, and available. A common complaint is about access to and the quality of the information received about a pension plan. One case in the files of the Pension Rights Center concerned a clerical worker who was working in a small doctor's office for over a decade and wanted to weigh her options regarding retiring versus working a few more years. She was verbally assured by her physician employer that she was covered by a pension plan, but when she inquired about the benefits and manner of applying for the pension, her employers and supervisors were vague and not forthcoming. No government agency will actively pursue these complaints without a lawyer's intervention, and Legal Aid, the agency that provides legal resources for the indigent, must deal with more pressing cases such as evictions and losses of food stamps.

The disappointments of these workers and others originated from four sources of moral hazard brought about by the desire to lower labor costs and skew benefits to a select few employees:

1. a psychological tendency of workers to overestimate the value of their own pension when information is spotty and difficult to understand;

2. the fact that bargaining power is required for workers to get a fair contract;

3. legal loopholes and policies that allow firms to use pensions for corporate purposes rather than worker interests; and

4. the conflicting roles of the firm as a provider of social insurance and a profit maximizer, which are especially disharmonious in hard times.

The moral hazard problems intrinsic to employer-provided social insurance and union limitations in curbing moral hazard problems, cause us to reconsider the efficacy of the highly subsidized (through tax favoritism) and regulated voluntary and private pension system.

The Importance of the Average Worker

The hypothesis that employer pensions are skewed toward an elite makes sense when pensions of the most fortunate worker are compared to those of the average workers. Standard economic analyses of pensions and much pension law often do not examine labor market outcomes by focusing on class differences. The models usually revolve around two agents, the firm and the worker. All differences in pension coverage and benefits arise, in the neoclassical mind, from choices made by each agent. If firms and workers receive different levels of benefits it is presumed to be the result of different choices or varying needs and desires. Fairness is subsumed under the sanctity of choice and worker diversity is swept away in the theoretical division of two equally balanced sides to a contract.

These ideas about pensions obfuscate how differences among workers, and the nature of the institutions that support the employer-pension system, operate so that workers with the most need but the least information, bargaining power, and income receive lower pension benefits than high-status workers. To focus on how institutions, information, and bargaining power determine the distribution of pension benefits a vocabulary is needed that defines equity and distributional fairness among various kinds of workers.

External Factors: Distribution of Pension Plan Coverage and Benefits

Pension income is skewed toward workers with the highest incomes (nonproduction workers, managers, CEOs) because of the synergy and interaction of the internal structure of pension plans and the external structure of the labor market. External factors such as unionization and labor market segmentation distribute plan coverage and jobs among workers; internal factors such as mortality, job tenure, and salary distribute pensions among workers in the same plan. The highest-paid workers in the labor force are covered by the best pension plans and, generally, the highest-paid workers in a plan will obtain a higher pension than a low-income worker.

But is this inequity unfair? Economists construct a language with which to talk about fairness by categorizing the distributional aspects of an income-transfer system in three ways: a regressive distribution, a proportional distribution, and a progressive distribution. If fairness is reduced to an issue of the distribution of resources and resources are reduced to measure of income, then assessing fairness is simple. Regressive systems, those that yield proportionally higher net benefits as incomes increase (or lower proportions as incomes fall) are most unfair. For example, state lotteries are regressive because working class and poor people spend a larger proportion of income on lotto tickets than do the rich and middle class.

In a proportional system the proportion of income received (or paid) is the same for every income group; a true flat-rate tax is a proportional tax. A progressive system is where benefits as a percentage of income fall as income increases. Simply put, if higher-income persons face a higher tax rate than lower-income persons the income tax system is progressive.

First, let us look at the employer pension system in terms of the regressivity of the benefits. Who receives a pension benefit and how much is it? Notably, in 1984, private pension income only accounted for 7 percent of total income to households containing a person over the age of 65, while Social Security provided 38 percent (Grad 1988: 94). For the average household (income between $10,000 and $19,999) with an aged head (65 and over), pensions provided 9 percent of all income, while Social Security provided 51 percent (Grad 1988: 95). In contrast, the highest-income elderly (households with more than $20,000 annual income) received a slightly smaller share of their income from pensions (their income share from asset earnings was almost twice the average), but their average pension was approximately twice the size of pensions going to the middle-income elderly.[4]

Private pension systems are largest for the elderly who need it least. Also, there is a great variation in the level of pension payments and in coverage. Although Social Security covers over 91 percent of the work force, the voluntary employer pension system does not come close to universal coverage. Between 1972 and 1987, the coverage rate for full-time workers actually fell from 50 percent for all private wage and salary workers to 47 percent in 1983 (Beller 1986: 105) and 46 percent in 1987 (Turner and Beller 1989: 397).

Coverage rates also differ greatly by industry. Almost all public sector employees are covered by a pension plan. Utility, communications, mining, manufacturing, and transportation have above-average coverage rates and retail trade and services have below-average coverage (Beller 1986; U.S. Bureau of the Census 1987; Employee Benefit Research Institute 1985: 93–113). In terms of the average worker, this uneven coverage is a bad sign, because the relatively uncovered industries are those with the fastest growing employment.

The average worker retiring with a pension in 1977 and 1978 (the latest comprehensive data available on distribution of benefits)[5] received an annual private pension benefit of $3,680; the median, however, was $2,650 (McCarthy 1986: 123). (Median income divides the group in half, 50 percent have benefit levels below the median and 50 percent have benefits above.) The mean pension in 1987 was estimated at $5,200 per year (Turner and Beller 1989: 5). Moreover, the distribution has a wide variance; one-fifth received benefits of less than $1,000 per year and almost one-fifth received more than twice as much as the median, sometimes much more. Three-fourths of retirees with pensions were men whose median pension was almost three times larger than the women's median. Only 8 percent of those who retired in 1977 or 1978 were nonwhites, but they had higher median pensions than whites. (What racial or ethnic group nonwhites are is not defined in the data set; see McCarthy 1986: 136.)

Among all the retirees who received pensions in 1977 or 1978, the median preretirement earnings (based on the last three years of employment) were $13,300. The average pension for this median group was approximately $3,080. Those whose preretirement income was more than 43 percent in excess of the median had pensions worth over 93 percent more than the median pension. Longer service alone cannot explain the big spread in pension incomes. The top preretirement income group only had four more years (15 percent more) of median service than the middle group (McCarthy 1986: 126).

Perhaps higher-income earners receive proportionally more pensions than average earners because they retire later. But age at retirement does not explain the spread; the median retirement age for both groups is 62 and the mean is 61. Examine table 4.1 to see how pension income widens the gap between the average income earner and the highest income earner. If plans were proportional to income, then the pension ratio would be equivalent to the income ratio. But pension plans and pension policy use

Table 4.1
Ratio of pension-related factors for the top earner and the median earner for recent retirees in 1977–1978

Pension factor	Ratio of top/median
Earnings while working (preretirement earnings)	1.43
Years of service	1.15
Retirement age	1.00
Pension amount	1.92

Source: McCarthy 1986: 123, table 1.

other factors, such as service and early retirement, to determine differences in pensions. If these were the only factors, then the differences in pensions should mirror differences in those factors. Instead we see, at least on the surface, that none of these pension-related factors fully explain the fact that pension income is skewed toward high-income earners.

The private pension system works to exacerbate the inequities already present in the labor market. The neoliberal politician and the neoclassical economist would explain this in terms of choices, which are greatly influenced by tax laws that give bigger tax breaks to high-income workers. One must assume that the top earner places a higher value on pensions than the average worker (Ippolito 1986b). Marxists would locate the existence of pension plans in the context of schemes to intensify production or lower labor compensation. An institutionalist presupposes that segmented labor markets and the structure of pensions explain the distribution of pension income. In segmented labor markets, in theory, almost every factor that distinguishes good jobs from bad is correlated with having a good pension plan. A good pension benefit requires a plan that is internally generous, and a good plan also depends on external factors such as favorable "pension-relevant" employment experiences including high pay, long service, full-time status, union representation, a large employer, and sufficient health to live long enough to collect a pension.

The connection between internal and external factors can be described in another way. The receipt of a small pension is difficult to interpret. A pension plan could be generous, yielding a large benefit for every year of service, but a person's employment experience may not have been sufficient to garner a generous pension. All workers could be covered by similar plans, but pension benefits would still differ because benefits depend on individual employment experiences such as service, earnings, and age of retirement (as is the case of Social Security). On the other hand, if all workers had the same employment experience, benefits would still vary because pension provisions differ greatly. In sum, pensions differ widely because the terms of a pension plan—the internal factors—vary enormously and the expected "pension-relevant" employment experiences differ by industry, occupation, size of firm—the external factors.[6]

Under the segmented market theory, the likelihood of bad employment experience is coupled with the likelihood an industry will have stingy plans. This means pension income would be more highly skewed than if markets worked according to the neoclassical theory of compensating wage differentials. This theory assumes that persons with low pay are compensated with higher pensions. If firms in sectors with the worst jobs (high turnover, low pay, and part-time jobs) compensated for the bad conditions with generous pension plans and firms with high-paid, long-term workers did not have to attract workers by offering generous pensions, then pension benefit levels and coverage would converge. But because markets are segmented, the worst plans are provided in the industries where workers have the worst pension-relevant employment experience. Pensions are complements to high wages rather than substitutes.

By crudely dividing persons who retired in 1977 and 1978 into two groups; the effects of employment characteristics and labor segmentation on the final benefit can be seen. The P group, which approximates a primary sector, consists of retirees from manufacturing and transportation industries and the S group, the secondary sector, comes from trade, services, and finance and real estate (FIRE). In 1978, the median preretirement earnings for group P retirees were 22 percent higher than the median for group S. (The ratio between the means is the same.) Group P's median and mean years of service were 31 percent higher than group S's, but the median pension for group P is over 200 percent higher than group S's (the mean is 153 percent higher.) Median earnings differed by a factor of one-fifth, service by one-third, and pensions differed by a factor of two (McCarthy 1986: 155).

This pattern holds when differences among all retirees are compared. The gaps among earnings, service, and age of retirement are smaller than the pension gap. Secondary sector workers consistently have worse pension-relevant experience than workers in primary sector industries. But differences in pension-relevant experience alone do not cause differences in pension income. Actually, private pension plans in the primary industries do not have more generous plans than firms in the secondary industries. McCarthy (1986: 147) evaluates the "generosity" of pension plans by calculating the replacement rate per year of credited service. This number is arrived at by dividing the mean replacement rate—the percentage of preretirement income replaced by the pension—by the mean years of credited service (the return per service year) (McCarthy 1986: 147). Credited years do not correspond with years of service in most cases.

In 1978, the ranking of industry pensions by generosity or rate of return per service year was not in accordance with the primary-secondary sector schema. For retirees just beginning to receive a pension in 1977 and 1978 the following pattern emerges: secondary industries, trade, and services exhibit the highest return per year of service, at 1.05 percent, manufacturing replaced 1.03 percent, transportation, communications, and utilities replaced 1 percent and FIRE is the lowest at .96 percent (McCarthy 1986: 155). Moreover, this ranking is not consistent when the pensions for all industry retirees at the time, not just those who retired in 1977 and 1978, are examined. For all retirees in 1978, manufacturing and FIRE replaced the same percentage of preretirement earnings at 1.16 percent. Trades and services replaced 1.09 percent per year of service, and transportation, communications, and utilities had the lowest rate, .76 percent (McCarthy 1986: 161).

This unexpected pattern prompts many questions. For example, why does FIRE have the lowest rate of generosity for new retirees and one of the highest for all retirees? One answer could be that new ERISA restrictions on vesting and eligibility might have affected FIRE more than the other industries if, in the past, banks and insurance companies extended pensions to a significantly larger group by reducing the generosity of the plans. Either there is no stable pattern of plan generosity across industries, or the "replacement rate per year of service" is not a reliable measure of plan generosity for other reasons.

In general, the replacement rate per year of service will be higher the more generous the benefit formula, but it is also higher if preretirement earnings are lower and there are fewer years of credited service. The rate also does not measure dispersion. The fact that the trade and services industries have the highest pension return per year of service may indicate that industries with the lowest-paid workers could have generous pension plans for the few employees who receive them. One cannot conclude that all workers in secondary industries have substandard pensions; some employees in these industries do well.

In trade and services, 12 percent of workers replaced over 50 percent of their incomes while in manufacturing only 3 percent did. The average retiree does much worse in secondary industries. One-half of retirees from primary sector plans replaced 25 percent of preretirement earnings, while one-half of secondary industry retirees replaced less than 15 percent of their earnings. To discover why pension plans vary more than earnings, an analysis of how pension plans work on a less aggregate basis, within sectors and within firms, is needed.

Internal Factors: How Do Pensions Affect Workers within a Plan?

The preceding analysis does not confirm the notion that polarization in the labor market means that high-status workers in high-status industries get the best pension benefits. Is there a causation that runs the other way? Pension plans seemingly contribute to the creation of "high-status" workers and the polarization of workers and total labor income.

The internal distribution of pensions depends on the plan structure and the structure of the work group. On the smallest scale, the plan level, plans that restrict the lowest-paid members from participating, or crediting service, will widen the gap between workers with the same years of service. Regressive formulas, which increase the replacement rate as earnings increase, also will widen the gap. Standard analysis measures regressivity on the basis of replacement rate, that is, pension income divided by preretirement income. Preretirement income is assumed to bear some relationship to payment to the pension fund. A true economic meaning of regressivity would have to take into account benefits per wage paid (or foregone) in exchange for the pension.

This is where theory helps because there is no direct measure of wages foregone. The theoretical analysis of pensions as insurance in imperfect markets suggests that pension plans may not serve as equalizing mechanisms, precisely because wages foregone, or the premiums paid, are not the same for all workers in the group.

Pension plans restrict participation eligibility by requiring a minimum number of years of service and full-time status. Age restrictions may also apply. The 1974 Employment Retirement Income Security Act allowed plans to restrict age eligibility to those twenty-one and over (age thirty in higher education). The 1984 Retirement Equity Act requires plans to include all full-time workers (those working more than 1,000 hours in a year) on the date of hire. These restrictions exclude newly hired workers (usually young and lower-paid) and part-time workers (usually female and low-paid). Thus these restrictions are one measure of the tendency of a pension plan to widen differences among workers. Secondary industries are more likely than those in the primary sector to have age and service requirements for plan coverage. On average, about 48 percent of all plans have restrictions on participation, but the percentage of plans with restrictions in the secondary industries ranges from 52 percent to 73 percent (Kotlikoff and Smith 1983: 176; Buchholtz 1989).

Benefit Formulas

One of the most regressive aspects of pension plan provisions is benefit formulas that favor high-income employees. Plans with regressive formulas constitute 32 percent of all defined-benefit plans. In 1977, most benefit formulas were based on earnings and service, although unions were much more likely to negotiate for formulas that are not related to earnings (64 percent of all union plans). Union plans constitute 13 percent of all defined-benefit plans but cover 60 percent of all participants (Kotlikoff and Smith 1983: 216).

Degree of regressivity is gleaned by simulating the experiences of hypothetical workers with thirty-five years of service and annual earnings ranging from $10,000 to $40,000, and then comparing the replacement rates (pension divided by the average earnings in the last three years of work) for each income group. Approximately 73 percent of all plans have proportional or regressive formulas; the replacement rate is higher, or the same, for high-income earners. A small percentage of plans, about 14 percent, is progressive, and the replacement rates are higher for low-income workers. The progressive benefits are explained by the high proportion of union plans that are not related to earnings—the so-called flat benefit related to service. These flat-benefit amounts are negotiated periodically to help pensions keep up with inflation. Progressive formulas are so-called flat-benefit formulas. The flat-benefit formula related to service pays a pension that is equal to a certain dollar amount multiplied by the number of years (or months) of service. Flat benefits not related to earnings or service proffer a set amount of pensions to all retirees.

Regressive formulas usually take the form of some kind of Social Security offset, or integrated, formula. Social Security integrated formulas work in slightly different ways, but essentially they deduct the workers' expected Social Security benefit from the firm's pension promise and the firm makes up the rest.[7] When Social Security benefits increase, the firm's share falls. And because Social Security benefits are progressive, meaning they replace a higher percentage of income for lower-income workers than for high-income workers, the employer pensions in these plans are the opposite; they replace more for high-income workers than for low-income workers.

Like average replacement rates per year of credited service, the extent of regressivity also does not fit the segmented labor market schema. Manufacturing and retail trades are less likely to have regressive benefit formulas, while a large proportion of plans in FIRE and in transportation, communications and utilities, have discriminating formulas, those that favor high-income workers. Large plans are least likely to have discriminating formulas (Kotlikoff and Smith 1986: 223).

Perhaps the largest determinant of a plan's progressivity is union status. Only 13 percent of defined-benefit plans are negotiated by unions, but 64 percent of those have progressive benefit structures, whereas only 15 percent of nonunion plans have progressive formulas (Kotlikoff and Smith 1983: 223). The proportion of participants in union plans is greater than the proportion of plans that are union negotiated, because union plans are larger than average. Table 4.2 classifies defined-benefit plan participants by the distributional effect of the plan's benefit formulas.

The replacement rates for each formula type are displayed in table 4.3. Although regressive formulas provide slightly higher pensions for low-income earners, they provide significantly higher pensions for high-income workers.

Benefit Formulas and Service

Another striking feature of some pension plans is the favorable bias for long-service workers and early retirees (Fields and Mitchell 1984; Lazear

Table 4.2
Percent of participants in defined-benefit plans by formula type and union status in 1978 (for hypothetical retirees with constant years of service[1])

Formula type	Percent of all participants	Percent of all union participants
Progressive[2]	42.8	59.0
Proportional[3]	11.6	7.7
Regressive[4]	31.9	14.9
Indeterminate and other	14.8	18.2
Total (rounded up or down)	100	100
Number of participants	28,481,524	16,994,014

1. Hypothetical worker is assumed to have thirty-five years of service and retiring at the plan's normal retirement age in 1977 (Kotlikoff and Smith 1983: 223).
2. Flat benefit based on service or on neither earnings or service.
3. Unit formula based on earnings or on earnings and service.
4. Social Security integrated plans (step rate or offset).

Table 4.3
Replacement rates and average pension of low- and high-income hypothetical earners in defined-benefit formulas (hypothetical retirees with constant years of service in 1978[1])

Formula	Replacement rates		Average pension 1977[2]	
	Level of earnings at normal retirement age			
	$10,000	$40,000	$10,000	$40,000
Progressive	26	7	$2,206	$8,825
Regressive	26	37	2,631	14,640
Proportional	23	23	2,523	2,523

1. Hypothetical worker is assumed to have thirty-five years of service and retiring at the plan's normal retirement age in 1977.
2. Participant weighted.
Source: Kotlikoff and Smith 1983: 223.

1983). Who do these features benefit? And why do most plans have defined benefits? What are the other pieces of the puzzle about formula distributional effects?

Formulas that are based on earnings and on service and earnings, approximately 78 percent of all defined-benefit plans, have a bias for long-service workers when earnings increase over time and benefits are based on the final years of salary, which most are. All non-union defined-benefit plans are based on earnings and service and 36 percent of union defined-benefit plans are based on earnings and service. Therefore, approximately 79 percent of all defined-benefit plans have some sort of long-term bias. This bias comes about because the vested benefit in each plan is based on the wage at the time of departure. Instead of having a pension based on forty years with an employer at a final salary, a peripatetic worker would have several pensions based on the same total of forty years, but at a variety of low salaries. Social Security avoids this bias by treating all employers the same. Fractional formulas that exist in an unknown number of plans constitute another bias. In these formulas a worker's pension is based on the fraction of years the person actually stayed with the employer, compared to the number of years until normal retirement age, usually sixty-five, at the age of hire. In other words, workers who leave the firm to retire, as opposed to younger workers who leave to work somewhere else, are rewarded. Do these provisions aid the dedicated secretary who stays on the job, or the high-income manager who remains with the firm?

One answer is that the disparity of tax savings by income group is exacerbated by these long-service biases (Congressional Budget Office

1987a). The tax gain for single people in the bottom income quartile retiring in 2019 is 1 percent, but for long-service workers with the same income it is 26 percent. For those in the highest quartile the tax gain is 9 percent for workers with less than twenty years of service and 29 percent for workers with the highest years of service. The Congressional Budget Office (1987a) concludes that this is because persons with long job tenure generally have higher incomes. Of course, this does not answer the question posed above: How does the long-service bias affect the plan's internal distribution of income?

These provisions attest to a strong favoritism benefiting long-service workers at any wage or salary. Ironically, the favoritism generally is not strong enough to affect a worker's decision to quit in search of another job during the first twenty or so years on the job (Gustman and Steinmeir 1989). The neoclassical interpretation of pensions rests on the notion that firms rewarded long-service workers in order to retain workers who learned valuable skills on the job. On the other hand, the generous provisions for early retirees prompted neoclassical speculation that firms wanted older workers to leave and make way for a fresh crop of employees. But 40 percent of defined-benefit plan participants can retire early based on their service, not on their age (Gustman and Steinmeir 1989: 9–10). The model of the pension contract as an efficient arrangement weighing labor costs against productivity may be too hollow, offering little resistance to the evidence of the actual structure of pension plans. At a Department of Labor conference on pensions in 1990, Emily Andrews, a prominent pension analyst, indicated that pension losses experienced by peripatetic workers do not worry her, as they reflect choices. This sentiment is certainly rooted in neoclassical soil, but it also reaches back to concerns about industrial feudalism and a celebration of worker mobility.

An historical and institutional view of pensions does better in explaining the favoritism toward long-service workers. Perhaps a lingering paternalistic attitude toward long-service workers, which harkens back to the early days of pensions, may also explain some of the bias toward long-service workers. The dedicated secretary and manager do better than the secretary and manager who leave before twenty years of service. But the difference between the two is not likely to be narrowed by membership in the same pension plan and equivalent degrees of dedication.

Defined-Contribution Plans and Internal Distribution

A notable trend in the world of pension plans since the passage of ERISA is the faster growth of defined-contribution plans than defined-benefit plans.

Defined-contribution plans place a certain amount (usually in terms of percentage of earnings) of monetary compensation into a fund that buys an annuity at the end of the employment, thus shifting the risk of fund performance onto the worker. An employer's contribution is straightforward, whereas the expected benefit depends on investment performance. In 1977, 77 percent of primary plans—the major plans—were defined-benefit plans covering 89 percent of participants, the remainder (less than 1 percent are neither) were defined-contribution plans. By 1983, coverage in defined-benefit plans fell to 70 percent of plans and 82 percent of participants, while defined-contribution plans grew to cover 29 percent of all plans and 17 percent of participants (R. Clark 1987).

Defined-contribution plans do have a distributional effect, but it is not as well studied as that for defined-benefit plans. Some defined-contribution plans are integrated with Social Security and have a regressive structure; firms contribute at one rate for earnings below a break point and at a higher rate (usually) for earnings above the break point. Break points usually have an historical relationship to the Social Security earnings base, but many are not as high as the Social Security maximum earnings base.

Defined-contribution plans are often driven by employer contributions, where the employer matches a worker's contribution. To the extent that higher-income workers save more, employers contribute relatively more on their behalf. Union defined-contribution plans (from the point of view of the employer) in multiemployer plans most often are related to earnings and service because the contribution is a flat rate per hour of work.

Other Internal Factors Affecting Distribution

In addition to formula structure, other internal factors influence the distribution of the final benefit among persons covered under the same plan with the same level of credited service. They are mortality, distribution of overtime, especially in the last few years of a career when pensions are based on hours of work or earnings, and deductions for leaves of absence, which may lower working mothers' and disabled workers' pension benefits. Until 1986, plans did not have to credit service before the age of twenty-two, or after the normal retirement age; those who started early could have up to five years of uncredited service. Part-timers could work part time for forty years and never collect a pension.

Federal law continues to regulate "discrimination" against low-paid workers in tax-favored fringe benefit plans. But the current structure of tax favoritism, the tax exempt status of employer pension contributions and pension fund earnings, skews the benefit structure in favor of higher-income individuals. The federal government subsidizes more of every pension dollar for a high-income earner than a low-income earner. Twenty-five percent of all couples in the highest income quartile who retire in 2019 will receive 46 percent of the tax gain from the tax expenditures for employer pensions (Congressional Budget Office 1987a). The bottom 25 percent will receive 9 percent. This is ironic. The very wedge the government uses to impose anti-discrimination rules against low-paid workers is a tool that benefits high-income workers more than low-income workers. Chapter 7 has a thorough discussion of the public policy implications. Here, the pertinent point is that pension regulation has a built-in bias against low-income workers, as well as a tolerance for plans that are highly regressive—those that exempt contingent workers, integrate Social Security plans, and have earnings-related formulas.

Women and Pensions

An enduring success of the women's movement has been the permanent imposition of a new point of view, of an ineluctable tendency to ask of all social problems: how does this affect women? In 1981, the first issue of a newsletter, *Women and Pensions*, was published, partially funded by the Ms. Foundation. It was part of the Women's Pension Project, which provided technical assistance to women's groups, operated an information clearing-house, and organized workshops and seminars. The project led to a focus on aging as a women's issue; after all, 62 percent of all people over the age of sixty-five are women and 64 percent of those over seventy are female. Policymakers and analysts had to face the gender consequences in all pension areas (Grad 1988: 1). Women are one identifiable group that benefits least from the marriage-related and employment-related pension system.

In 1984, women working full-time earned sixty-two cents for every dollar a man earned (Bergmann 1986: 67) but received on average fifty-four cents for every dollar in pensions a man received. This ratio compares men and women who receive pensions; however, the likelihood of women receiving any benefit is smaller, so that women receive 22 percent of all pension income and men receive 78 percent. In contrast, women receive 34 percent of Social Security income (U.S. Bureau of the Census 1987: 9). The sex-pension inequality grows larger as the importance of each level of pension-status becomes more meaningful. Sixty-seven percent of working women are eligible to participate in a public or private plan compared to 70 percent of male workers who are eligible, and women's coverage is 94 percent of men's. However, only 48 percent of all women workers actually participate in a plan compared to 61 percent of men who do, so women's rate of participation is 79 percent of men's. Only 32 percent of women workers, compared to 43 percent of men, are vested and eligible for future benefits; the vesting gap is 74 percent (U.S. Bureau of the Census 1987: 2).

The sex-pension inequity is caused by factors both external and internal to pension plans. Externally, women are less likely to be covered because they are extensively employed in generally noncovered, secondary industries. The plans that do exist in these industries are more likely to have minimum age and service requirements for eligibility, which tend to exclude women because of their employment behavior; more frequently they are found in part-time status, or working for a smaller employer. So that even when women and men are in the same industry, men are more likely to be covered and vested. For example, 51 percent of men in wholesale trade were covered, while only 26 percent of women were (Miller 1988).

Former House of Representatives member Geraldine Ferraro, just before being nominated as Democratic candidate for vice president, celebrated the passage of her sponsored legislation, the Retirement Equity Act (REACT) of 1984. This legislation embodied many of the changes in ERISA sought by the Women's Pension Project and other advocacy groups. Among other things, REACT lowered mandatory eligibility rules and vesting standards. Unfortunately, according to a 1980 study, these aspects of pension plans were not the most important factors in causing the pension-sex gap. One external factor, the fact that women's employers tend not to provide pensions, and one internal factor, the widespread use of regressive formulas, were the most significant factors in causing women to receive fewer benefits than men. These reasons were more important than women's higher probability of turnover, eligibility restrictions, or part-time status (Cohen 1983). In fact, REACT probably will put more money into men's pockets than women's. This perverse result demonstrates how deficient understanding of the internal workings of a pension contract can mislead policy solutions, or mistake their likely result.

Distributional equity in pension plans needs to be analyzed on a deeper level, deeper because distribution cannot be measured as easily, or as accurately as is the case when examining pension benefits received by income class or industrial sector. To assert that women do not receive enough in pension benefits is easier than determining if women get as much as they pay for; in other words, do women get their fair share of pension benefits? In order to look at both sides—the payment and benefit side—of an income transfer, or an income insurance scheme, one needs an analytical framework, a description, a notion about what the nature of the contract is—how something is exchanged for something else.

A Theory about the Pension Contract

The 1974 ERISA legislation entitled workers to a plethora of information about their pension plans: documents the company sponsors file with the IRS, the actuarial statements, the accountants' reports. For the first time, an accessible, formal, and written plan document had to be filed with the Department of Labor and the Internal Revenue Service (IRS). The provisions were viewed as steps toward curbing the practice of firms and plans arbitrarily doling out pensions to a select few retirees (as well as pension funds to a select few investments and investors) and to provide information so workers can better plan for retirement by anticipating their pension income. The "buyer beware" approach to consumer activism and the "worker's right to know" approach to such things as occupational health and safety are consistent with the information and disclosure provisions in ERISA. Legislating the dissemination of information helps temper the need to regulate. The government's requirement that pension eligibility and funding status be public knowledge is a significant change from the informal plans of the early part of the century when employers declared the amount of a pension on the day of retirement.

Superficially, the existence of a pension contract that specifies the rules everyone must abide by in order to receive a pension seems fair. Everyone knows the requirements and every worker in the plan is governed by them. But what do people give up in being covered under the plan and receiving a certain promise? Do certain kinds of workers, distinguished by earnings or employment status, give up different amounts? Does everyone give up a "fair" amount of wages for their pension promise? The answers to these questions depend on how the pension contract is made.

Fairness is subjective; how to estimate payment for every dollar received is objective. A structure wherein every worker gives up the same proportion of wages for each dollar of pension would be a proportional structure. A progressive contract is one where workers give up more wages as income increases for every dollar of pension received. A regressive-benefit structure means workers give up a smaller proportion of earnings as income increases for a dollar amount of pensions. This could happen if higher-income workers paid less for every dollar of pension or forewent the same amount as pensions increased. A very regressive system would be one where not only do workers pay less as incomes increase, but pensions increase with earnings. This would mean that pensions (for the same year of service) would have a higher pension-to-payment ratio as earnings increased. Which structure is preferable is not a concern here; the issue addressed is that the structure is obfuscated by the peculiar nature of a defined-benefit pension plan.

Directly determining the true economic progressivity of a defined-benefit plan is not possible. The wages workers may give up in exchange for a future defined-benefit pension (from a plan that is not funded by specific employer contributions) are not measured directly. An analytical framework is needed to estimate whose wages are given up for what benefits.

Who Pays What for the Pension Promise?

The analytical framework that best describes the pension system is an insurance model. Pension plans are not savings plans; one is entitled to a pension based on experience and membership, not contributions or premiums paid. The premium structure and payout rules can be structured in favor of high-income workers, a select few. Employer-provided pensions could be the most regressive element in the labor compensation packages of U.S. workers.

Employer-provided pensions are insurance plans fashioned in the labor market—a market whose outcome depends on information and power. Workers with the most information and bargaining power generally do better in the labor market than those with less. Experience with pension plans is no different. Workers with the most bargaining power and information will tend to pay less for a pension promise than those with less information and bargaining power. For union plans, the bargaining environment will largely determine the distribution of information and market power among workers and between workers and employers. In nonunion plans, bargaining power is more individualized. One consequence, as we saw in table 4.2, is that nonunion plans are more likely to have regressive formulas than union plans.

The dominant framework policymakers use to understand pension contracting is the neoclassical theory of compensating wage differentials. The framework is used to answer the question, what do workers and firms pay for a pension promise? According to the compensating wage differential theory, under conditions of perfect information and competitive labor markets, what workers forego for their pensions is just that amount that would make workers indifferent between one more dollar of pension and one more dollar of wages.[8] Firms save on labor costs by providing a benefit workers tend to overvalue. Some workers may tend to overvalue their pension plan more than others; thus, they demand less wages than they should. This group subsidizes the pensions of others. In addition, the annual cost of a particular promise to the employer can vary according to actual assumptions and funding methods. Pensions are sources of flexibility for the firm in hiring, negotiating labor contracts, and the ability to make corporate financing decisions.

Pensions are also a source of flexibility and survival resources for unions. By bargaining for pensions, unions reaffirm their ability to deliver valuable non-wage programs with the great benefit of having the costs paid for on an installment plan. Defined-benefit pension promises are like home mortgages; the promise of owning a home is costed at a particular dollar amount per year. Unions also can use pensions to attract and retain union members. Pensions are a variable in bargaining and are an organizing tool.

The value of a pension promise won in bargaining is determined simultaneously by individual workers' perceptions, the union's interpretations, the employer's strategies, and the actuary's instructions and legal restrictions. It is much more vague and flexible than, say, a 5 percent increase in wages.

The institutional analysis of pensions as unfair insurance contracts rests on the notion that the costs and benefits of a pension promise are vague and flexible. Unlike other aspects of employee compensation, the cost of the pension promise can vary widely, while the value of the promise to the worker remains stable.

There are two values (at least) of a pension promise: the employer's valuation of the cost of a pension promise and the worker's valuation of the benefit. The employer's cost of promising one dollar of a defined benefit promise is a function of various factors: the managerial and actuarial practices in funding the plans and the employment and demographic characteristics of the workers in the plans. Pension-related employment experiences are length of job tenure, salary profiles, morbidity, and mortality. Employer's defined-benefit pension costs can vary according to inflation and its relationship to salary growth, years of service of the group, fund performance, future increases in Social Security, and other contingencies that determine pension costs. Employers have little control over some of these contingencies—inflation, mortality, morbidity (to some extent), and workers' attachment to the firm—and more control over others——funding status, salary growth, and layoffs.

Workers' estimations of their pension promises depend on the information available and their employment and demographic characteristics. These characteristics can affect the workers' calculations and proclivities to base decisions on these calculations and how workers value future income. Because individuals have cognitive dissonance, people tend to overvalue their benefit. When people are asked to estimate their probability of death, termination, sickness, or injury, the result will likely be rosy and pension expectation relatively large. If people adjust for inflation when making their calculations their estimates will be larger than their employer's, which do not include inflation adjustments.[9] Moreover, the workers' calculation problems are made worse if the plan is difficult to understand, the employer or union misrepresents the plan, or workers do not take into account the firm's ability to terminate the fund.

There is no reason to believe that the employer's and the employee's estimate will be the same, nor that two workers with similar characteristics will have the same value for the same pension promise. Management and the union (where relevant) do not only collect information from workers and each other, they provide information and seek to influence opinions and knowledge. Unless the union is very sophisticated and well-staffed, management provides all the cost estimates of even the union's proposed amendments to the plan.

A personal experience illustrates the most benign form of pension information problems. In 1987 I asked a steelworkers' bargaining committee in northwestern Indiana to calculate the pension due a hypothetical worker under their pension plan. All of the members of the bargaining committee were union officials who had considerable bargaining experience and relations with management were extremely good. All seven members had different estimations of the hypothetical pension. They acknowledged that retiring members had complained that their final benefits were not what they had expected, but the union always deferred to the personnel manager's calculations.

The employer's information about the pension to union members rarely reports the employer's present cost; the information usually contains projected benefits based on unrealistic job-experience assumptions for many workers, especially those with high turnover rates. The employer can also create a gap between the workers' estimations and the real costs by eroding the funding standards of the plan. This aspect of moral hazard, changing funding standards, is discussed in chapter 5.

The Uses of Ignorance

How does the asymmetric distribution of bargaining power, information, and cognitive dissonance affect the distribution of pension benefits? The environment in which pension contracts are made allows an employer, union, or regulator to provide pensions to a select group, for whatever reasons—encouraging specially trained workers to stay with a firm, encouraging loyal, hardworking service, or currying political loyalty. Employer pensions allow a firm to have lower costs if the risk-sharing community, the community that bears the burden, the risk, that some workers will retire without adequate income, is large, but the number of beneficiaries is small.

Pension experts Merton and Joan Bernstein (1988: 125) summed up the inadequacies of the voluntary pension plan system's ability to provide income security:

Who will be the winners and losers can be guessed roughly. Likely winners are in the group of those who have the best jobs for most of their working lives, or at least for long periods just preceding retirement (the period that one can least foresee), who are employed in stable companies or stable industries, whose personal health holds up, whose own skills remain in demand, who command good pay, and who make or influence their enterprises' decisions about pensions. Likely losers are those with the least control over their economic fate, the less well paid, nonunion employees, large groups of minority workers and women, part-time workers (again with overrepresentation of women and minorities), and those with jobs in unstable and or rapidly changing industries, companies, and regions.

Beneficiaries can be limited to the select group if members of the group have unequal power or distorted information. If the characteristics that would tend to lower the costs to the employer of covering a certain worker—high morbidity, low salary growth, low length of job tenure—are related to reasons a particular person would overvalue their promise, or to reasons why a person would not be in a position to protest, then an employer can redistribute pension benefits among workers without incurring rancor, or wreaking havoc. If there are two groups of workers and the demographic and employment characteristics of one group are such that the actuarial cost of promising one dollar per year of pension to that type is less than for the other type (for example, because they are women and will not stay as long on the job, or they are part-time and seasonal workers) the employer will adopt a pension plan that exploits the overvaluation of that group. The group could have less bargaining power.

If all workers miscalculate the value of the pension, or are forced to accept less than the maximum amount the employer is willing to pay, then the employer pays less for the supply of labor services from workers and the employer will pay less than if labor remuneration was only wages. The subsidy goes to the employer. A firm can compensate an entire group of workers for less than the maximum it is willing to pay when pensions are provided and workers tend to overvalue their pension or firms have some monopsony power. Unions may encourage this overvaluation to avoid a strike, maintain an ongoing relationship with the employer, or distribute benefits to certain workers.

For example, low-income workers, aware of their needs to supplement Social Security, may value their promise more generously than their employer because of cognitive dissonance or because they do not perceive the high turnover assumption the employer is using to estimate their pension. Cognitive dissonance could be worse among low-income workers, who have less choice than the employer, than among high-income workers who do have a choice among employers. In these cases, the employer's low cost is correlated with a high-employee estimation.

Survey data show that workers often make crucial mistakes when asked to describe their pension plans and estimate their worth. The President's Commission on Pension Policy (PCPP), formed by the Carter administration in 1979, surveyed workers and their employers and actuaries about the worth of each worker's pension promise. After it proved too difficult to collect three estimations, the PCPP decided to rely on the worker's estimation. Table 4.4 shows this reliance was a big methodological mistake. Worker estimations were higher than those of the employer or actuary.

The workers' evaluation of their projected benefits—the amount expected if a worker stayed with the firm until retirement—is 77 percent higher than the employer's estimate. (The estimation requires salary assumptions if the benefit is based on salary.) Worker evaluations of accrued benefits—those that would have to be paid if the plan terminated immediately, and which are based on past service—are four times greater

Table 4.4
Asymmetric estimations between workers, actuaries, and employers, 1980

Variable	Sample size	Mean ratio
Worker-employer projected benefit	49	1.77
Worker-actuary accrued (legal) benefit	46	4.31
Worker-employer accrued (legal) benefit	22	1.21

Sources: President's Commission on Pension Policy 1981; Ghilarducci 1984.

than the actuary's estimate, but only 22 percent higher than the employer's estimate. On average, it is estimated that the accrued benefit is one-half of the projected benefit. Therefore, at the time of termination, the average pension plan participant is estimated to receive about 50 percent of his or her projected benefit and 25 percent of what he or she expected at the time of termination. This is important, because the 1.6 million individuals who experienced a plan termination were paid an actuary's determined benefit, regardless of what the employer believed workers would get.

After controlling for union status, tenure on the job, and education in regression analysis, I found that women were more likely to overvalue their benefits than men. This is not because women are more optimistic about their retirement income; in fact, women are more likely to feel their overall retirement income will be inadequate (Ghilarducci 1984). Women's over-valuation of their employer benefits must be due to either their overestimation of their eventual service and earnings, or a distortion of information that stems from the plan itself. Cynthia Cohen (1983) found that women's disproportionate coverage in Social Security integrated plans explained why women's pensions were smaller than men's. In integrated plans employers promise a certain benefit; only the fine print reveals that Social Security is deducted from that promise. The fact that firms end up providing less of the final pension than they promise under Social Security integrated plans means that people in these plans (disproportionately women) tend to overestimate the employer's share.

Olivia Mitchell (1988) has also shown, using a more recent survey from the Federal Reserve Bank, that many workers do not know crucial details about their pension plans, such as what type they have and other pertinent rules. Unfortunately, the survey Mitchell used also presumed workers could value their pension accurately.

Ignorance and the distribution of ignorance matters. If some people have a propensity to overvalue their pension plans, then those people who trade off pensions for wages are making disadvantageous trades; for instance, women and workers with less-than-expected tenure are giving up too much in wages for coverage in a pension plan (Ghilarducci 1990).

In summary, if workers tend to overvalue their pension plans and have different degrees of market power, then employers with pensions can have the same labor supply with less labor costs than if they only paid wages. There is nothing surprising in this conclusion. It is merely the transfer between parties that takes place in a group insurance plan where information and bargaining power determine who will be harmed by conditions of moral hazard.

Union Success and Limitations in Curbing Pension Moral Hazard

The "business" union—one that bargains for improved working conditions, pay, and protection from employer exploitation—has a particular, preordained role in pension bargaining. This genre of union seeks to increase benefits and attempts to curb moral hazard. To some extent, this is what unions have actually done with regard to pensions, although union pension strategy has mainly been reactive to company initiatives. Many of the newly organized large employers in the 1930s and 1940s already had pension plans in place: the telephone company, utilities, and basic manufacturing. Not until workers struck over the right to negotiate over their employers' pension plans and the Supreme Court in 1949 deemed pensions mandatory subjects of bargaining did unions have a significant say in the structure of their employer pension plans.

Indeed, unions have made a mark on employer pensions. Union plans have a significantly more progressive benefit structure, which reflects union's compressing effect on pay in general. Unions reduce moral hazard somewhat by curbing the firings and layoffs of older workers through which firms intend to lower pension costs. Moreover, unions recently have succeeded in negotiating a say in plan termination decisions. Unions, notably the UAW, have taken pains to gain expertise in pension matters. (For many years the UAW was the only union to have a staff actuary, who often helped other unions.) The AFL-CIO education department and George Meany Center sponsors programs to teach negotiators the rudiments of pension plan design and funding.

Forty years ago, large industrial unions wanted a more proactive role in the employer pension system. They sought joint control of pension funds in the 1940s but met powerful employer resistance. Lack of union strength and information can prevent the union from restraining the moral hazard. Realizing the limitations of their own knowledge and power, the labor movement, somewhat united, supported aggressive federal pension regulation and declared the passage of ERISA a victory for unions and labor. This legislation, which requires minimum standards that unions otherwise would have to negotiate, potentially makes pension bargaining easier (though most collectively bargained plans had, by 1974, met ERISA-required funding standards and vesting and service rules).

But, as discussed in chapter 3, describing the role of unions in the employer pension system as one of minimizing moral hazard by providing information and exerting bargaining power would not take into account the inherent complexities. Sometimes, to meet other goals, unions have to take advantage of the moral hazard, to build a strategy around the vagueness and flexibility of the benefit promise and the cost of a promise.

My regression analysis indicates that unions do not significantly affect the accuracy of a worker's valuation of her or his employer pension. Unions have reasons to keep the valuation of the pension promise vague. Unions may want to cater to senior workers, because they are more loyal union members and are more active in the union (this is similar to Freeman's observation). Unions also need to survive as voluntary political organizations. A union survives by settling contracts and maintaining a stable relationship with the employer. Because of the ambiguity surrounding pension estimation, a contract with pension provisions can look more lucrative than it is (Root 1982).

The ambiguity may serve union's interest at times, but information and accuracy are most often under the control of employers. ERISA requires employers to provide pension plan information to the union (often with a two-year lag) regarding the funding decisions made, but only the most sophisticated unions are able to ascertain whether the funding was sufficient. The interest rate assumption, amortization decisions, and so on, are rarely discussed at the negotiating table and are the responsibility of the company experts. The company is also the agent that has the bulk of the responsibility to explain the plan's provisions to workers. In order to deflate expectations about pension benefits, the union could launch its own education program, separate from the personnel department, but the discussion in this chapter and the environment of collective bargaining suggest that this would be a time-consuming, expensive endeavor and would be construed by management as hostile. Moreover, workers would regard the bearer of bad news—the union—with suspicion.

In seeking national legislation unions recognized the structural limitations and contradictions in their own enforcement of the pension plan contract. Almost 60 percent of pension participants are in union pension plans. This means pension plans are crafted in a political economy that is only remotely related to a market where individual workers determine the trade-off between pensions and wages.

Moral Hazard in Defined-Benefit and Defined-Contribution Plans

Would pension moral hazard disappear if all employer-provided pensions converted into defined-contribution plans? Defined-contribution plans are much simpler to administer, the contribution rate is clearly defined, the relationship between the fund's earnings and expected benefits is in plain view. The information problems for defined-contribution plans are much less prevalent than for defined-benefit plans. So, why do firms and unions prefer defined-benefit plans? Why do unions and firms worry legislators each time pension reform is introduced about detrimental effects on defined-benefit plans?

"Peace of mind," "security," and "protection from risk" are common phrases used to answer these questions. Economists have argued that workers prefer defined-benefit plans because workers know exactly what their pensions will be when they retire, and that their dependence on the final years of salary in defined-benefit plans will help adjust the pension to wage and price inflation. They argue that defined-benefit plans exist because employers are less averse to risk than workers and workers prefer defined-benefit plans to defined-contribution plans.[10]

The choice of the structure of employer pensions does not, however, reside with the worker. When the unions lost their bid in the 1940s to jointly control single-employer defined-benefit plans, unions most often chose to bargain for benefits and allow employers to administer and bear the risk of financial uncertainty. Economists have gone to great lengths to demonstrate that this reality can be explained in individual-based theory. Union leaders are less ethereal in describing the prevalence of defined-benefit plans. They argue that if employers control the fund they should bear the risk of malperformance. If the workers bore the risk, employers would have little incentive to administer the plan with care.

Ironically, the most frequent and fatal risks to pensions have been those that are not protected by being a defined-benefit plan and are not borne by the employer. In the last forty years, pension plans mainly have been curtailed or terminated, not because of poor investment performance, but because of poor management and other factors leading to bankruptcies and mergers. These costs have been borne entirely by workers and the government insurance plan covering pensions, the Pension Benefit Guaranty Corporation (PBGC).

The distributional features of defined-contribution plans are not as well studied as those of defined-benefit plans. Yet, many defined-contribution plans have Social-Security-inspired, step-rate contribution schemes that usually are regressive. Contributions are made at one rate up to a certain earnings amount and then are increased for earnings over that amount. For many plans the earnings level approximated the earnings cutoff for Social Security taxes. Defined-contribution vesting and eligibility restrictions can also have the similar, but milder, distributional effects as those in the defined-benefit plans, in regard to favoring long-term workers. The informational advantages are not so large that they overwhelm asymmetric power relationships.

Firms prefer defined-benefit plans partly because of the capacity to reward a select group of employees for long-term service. Pension economists have called this reason "incentive effects" (Bodie et al. 1988; Kotlikoff 1988). The defined-benefit form is more desirable to paternalistic firms, which operate under a feudalistic or manorial model of employee relations (Kerr 1954). The firm promises a benefit; it heroically guarantees it in the face of vagaries of the investment markets. A defined promise adds a benevolent mystery to the provision of the pension. In contrast, the defined-contribution plan is crass in its bold revelation of how much an employer pays to fund the plan. Even before unions negotiated benefits, firms sponsored defined-benefit pension plans. Industrial unions generally have gone along with the scheme and negotiate for improvements in the promise of the single-employer defined benefit.

Portable Pensions, SEPs, and Distributional Equity

In 1987, the Committee for Education and Labor in the House of Representatives held hearings to consider portable pensions in response to pension plan terminations, women's lack of coverage, and inadequate retirement income. Bipartisan support for portable pension legislation emerged in 1986, with bills sponsored by Representative William Clay (D, Pennsylvania) and J. Danforth Quayle (R, Indiana).

Portability is not a highly controversial topic. Many employees have portable plans: university and college professors in Teachers Insurance and Annuity Association-College Retirement Equities Fund (TIAA-CREF), construction workers, mine workers, and so on. The debate is whether portable plans should be made mandatory or be based on a voluntary scheme with tax-break carrots. The PCPP showed renewed interest in the European model for mandatory pension coverage in 1981. The PCPP's proposal was to require firms to contribute 3 percent of earnings per year into a portable pension plan. This would differ from Social Security because workers could plan when to spend the account with a tax penalty. A portable pension system would be more like a forced savings account than a pension plan, especially for lower-income workers who are more likely to use savings for emergencies and other purchases, rather than retirement.

The tax laws have set up a system of voluntary portable "pensions." The experience of these plans should reveal something about what a mandatory portable pension system should avoid. What problems are inherent to the pension idea, or to the voluntary status? In a voluntary world where persons receive tax breaks for contributing to a "portable pension" plan, the retirement income scheme becomes more biased in favor of the highest income earners, especially because they shelter a much larger percentage of their income from tax.

Since 1978, employers could set up portable pension plans, called Simplified Employee Pension plans. The law attempts to prevent sheltering too much income from tax, or benefiting high-income workers by limiting firm and worker contributions each to 15 percent of income or $30,000, whichever is less. For the majority of firms with less than twenty-five employees, the restrictions are less because employees can supplement the firm contribution—up to 15 percent of earnings. This means the tax expenditures are regressive; the higher earner gets a larger proportional tax break for every dollar deferred from tax. A manager earning many times more than her or his secretary can defer the same percentage amount at a higher-income tax rate. For small companies the tax incentives are even more regressive, since the manager is more likely than the secretary to afford to save 15 percent of his or her income.

For example, a manager in a small firm who earns ten times more than his secretary (not an unusual ratio), $200,000 compared to $20,000 per year, can have tax-deferred contributions equaling 30 percent of his income (officially 15 percent from the firm, 15 percent from his earnings), a total of $60,000. His secretary probably will not contribute because of her low income, so the firm will put 15 percent of her income into a Simplified Employee Pension (SEP), a total of $3,000. The manager will save $16,800 (assuming the firm would have paid its share to him in the form of wages) and his secretary will save $450 in taxes (this assumes the manager pays 28 percent income tax and the secretary pays 15 percent). The manager earns ten times more than his secretary, but the tax incentives for pension plans allow him to save thirty-seven times more in taxes.

Now, let us say that the secretary and her boss both face an unexpected property tax hike. The secretary has no extra funds and must cash in some of her SEP to pay taxes, while her boss is able to pay the extra taxes out of spending income. She saved $450 by contributing $3,000 to her SEP, but had to pay 25 percent (15 percent plus a 10 percent penalty) on any income withdrawn. She had to take $1,250 out of her SEP to pay a $1,000 property tax bill and ended up paying $250 in taxes. She ends up with a tax break of only $200, which is eighty-four times less, instead of thirty-seven times less, than her boss's tax savings, because her lower income did not have a cushion for unexpected expenditures.

The advantages of the SEP are that everyone is covered and can take her or his money at the point of departure with the firm. The pension does not tie the employee to the firm as much as a voluntary employer-based pension does. A mandatory pension system that specifies a fixed-percentage contribution does eliminate much of the moral hazard in pension plans due to the asymmetric distribution of bargaining power and information. But if workers can cash their funds in at will and the tax benefits increase as income increases, then the goals for a progressive or proportional retirement income security policy are more difficult to attain.

In the spring of 1991, Secretary of Labor Lynne Martin proposed to expand SEPs to firms of all sizes to simplify plan administration. The plan is called POWER (Pension Opportunties for Workers Expanded Retirement). Under the plan, workers can contribute $4,200 annually before tax and firms can match that amount up to $2,100.

Critics claim that the proposal does not go far enough because the system is voluntary. Representative William Ford (D, Missouri), Chair of the House Education and Labor Committee, commented on POWER as follows:

No one has ever been able to create a proposal that was truly portable. . . . The only thing that comes close is Social Security and only because it is mandated. (U.S. Bureau of National Affairs, 1991)

Outcomes and Contradictions: Toward a Mandatory Pension System

The pension system is stubbornly regressive when viewed from the perspective of the labor force as a whole. Pension benefits are more skewed than earnings and relevant labor market experience, such as years of service or retirement age. I used a metaphor to describe the contracts workers make with firms when covered by company-sponsored pension plans. Pension plans are insurance and deferred wages are premiums. For the system to work well and fairly, workers need objective estimates of the probabilities of the disasters that can, and will, befall them and affect their pension benefits—death, layoff, firing, injury, fund termination, plant closings, even quitting. Workers are overly optimistic about the size of their eventual benefit and employers are not neutral insurers. A fair insurance contract also requires that no party can change the contract after it is made. In pensions it is the insurer, the employer, who can change the contract after it is made, by decreasing funding levels or reneging on implied salary growth. What is moral hazard from the point of view of the pension contract is good business from the point of view of the corporate finance department.

According to the insurance model of pensions, firms want pensions because they can be used to divide the work force and the existence of moral hazard makes pension plans flexible forms of labor compensation. Therefore, pension coverage will fall as firms have less need to divide workers and less ability to exploit moral hazard. In Marxist terms, this phenomenon can be explained as a consequence of the changes in the social relations of production, where the segmentation of the labor force becomes more entrenched and unions less empowered.

The fact that pensions may be the most regressive aspect of labor compensation, and that they are a small portion of total retirement income, will cause pressure for more government regulation, especially if pension plans are a means by which women and minorities subsidize higher-paid men within a work force and are a huge tax loss for federal revenues. The IRS regulations, which originated in the 1920s, and legislation such as 1974 ERISA, the 1984 Retirement Equity Act, and the Pension Reform Act of 1987 sought, in part, to expand coverage and limit the grossest regressive redistributional elements in pension plans.

Furthermore, there has never been any trend toward universal coverage under a pension system that supplements Social Security. The industries that did not provide pensions in the 1940s have shown no signs of expanding pensions now.

The President's Commission on Pension Policy (1981) recommended a mandatory defined-contribution private pension system. The proposal called for the employer to contribute a flat-rate amount (the PCPP proposed 3 percent of salary) to an account that could only be used for retirement benefits. The contribution would be mandatory, so it would automatically be portable. Workers in certain industries already have these types of plans, but the portability is restricted to certain industries. In addition, 91 percent of all U.S. workers are covered by a similar plan already—the Social Security system. Social Security financing has one crucial difference. It is not advance-funded (except for the retirement trust fund surplus accumulated in the late 1980s and 1990s for baby boom retirees). When the valuations of the insurer (the company) and insuree (the worker) are very different, the mandatory pension system proposal would make occupational pensions proportional in terms of contributions and eliminate the moral hazard inherent in this form of social insurance.

A long history of private social insurance in the United States and entrenched interests in the voluntary pension system stand in the way of an ideal pension system. A universal tier of pensions, one that is occupation-ally related and supplements Social Security, would be more equitable and would serve most workers better than the current private-public mix. If a new Social Security system is advance-funded and administered by a public board of investors, it would go a long way toward solving the capital market worries over eliminating the tax benefits for employer pensions.

Concerns over the pension system's inadequate coverage persisted throughout the 1980s, but the capital market dimension of the private pension system almost overwhelmed the interest in pension benefits, in favor of interest in pension funds themselves.

5   Corporate Uses of Pension Funds

"Most employers try to do the right thing," remarked Karen Ferguson, director of the Pension Rights Center.[1] Ferguson's assessment is noteworthy because she directs an organization that each month receives hundreds of letters and calls from workers, pensioners, and their advocates—Ralph Nader, the American Association of Retired Persons, unions, and private attorneys. The Center fields questions and complaints that range from the dismay of a retired garment worker who receives $100-a-month pension benefit for thirty years of employment, to concern from lumberworkers that their pension plan will terminate, to suspicions of a plumber about unwise and illegal investments made by his pension fund trustees. Although most employers attempt to meet legal and moral obligations involved in the pension contract, the employer-based system, at the very least, causes anxiety and a demand for legal and advocate vigilance.

Doing the "right" thing is increasingly complex: Using pension funds to do right for the shareholders is becoming more and more in conflict with what is right for employees. And when pension contributions and earnings are tax exempt, a manager must do the right thing in the eyes of the Treasury department and the IRS.

The structure of pension plans and the distribution of pensions in the labor market leads to the highest-paid workers receiving the best pensions and the lowest-paid workers receiving little or none. According to bargaining theory, this distribution results from a situation where power and information are not distributed equally among workers. This asymmetric distribution of information and power can also lead to a transfer of income from workers to firms. When workers do not share information and do not have enough power to offset the ability of employers to change the pension contract after it is made, then workers will forego more wages for the pension actually received. In theory, workers without sufficient power or information could transfer the value of their productivity to more-favored or more-empowered managers and executives, or to shareholders, through their pension plans.

Pension Contracts and Firm Default

What are the mechanics of this transfer? A firm does not usually lower pension benefits directly, by explicitly worsening the generosity of the benefit formula, vesting, and participation requirements. But defined-benefit pensions are peculiar institutions. Often the worth of a pension, such as periodic cost-of-living adjustments for retirees, is an implicit part of the written pension contract. Intangibles such as security and safety become tangible only when the dangers of termination and default are explicit.

From an individual's point of view, pensions exist in a nether world of contingent claims where the unforeseeable, the unthinkable, and the unpleasant are not predicted, considered, and confronted. To assess the real value of one's defined-benefit pension promise a person must accurately predict the time of one's own health, death, firing or layoff, spouse's mortality and morbidity, the future of the firm, inflation, macroeconomic growth, and the strength and integrity of the firm's attachment to its workers. The contingencies upon which the pension promise depend are vast and determine the actual value of any particular defined-benefit promise. Because pension plans are essentially voluntary, an important determinant of the value of the pension benefit is the commitment firms have to their work force.

When Random House publishers bought Crown Books in 1989, the Crown pension plan was terminated, as were several long-service employees. A fired veteran of Crown consoled herself with the expectation that her lump-sum pension payment would be enough for a down payment on a New York City condominium. Instead, she received two months' severance pay and a $4,000 pension disbursement for sixteen years of service. It was not until the time of our interview that she heard an explanation of the principles of present value discounting and why the lump-sum payment was so much less than she expected.[2]

The mergers and acquisitions activity of the 1970s and 1980s and the global restructuring of U.S. business have permanently changed the nature of a firm's attachment to its work force and the integrity of the pension promise. The pension problem of the occasional failed firm of the 1950s and 1960s is insignificant (except in steel) compared to the problems caused by corporate restructuring. The loyalty aspect of pensions has switched focus;

no longer is it worker loyalty to the firm that is at issue, but a firm's loyalty to its worker.

The rash of terminations of healthy pension plans since the 1980s, a phenomenon often triggered by a corporate takeover or leveraged buyout (Mitchell and Mulherin 1989), represents the kind of drastic shortening of the relationship between some firms and their workers that changes the nature of the pension contract. Over 12,000 defined-benefit plans have terminated in the thirteen-year period between 1975 and 1989, which is more than the number terminated in the twenty-four-year period between 1950 and 1974 (Ippolito 1986a). The largest number of terminations occurred in 1985 and the greatest amounts of money reverted to their corporate sponsors in the following year. In 1986, in the largest termination to date, Exxon took advantage of an about-to-expire tax credit and terminated its pension plan, reverted the surplus assets of $1.6 billion to the corporate treasury and used the tax credit to avoid the corporate income tax on the "newly found" cash.

The increased rate of terminations coincided with particular macro- and microeconomic events, namely the globalization of U.S. business and corporate restructuring. Unfortunately, the rate of pension plan termina-tions has increased as the importance of pensions to workers has grown.[3] Social Security benefit increases are not planned or even discussed, and aggregate savings, some presumably for retirement, have fallen, because real incomes have fallen. As workers become older—the greying of America continues to be a marketing trend—the subjective valuation of any pension promise increases. The pension also increases with job tenure. In fact, a defined-benefit promise based on final salary represents some semblance of a cost-of-living protection until retirement. Moreover, in the past, firms with surplus pension-fund assets, or what the industry calls an asset cushion, paid a cost-of-living adjustment (COLA) to retirees, although such a promise was ad hoc and rarely made formal. The asset cushion was created by maturing funds, a soaring stock market, and higher interest rates that reduced the value of projected liabilities. But, in the 1980s, instead of making additional COLAs, firms increased the rate of pension terminations and reversions.

It was not just the economy that induced firms to increase terminations and use pension funds; the political and legal atmosphere also contributed. The Reagan administration helped by narrowing the meaning of legal pension liability under pressure from the business community, which claimed that restricting access to the surplus assets would militate against the formation of more plans.

Workers forego wages in anticipation of an inflation-protected pension, based on future union negotiations or salary increases. But, at termination, workers only receive an annuity based on so-called accrued benefits, or a lump-sum payment equal to the annuity value. Therefore, employers who terminate their defined-benefit pension plans during times of anticipated inflation face uniquely large advantages. Anticipated inflation makes annuities cheaper, because insurance companies are able to use a higher interest rate assumption to calculate the present value of a future payment. And the opportunity gains from discontinuing a promise of a pension based on future earnings (likely inflation-adjusted) are greater during times when inflation is below the anticipated future level. In fact, legal liabilities fell and pension earnings increased, while stock markets boomed and interest rates climbed in the late 1970s and 1980s.

In the last fifteen years corporations have adopted sophisticated financial models and tactics to fold pension funds into larger corporate finance strategies. Again, the exploitation of the moral hazard inherent in a contingent claims contract, the pension contract—changing the terms of the agreement after the contract is made—is a symptom of larger changes in the economy. Corporate use of pension plans has evolved from personnel devices to factors in corporate finance strategies. The metaphor of pensions as financial intermediaries, wherein firms mediate workers' preferences to consume now or later, is made less relevant by the adventuresome practices of healthy, ongoing, nondistressed firms to terminate pension trusts and use trust funds creatively, for their own purposes, since the late 1970s.

These creative uses have allowed firms to function as an autonomous party to pension contracts. Firms are increasingly able to change the contract after it is made by terminating a plan, which may be replaced by an inferior plan or in some cases with no successor plan. Between 1979 and 1983, 20 percent of participants in terminated plans had no successor plan and the fate of 33 percent of the participants was unknown. If one-half of these participants had no new plan, over one-third of all terminations had no successor plan (Ippolito 1986a). Until the early 1970s and even after well-publicized failures of pension plans, "the reputation effect," the presumption that firms will not cheat workers for fear of alienating skilled applicants and current employees, was deemed sufficient to deter pension-fund shenanigans. (The Studebaker Corporation of South Bend, Indiana, which closed its plant in 1964, leaving most employees without funding for their entitled pensions, is one famous example of a failed plan.) Policy-makers, not content to rely on the strength of the reputation effect, passed the 1974 Employee Retirement Income Security Act to help balance the power in the pension contract between workers and firms. The feeble funding positions of plans—more than half of funds had pension assets worth less than the liabilities—were the burning issues of the day.

Since then, pension management has grown more sophisticated, pension funds have grown in size, and the position of U.S. corporations in world markets has changed dramatically. There is an increasing dissonance between the concept of pension trusts as irrevocable payments to workers and pension funds as an underexplored corporate resource.

Government and the Corporate Use of Pension Plans

The use of pensions as corporate financing resources is peculiar to the United States (and to some extent Britain). As explained previously, the United States distinguishes itself by not conferring entitlement of substantial social insurance to its residents. Instead, it is employers, substantially subsidized by favorable tax treatment, who confer a large part of social insurance. The government issues tax incentives to the system and directs firms through a complex system of regulations promulgated by Congress, the Courts, the Internal Revenue Service, and the Department of Labor, in order to steer firms away from self-interested use of their workers' pensions. Private pension contributions and earnings are exempted from corporate income tax and deferred from individual income tax until retirement. In 1989, this was the largest available tax loophole and was worth $50 billion (Munnell 1988). In return for the tax exemption the federal government gained the leverage to regulate the system and seeks to prevent corporate abuse, a possibility that stems from the employer's sole control of administration, financing, and structure. Firms have sole control of a plan as long as it meets ERISA standards or the plan is covered by a collective bargaining agreement and held in joint trusteeship.

ERISA's fundamental purpose was to ensure that pension promises would be fulfilled. At the very least, the law was written to minimize moral hazard from underfunding and faulty and incomplete information. More optimistic assessments of what the law was supposed to accomplish included a hoped-for broadening of pension entitlement to workers who change jobs by mandating vesting periods. ERISA established minimum plan rules (but not benefits). It also helped secure pension promises by making pension liabilities an explicit corporate debt, mandated payment schedules, established the Pension Benefit Guaranty Corporation (PBGC) to insure pension promises (the PBGC acts somewhat like the Federal Deposit

Insurance Corporation), and strengthened reporting and disclosure requirements.

The legislation also mandates that the employer-pension plan be managed in the sole interest of the pension plan participants. Practically, this means the plan should be managed as a "prudent expert" would, one whose sole interest is that of the participants. Because, by definition, expertise and prudency are whatever passes for standard practice by members of the pension industry, the law requires the industry to abide by the standards the industry itself defines. The prudent person rule sanctions management practices that would be used "in the conduct of an enterprise of a like character and like aims" (Gray 1983: 54).

This provision settled an important controversy among regulators about whether each investment vehicle had to yield a maximum return for a given risk, or whether the fund was to be scrutinized for its total, risk-adjusted rate of return as well as its coordination of expected earnings and withdrawals. The prudent expert rule represents a choice for the holistic concept (Gray 1983). This standard has, however, become a way by which employers gain latitude, thus advantage, in establishing pension funding levels as accounting procedures.

Although ERISA and since the 1940s, the tax code (Altman 1987), clearly require that pension funds be managed for the sole benefit of plan participants, the hospitable business environment under the Reagan administration and a general waning of corporate trepidation about how strictly ERISA would be enforced encouraged corporations to include their pension funds in their financial strategies. Recent articles in the academic financial press and a title of a 1986 book reveal the temptation and tactic; from its dust jacket, "Pension Funds and the Bottom Line is the first book to treat the employer retirement system as a separate corporate entity. This new framework enables pension managers to integrate the pension fund into the overall business strategy of the corporation" (Ambachtsheer 1986).

In 1983, an IRS ruling (83-52, 1983-1 C.B.87.) accommodated firms whose pension funds were increasing and liabilities falling (Ippolito 1986a) by ruling that "surplus assets"—those that are deemed superfluous and belonging to the company—were all the assets that might at any one point in time be in excess of current liabilities. The ruling made the termination of pension plans more lucrative by interpreting the Treasury Department's clarification of the Internal Revenue Code's prohibition against an employer's use of pension assets until all liabilities are paid. Section 1.401(b) of the tax code is based on the legislative history of tax law in 1939 and it permits "the employer to recover at the termination of the trust and only at the termination of the trust, any balance which is due to erroneous actuarial computations during the life of the trust." The Treasury regulations, which stem from the 1939 tax law, posit that excess assets arise when the actuaries are wrong about predicting the growth of the fund or plan liabilities. The 1983 ruling presumes that an actuary made a mistake merely if the present value of pension liabilities exceeds the assets. Therefore, all excess assets by definition are due to an actuary's mistake. Thus, all excess assets belong to the employer, regardless of whether the surplus was caused by a better-than-expected fund earnings or by freezing the benefits before the actuary expected them to be frozen, which happens when plans terminate. Because firms can only get access to "surplus assets" through terminations, this ruling opened the way for thousands of plan terminations and reversions.

In 1984, in a move that further encouraged terminations, the Department of Labor (DOL) and the PBGC issued termination guidelines, giving these practices federal imprimatur. The guidelines came about through the efforts of the Celanese Corporation when, in 1984, it wanted to terminate its pension plan and recapture over three billion dollars of excess assets, but the firm was skittish of the publicity consequences (perhaps a vestige of the reputation effect). Although the law allowed terminations, the company lobbied for and obtained the Department of Labor's approval. The Reagan administration's philosophy was made clear in subsequent IRS and DOL actions. They argued that because pension plans are voluntary and firms bear the costs of the risk of having to pay a promised benefit, firms need the benefit of the option to terminate "overfunded" defined-benefit plans. In an interview seven years after these decisions, William Niskanen, former chair of President Ronald Reagan's Council of Economic Advisers who formulated the philosophy and shepherded the termination guidelines through the Department of Labor and the Pension Benefit Guaranty Corporation, said of Celanese and the other corporations who wanted the guidelines, "They didn't have to do much persuading. Many corporations seemed taken aback that we didn't need to be convinced" (Tackett 1989).

The Treasury and other pension advisors grew alarmed at the increase in terminations in the following years. The cause of alarm was not so much the gross reneging of pension contracts and the loss to workers, but the drastic loss of tax revenues when firms usurped funds that were collected tax free. In 1987, a 15 percent excise tax was imposed on any captured "surpluses," yielding the government an estimated $1.6 billion in increased tax revenue. These legal developments occurred at the same time that economic developments—increasing foreign competition, globalization of capital, the collapse in oil prices, and the shortening of the corporate time-horizon—required companies to devise new corporate financial strategies.

Corporations have increasingly turned to pension funds to meet a variety of cash-flow needs in the face of the sagging stock market in the 1970s and hostile and friendly takeovers and acquisitions in the 1970s and 1980s.[4] Using internal funds for any purpose rather than external funds— banks, the stock market, the commercial paper market—is cheaper for the firm, especially if high-quality borrowers are not as highly rated as they would be if lenders had as much information about the firm as the firm itself. The argument is that once a company turns to the external market for money the value of the firm is discounted because lenders suspect that a firm wants to borrow because it is in trouble, despite the financial statements or actual condition of the firm. (VanDerhei and Harrington 1989). Ironically, this has resulted in corporations becoming the vanguard of innovators in the so-called "non traditional" or "alternative" uses of pension funds, an issue covered in chapter 6.

Corporate Uses of Pension Funds

There are four primary ways corporations have used pension funds to meet their own financial needs. Sometimes these uses are in direct conflict with worker needs.

First, firms can shelter profits from tax, or engage in "tax arbitrage" by funding their pension plans with amounts over the minimum ERISA contribution. Tax motivations are not the only reasons for maintaining excess assets or a pension cushion. Actuaries advise firms to fund implicit promises, such as post-retirement cost-of-living clauses, and to have a margin in case of earnings fluctuations. A cushion also helps a firm pay for subsequent improvements in the benefit formula. Periodic and predictable benefit formula improvements were the usual method by which employers (especially those engaged in collective bargaining) who sponsored flat-rate defined-benefit plans kept the promise in line with salary increases. Moreover, some firms might purposely overfund the pension plan in order to attract bidders, which would benefit shareholders, but not usually workers or beneficiaries unless the firm used the increased share value to improve the productivity of the firm.[5] In the 1970s, overfunded plans generally served as insurance for current and future participants and minimized tax liabilities for shareholders. In the 1980s, overfunding served corporate financial purposes.

Second, firms can terminate overfunded plans in order to fend off takeovers and improve cash flows. Business advisors warned companies in the 1970s that overfunding a pension plan to terminate it would be irrational, because the overfunded amount would end up going to workers and not to firms.[6] But this advice did not take into account or anticipate the pro-business IRS ruling in 1983. These legal developments, combined with a booming stock market, which increased the size of pension funds, and the economic changes that made firms increase their demand for liquidity, are among the reasons corporations are changing their attitudes toward pension funds. Under these conditions, terminating an overfunded plan and reducing contributions to use the cash is a rational business decision.

Third, firms can underfund plans in times of financial crises, knowing that the existence of the PBGC "put," or guarantee, places a floor under the value of corporate equities when extreme underfunded liabilities exist (Estrella 1987). A firm, especially an indebted firm, can protect creditors at the expense of shareholders, workers, and the PBGC by underfunding the plan.

Fourth, firms can engage in self-dealing because of the paucity of enforcement of pension-fund practices. Large firms can instruct their pension-plan managers to invest in the corporate sponsors' stock—a questionable practice refused by many sponsors. Small firms engage in different kinds of fraud—low-interest loans to relatives, or verbal promises of unfunded benefits to loyal employees. Another consequence of corporate sponsoring of pension plans cannot always be called self-dealing—the term has pejorative connotations—but the outcome is an enhancement of corporate interests through the development of a community or network when a firm goes about hiring consultants and money managers to administer the plan. A controversial and almost illegal result of corporate involvement with pension-fund managers occurs when corporate sponsors pressure their "independent" pension-fund managers to vote their proxies in a way pleasing to management. The interdependencies cause the principal problems facing government enforcement of pension investments to grow larger and more complex. Corporate tactics to incorporate pension funds into the "bottom line" are discussed below.

Pension Funding and Good Business Practices

The tax-exempt status of employer contributions and fund earnings creates incentives for funding the pension above the minimum standards. The motivation is similar to the reasons for funding life-insurance policies with investments rather than cash—to pay for a known large pension liability with earnings rather than cash flow. An asset cushion also is recommended for any fluctuations in earnings and to meet obligations not explicitly accounted for by the actuary, such as ad hoc benefit adjustments for retirees and expectation of future increases in the benefit formula.

One theory about optimal funding is the tax-based argument of Tepper (1981) and Sharpe (1976). The firm would hold otherwise highly taxed holdings in a pension and fund the pension plan above the minimum required by law. That money earns a tax-free rate of return and the firm gets a tax deduction for issuing the debt. The tax arbitrage, overfunding strategy works because a firm, appropriately working for the interests of shareholders, compares the returns to pension-fund investments to the rate of return on alternative investments. Because pension-fund earnings are tax deductible they are preferable to investments that would make less than the rate-of-return divided by the corporate tax rate. For instance, if the corporate tax rate is 50 percent, a taxable asset would have to earn 16 percent to be comparable to an 8 percent asset in the pension fund. Overfunding a pension trust is especially attractive during times of inflation, because the corporation pays its debts in cheaper dollars. The main drawback to overfunding, advocates of this view point out, is that the pension-fund assets were held in trust as collateral for pension liabilities, for workers only. The strategy of overfunding pension plans was cautioned against if the chance of terminating the plan was high. The concern was that all funds left over from a terminated pension fund had to go to workers anyway, so firms were advised against overfunding if corporate reorganization, for instance, was likely. Pension experts Tepper and Paul (1978 : 50) assume in their advice to companies that so-called excess assets would be used only for participants:

The larger the investment of corporate assets in the pension fund the greater the loss is likely to be in a termination situation if the assets exceeded the amount required to match the PBGC guaranteed benefits and the excess turns out to be irrevocable.

This drawback was seen as being somewhat mitigated, because the firm has "access" to the money by virtue of its ability to use the excess as credit; in times of financial need a firm would merely reduce pension contributions (Black 1980; Tepper 1981).

The theory proposed a clearly rational way for firms to act. The problem was to explain the divergence of reality from the theory. Some firms had underfunded plans and none held only bonds, the most taxable asset, in their pension plans. The tax-arbitrage view gave way to the now more acceptable view of corporate pension funding, the risk-offsetting theory. This theory proposes that firms do not seek to only maximize shareholders' interests by reducing taxes, but must also maximize creditors' interests by reducing the chances of loan default. Moreover, firms need to maximize return and minimize risk. The pension-funding strategies of firms must take into account the overall level of risk and profit in the corporation. Benjamin Friedman found that highly indebted firms tended to have underfunded plans, shifting the risk of bankruptcy to the Pension Benefit Guaranty Corporation (PBGC) and shareholders. Firms with variable profits tend to have more conservative pension-funding practices (Friedman 1983).

In addition to altering the level of pension funding, firms had great leeway in accounting for pension liabilities and assets by adopting funding methods and manipulating actuarial methods and assumptions. For example, until 1987, there were no limitations on interest rate assumptions that the firm-hired actuaries assumed the pension fund would earn. A high-interest-rate assumption leads to a small required contribution. If the fund is assumed to be a low-earner in the future, the firm must contribute a larger amount.

Theoretically, firms could vary interest-rate assumptions to conserve cash or shelter profits (Tepper and Paul 1978: 51).

Actuarial policy can be varied widely to accommodate the funding decision. The actuary can select from a number of acceptable funding methods, each generating a different value for allowable funding limits. The manner in which the actuary treats inflation, the method he uses to value the assets of the plan, and the degree of conservatism he employs in the valuation are parameters that can legitimately be varied to accommodate the company's funding policy.

The theory is supported by the empirical correlation between a corporation's interest-rate assumption and their cash-flow needs (Ghilarducci 1984; Bodie et al. 1987). At 5.5 percent, the IBM corporation, one of the most profitable Fortune 500 firms, had the lowest interest-rate assumption of 200 firms from 1981–1984. On the other hand, tire companies—an industry beleaguered by plant closings and loss of market share—used on average an 11.3 percent interest-rate assumption. This means that the same pension liability cost 12 percent more (the discounted value) at IBM than it did in the rubber tire industry.

In other cases, General Motors (GM) raised its interest-rate assumption used to discount pension liabilities to 7 percent from 6 percent in 1981, creating two-thirds of its profits that year. In 1989, GM increased its first-quarter profits by 10 percent by increasing the investment return assumption and reducing the mortality assumption—assuming retirees would die two years sooner. Ford Motor Company also increased its 1990 first-quarter profits by 5 percent by changing pension assumptions (Burr 1990: 43). Inland Steel, Eastern Airlines, GATX, and Santa Fe are other companies that explicitly changed interest-rate assumptions to reduce contributions (Pensions and Investment Age 1984: 58, 14). In 1984, the Milwaukee County Employees plan was able to cut its contributions by 40 percent, even though the plan reported losses by changing actuarial interest-rate assumptions (Burr 1984). In fact, 30 percent of a sample of major U.S. corporations changed the interest-rate assumption used for pension liability disclosures in 1983 corporate reports (Pensions and Investments Age 1984). Another source of pension-funding flexibility was a firm's choice of actuarial funding methods. Front-loading by funding for projected benefits based on projected earnings is a savvy financing strategy if the firm can afford it, because corporate profits are protected from tax and the principal of the fund earns interest. If a firm wanted to save cash and minimize contributions, another actuarial method would allow funding the liability accrued each year, although as employees grew older the liability would increase tremendously.

These pension-fund financing methods engendered little controversy. Researchers reassured themselves that investors were not fooled by these practices, because stock values are affected by the amount of pension liability (Mork and Feldstein 1983). This view is acceptable, because it is rational model of corporate behavior that sees a corporation as one that maximizes and balances various interest groups—creditors, shareholders, and workers. Although the firm's pension management was not in the sole interest of the participants, that is, participants were not insulated from corporate interests and the fund seemed to be in violation of ERISA, no watchdog protested because participants seemed unharmed.

An obvious loser when pension funds are deliberately overfunded is the U.S. Treasury, but the Treasury's loss was seen to be in concert with public policy to encourage private pension plans. In the 1980s, however, the Treasury sought to shore up its interests and obtained legislation that restricted the tax-sheltering ability of pension funds by limiting interest rate manipulations and overfunding limitations. In 1980, five years after ERISA passed, unions, the courts, and Congress began to challenge corporate management of pension plans. Economic and political events made the thin line between pension funds and the corporate balance sheet an exposed nerve.

Overfunding and Terminations

Between 1980 and 1989, firms terminated more than 2,000 pension plans and used $20 billion in "excess" funds for their own purposes. Pension funds provided a source of direct capital to firms throughout the turbulent 1980s and 1.6 million individuals who experienced a plan termination were paid an estimated 50 percent of what they would have received had their plans remained intact, because firms terminated "overfunded" plans, paid off legal liabilities, and used the extra cash (Ippolito 1986c).

The best way to understand the concept of "surplus" is to understand not what creates the surplus—the assets in excess of legal liability—but what defines the legal liability. The legal liability is the liability to the plan at the time of termination, not the liability if the plan is to remain ongoing. Professional codes of conduct require that the actuary make funding recommendations based on the assumption that the plan is ongoing, not one that will terminate and only have to pay, and fund for, "legal," otherwise known as accrued or termination, liabilities. The former will be larger than the latter. At termination this is essentially what creates the surplus. The actuary reports various types of liabilities: liabilities for vested and nonvested employees and for their past and expected service. At termination only one liability becomes relevant, the liability for vested past service.

There are a number of reasons for healthy pension plan terminations: a fundamental change in the relationship between workers and firms and increased need for cash due to the furious trend toward corporate takeovers and acquisitions. Terminating the plan and paying off the "legal" as opposed to the larger "true" liabilities meant that corporations could harvest "overfunded" pension plans.

A firm can avoid unfriendly takeovers by terminating the plan and using excess assets to buy outstanding stock, or by directing the pension plan to buy up the sponsor's stock. Pension funds can also act like well-behaved stockholders, or white knights with their excess cash. Pension administrators can fend off hostile takeovers by allowing the fund to accept a firm's bonds, stocks, and real assets in lieu of cash contributions. Terminating a newly acquired firm's pension can help reduce the hefty debt incurred for the acquisition. When a German company acquired the Great Atlantic Tea Company, it terminated A&P's pension to usurp $250 million in excess assets. An out-of-court settlement required A&P to distribute some of that to participants. Fifty million dollars, only 20 percent of the excess assets, was distributed.

The terminations and reversions have been allowed, despite protestations in court and in Congress, because of how "surplus" is defined.

Liabilities are defined as those that represent accrued pension liabilities as of the date of termination. They do not include the pension value that would have been paid based on future salaries—the projected pension liability. Moreover, firms had leeway in deciding how annuities could be valued. Some overfunding represents deliberate attempts to shelter profits from tax and to prefund pension-benefit obligations for either past service or anticipated increases. But the 1983 IRS ruling deems that all causes of surplus stem from erroneous actuarial assumptions that assumed earnings would be smaller.

This provision in the tax code was intended to prevent punishing firms for achieving better-than-expected rates of return on their pension fund. The argument is that if firms bear the risk that the stock market will be worse than expected, they should reap the benefit when it is better. Yet, as lawyer Norman Stein argues, actuaries are instructed to predict investment earnings and liabilities based on the assumption that a pension plan will continue. Most plans front-load payments, using a tax-favored reserve to prefund projected liabilities. Thus, most surpluses do not stem from unanticipated earnings, but from good business practices.[7]

Moreover, Federal Reserve economists Arturo Estrella (1987) and Mark Warshawsky (1989) interpret the situation as instances of actuaries using conservative assumptions about the plan's earnings in order to pad the fund against implicit expenses (the projected liability from future salary increases), which companies do not want made explicit but actuaries realize are there. This professional decision is in accordance with Stein's assertion that actuaries operate under the assumption that the plan will continue. What was merely a shortcut adopted by an elite group of professionals—the practice of using low-earnings assumption to compensate for unacknowledged but real future salary increases and implicit COLAs— has become the basis for massive redistribution of assets from implicit ownership of workers to firms.

Pre-ERISA firms merely had to assert that the pension fund was held in trust for participants in order to maintain the tax-deferred status of the pension trusts. In 1966, the Accounting Principles Board issued guidelines on appropriate pension accounting. They required firms to report normal cost, the amount accrued that year for current employees, but not unfunded liabilities. Although facing increasing restrictions in the 1980s, firms could also use a wide range of actuarial assumptions, causing firms with identical liabilities to report vastly different asset-liability ratios. The variation comes from the liability calculations. In 1980, the Financial Accounting Standards Board (FASB) continued to tighten pension accounting procedures and required firms to report accrued liabilities and assets in a footnote to company reports. The FASB is the agency that standardizes corporate accounting in order to achieve its stated goal to improve financial markets by providing information to all corporate bidders, equity buyers, and lenders. The option to vary the calculation of the same liability for pension-funding purposes remained.

In 1985, the FASB issued Statement 87, effective in 1987 and Statement 88, effective in 1988. These statements required a more detailed footnote report of projected liabilities (those including future salary increases) and regulated interest rates to the settlement rate or the PBGC rate, which was often much higher than the assumed interest rates. Remember, lower interest rates make liabilities look larger and thus require larger contributions. The major goal of the changes, FASB Statements 87 and 88, is to rigidify rules regarding expensing and corporate valuation. It is important not to confuse pension expensing with funding. The corporation keeps two sets of pension records: the traditional actuarial valuation report and the FASB 87 expense determination for purposes of corporate accounting. The FASB rules did not affect pension funding, which remains flexible. Firms can choose funding methods based on cash flow, investment returns, and other concerns and legal limitations.

The FASB rules will make pension expensing, the appearance of pension costs, more volatile each year. Moreover, the reported differences in funding health among plans will grow wider. Generally, underfunded plans will appear more underfunded and the overfunded plans will appear more overfunded. The growth in disparity occurs because a pension debt (liabilities minus assets) and a pension surplus (assets minus liabilities) must be amortized, accounted for, in a much shorter period of time.

Some of the FASB changes are directed at the collectively-bargained plans that are underfunded. "FASB is recognizing an economic reality: in many instances, employers and unions have agreed to generous pension benefits but have inadequately accounted for the cost" (William Mercer-Meidinger, Inc. 1985). Under the new rules, collectively bargained pension improvements for past service or for future increase must be accounted for immediately, rather than amortized over a thirty-year period. This may be prudent policy with regard to the percentage of plans that are underfunded—such plans are concentrated in the steel industry—but it does not address the inconsistencies and problems in plans that are reported to be overfunded.

Mark Warshawsky (1989) demonstrates how much accounting practices matter, if economic concepts, rather than accounting standards, are used to judge the extent of so-called overfunding. The overfunding perception was created by the commonplace notion that pension funds did well in the booming stock market of the 1980s because assets grew faster than liabilities. Warshawsky shows that the *reported* average percentage of assets exceeding liabilities grew from 17 percent in 1981 to 35 percent in 1985. The overfunding picture can change drastically with slight changes in actuarial assumptions and conceptions of the pension liability.

In 1986, if the liabilities are calculated to include the effect of projected salaries on benefits, then the average funding ratio of a sample of ninety-six large firms is 117, or 17 percent overfunded, rather than the 51 percent overfunding ratio reported by the companies (Warshawsky 1989: 10). In addition, the variations of liabilities calculations of a sample of plans can be seen by comparing the liabilities of the same plan estimated three other ways. The first method estimates the liabilities using a typical interest-rate assumption (before 1987) and excluding projected salary increases. The second method of estimating projected liabilities assumes that increases come only from salary increases, not increases in service, and the third method adds the cost of indexing the final pension for 50 percent of any inflation loss. The first estimate yields a liability of $132 million, the second $151 million, and the third $180 million.

The incisive lesson from Warshawsky's simulations of various methods of calculating the same liabilities is that there is much less cushion, less excess, than reported funding ratios (assets divided by liabilities) would lead one to believe.

Underfunded Plans and the Role of the PBGC

The third way firms have incorporated pension fund strategies into corporate financial strategies is to purposefully underfund the pension plan. Many times a firm underfunds because of poor industry profitability and excess indebtedness. This is contrary to the theory that pension plans are managed independently of the corporation. Firms may underfund because they are conserving cash for a myriad of purposes, ranging from cash-flow needs due to acquisition activity, debt maintenance, or a sluggish product demand. Pension expenses may have risen suddenly because of a sudden reduction of the work force. The firm may also underfund because it is somewhat protected from liability at termination by PBGC insurance. The firm may have low taxes because of tax credits and therefore sheltering cash from tax is not important. All these conditions described the steel industry in early 1980s, the industry that has exposed the PBGC to more real and potential liability than any other. On the surface the problem of under-funded plans looks like it is caused by poor industry earnings. Harvard economist Benjamin Friedman (1983) found that firms with unfunded plans were likely to have both high profits and high debt. This is evidence that simple theories cannot be used to explain how companies best serve their interests when making pension financing decisions. What is clear is that the fund is not managed solely for the benefit of the participants.

The following are two examples of how steel firms managed to create some of the largest unfunded liabilities faced by the pension system. These cases show that some firms have incurred more debt than allowed by ERISA by obtaining IRS waivers and exemptions and contributing stock from shaky companies to their pension fund. In 1983, three years before the PBGC terminated the LTV Steel Corporation pension plans and assumed the insured liability, the IRS allowed LTV to legally underfund its plans below the ERISA minimums. Earlier government action also weakened the fund. In 1982, the company contributed two million shares of LTV preferred shares to its pension plan, which represented 25 percent of its contributions that year. This move reportedly was to conserve cash for planned corporate acquisitions and left the fund with LTV stock that soon lost value (Webman 1983). Although Boston Federal Reserve vice president Alicia Munnell warned in 1982 that certain steel companies, LTV included, were endangering the health of the Pension Benefit Guaranty Corporation, the IRS waivers and the tolerance of questionable funding practices revealed acceptance of the financial community and the regulators that the pension fund is inextricably tied to the fate of the company. The sponsor does not steward a trust for the sole benefit of the participants—as ERISA mandates—but incorporates it (with the regulators' approval) into the operation of the corporation. In 1986, when the PBGC terminated LTV's plans and assumed the insured liability, it excluded early retirement benefits and those exceeding the maximum. Some workers received $400 less a month when the PBGC took over the plans.

In a second case, Wheeling-Pittsburgh filed for bankruptcy in 1986 and incumbered the PBGC with over $400 million in pension liability. In 1984, after receiving a $50-million waiver from the IRS, Wheeling-Pittsburgh requested a partial waiver of its 1983 contributions, although the IRS had conditioned its 1982 waiver on payment for 1983. The IRS did not rescind its 1982 waiver and approved the 1983 request. The firm also raised its interest-rate assumption and issued nonconvertible preferred stock—a stock with no established market—just for the contribution to the pension fund. All these actions, of course, limited the cash contributions to the plans. An example of the sentiment that corporations should use the pension fund for their own benefit is well expressed by an attorney commenting on the Wheeling-Pittsburgh practices. Chemoff (1984: 76) summed up the attorney's remarks, writing, "it is hard to second guess firms that try to keep afloat by contributing securities in lieu of cash"; and, in a direct quote, "There is something sanctimonious about standing on the side lines and pointing a finger at these boys."

What both cases suggest (and what the attorney is saying) is that the law cannot be interpreted strictly. Somehow it has been found reasonable to expect (and even welcome) corporations to manipulate their pension plans when survival is at stake.

ERISA and the creation of the PBGC, in part, were prompted by outrage and concern for workers left behind without promised pensions because of a firm's economic distress. The federally sponsored insurance system was to act like other kinds of social insurance—unemployment insurance and worker's compensation—to protect workers from some of the risk and vagaries of participating in a capitalist system. The provision of insurance immediately raises the possibility of moral hazard, of firms increasing the risk of loss because insurance exists. So ERISA restricted the holdings of corporate assets to 10 percent and required advance funding. The existence of the PBGC also created an asset for the company. Treynor et al. (1976) first coined the term "pension put" to illustrate the asset the corporation gains when the PBGC insures 30 percent of assets. Gersovitz (1980) and Feldstein and Seligman (1980) found that corporate share prices were sensitive to the amount of protection the PBGC guarantee afforded a firm. The major form of moral hazard was presumed to be the underfunding of plans and the holding of imprudent or undiversified assets, mainly the corporation's stock or debt.

In the 1960s and 1970s a lagging stock market and celebrated cases of terminations and newly pensionless workers made the underfunded, unprotected plan the focus of pension reform. In ERISA, government policy worked in two directions. It bestowed an asset on a firm with underfunded pensions and it required that a firm fund a promise that otherwise may never have been secured.

In the 1980s and 1990s attention has been focused on the terminations of healthy overfunded plans, a phenomenon ERISA clearly did not foresee. This concern has brought into question the role of the PBGC in creating incentives for healthy terminations. When the Facet Company terminated its plan, it followed PBGC guidelines and paid 30 percent of its net worth to the PBGC. This was not a distressed termination; it was a mere exercise of the pension put—the implicit asset the PBGC provides companies by limiting their liability to only 30 percent of net worth. This prompted the PBGC to win legislation in 1986 that limits this practice, unless a company is distressed. The 1986 legislation added to the firm's liability in case of an underfunded termination. Not only can the PBGC claim 30 percent of the firm's net worth—this claim having first priority in bankruptcy court—the PBGC also has a lesser status claim for 75 percent of the liability not yet recovered. The firm can still push a portion of the liabilities onto PBGC, and this amount increases, of course, when net worth falls.

Arturo Estrella (1987: 270) shows that both the protection created by the PBGC coverage of nonfunded liabilities and the firm's ability to take "surplus" assets from the fund at any time represents a corporate asset, a pension call option. He calculated the implicit value of this call option and showed that as overfunding decreases the incentives to continue the plan rise.

The old problem of underfunded plans, coupled with the phenomenon of healthy terminations, haunts the private pension system as a form of private-public social insurance. When an overfunded plan terminates, the "good risks" in the pool of insured participants are reduced. Until 1988, when the premium was almost doubled, the PBGC always experienced increasing deficits. The deficit was easy to calculate, but the actual exposure of risk was a bit more difficult. One way to calculate the exposure is to examine the underfunded status of the insured plans. A Congressional Budget Office report showed that over 80 percent of plans are overfunded and 20 percent underfunded. Many analysts, including Warshawsky, would qualify the terms "underfunding" and "overfunding" because accounting practices vary so much that one practice can determine that a plan is overfunded while another can determine that the same plan is underfunded. In his study, Warshawsky (1989) showed that reported funding positions overstate the health of the pension funds. Using the FASB 87 rules that require the calculation of projected liabilities rather than termination liabilities and added liabilities incurred to fund a 50 percent cost of living increase, if pension funds in 1981 through 1985 are examined, the percentage of funds that are underfunded would jump from 41.3 in 1981 to 67.3 percent and 21.1 percent in 1985 to 64.3 percent. Pension contributions have declined since 1980, thus endangering the PBGC even more.

The main point should not be lost. The problem with the PBGC may not be due to just inadequate premiums or regulation. In regard to the entire PBGC and private pension idea, it may be that the moral hazard inherent in private pension funds cannot be sufficiently reduced. Because most of the

PBGC's liability comes from the steel industry, the actual effect of the PBGC's takeover of pension liabilities changes from pension insurance to a form of industry bailout and covert industrial policy.

Exemptions for prohibited transactions also have let firms go beyond ERISA guidelines and use pension funds directly for their own purposes, such as investing in more than 10 percent of a company's stock.

Self-Dealing

Without terminating a fund, corporations can use their funds strategically. In the early 1980s, Boise-Cascade Company sold 15.6 million acres of timber land to their fund and then leased the acreage back. Burroughs used its pension plan to buy Burroughs-owned manufacturing plants for $30 million. Burroughs (which later merged with Sperry to form Unisys) leases the facilities from the plan with payments that the company admits are generous. The company avoids cash contributions to the plan because the plan earns a large amount of cash from the leases. Burroughs may not have secured such an arrangement on the open market; the plan was used as a captured buyer or creditor. Furthermore, the Department of Labor is not required to scrutinize the trade, because a sale and leaseback is not a "reportable event."

In 1986 the Sherwin-Williams Company obtained Department of Labor approval to borrow $65 million from its pension plan in order to forestall a takeover. Sea First directed its pension plan to buy its stock at inflated prices in order to forestall a takeover.

In June 1989, the inspector general of the Department of Labor released an internal study of 168 pension plans in 1988-1987 that showed that independent auditors did not disclose $6.7 billion in misused assets, or that 50 percent of the audits were incomplete. The report also raised the specter of the possibility of another Savings and Loans-type crisis—the uncovering of fraud and mismanagement that led to the collapse of a substantial amount of the savings and loan industry in the late 1980s—in the pension industry. The inspector general proceeded with criminal charges against some plans, until his authority was challenged by the Justice Department. The Department of Labor then sought, through Congress, to expand the responsibilities of the public accountant, to require that person to identify violations of the law, report the violations to the Labor Department, and be subject to sanctions for inadequate audits (U.S. Department of Labor 1989; Ferguson 1989). As the Pension Rights Center accuses, however, the accountant is deemed independent even if the accountant is retained or engaged in other business by the pension sponsor. Small plans—those with 100 or fewer participants—are likely to have company owners serve as plan fiduciaries and would not be covered by these recommendations.

The potential for pension investment fraud has always been recognized by the relevant governmental agencies; in fact, the infamous case of the Teamster's union pension-fund scandals in the 1950s, at one point, made fraud the centerpiece of the public's interest in pension-fund reform. The stewards of the private pension system must diligently assess the magnitude of the problem in detecting illegal behavior, as well as the incentives for self-dealing, especially when it is done at the expense of workers, retirees, the government, and other interests and firms.

Illegal Activity

ERISA challenged and sought to forestall what were once acceptable, prudent business practices and the necessities of doing business in order to protect pensions. Section 510 of ERISA protects workers from discriminatory treatment due to their participation in a pension or health and welfare plan. This section anticipated cases where workers who might require expensive health care, or are just about to retire or vest in their pension, would be fired to avoid these costs, and where older workers, as a group, would be discriminated against because of their relatively high costs of participation in pension and health plans. In partial compromise, corporate lobbyists were able to obtain ERISA's permission to exclude employees over the normal retirement age (usually 65) from participating in a pension plan. This was disallowed by amendments to the Age Discrimination Act in 1988.

In the 1981 case against the Continental Can Company (CCC), mentioned in chapter 4, the U.S. federal court found that the company had constructed an elaborate system that kept track of employee eligibility for generous early pensions. In order to facilitate much-needed cutbacks in plant capacity, the corporation saved costs by denying pensions to some employees. This was a secret accounting system that the company did not deny developing. CCC's defense was bold; it claimed that the existence of the system was legal and that the company was innocent of wrong-doing, because the system was not used and pension costs were not important factors in the company's administrative costs.

In 1987, the Steelworkers Union knew the industry was declaring that a few mills were temporarily closed, when, in fact, they were never to be reopened, in order to avoid making laid-off workers eligible for retirement benefits.[8] Perhaps the union is not challenging these actions because the pension claims would be a strain on already troubled pension funds, there is hope that the mills will be reopened, or the costs of litigation are not worth the expected benefits. But there are cases in the files of the Pension Rights Center of persons that claim their employers fired them or, more commonly, did not give them the usual number of hours at the end of their career in order to save on pension costs.

Pensions costs are incorporated into the investment decisions of firms. Some of this incorporation is illegal, some is a violation of social conventions and implicit contracts between workers and employers, and in other instances, pensions are a cost prudent investors avoid.

In sum, there are legal loopholes in the ERISA legislation. Firms have used pensions for taxes, for cash, and as receptacles for stock. Pensions are a catch-all, a crutch propping up the financial strategies of firms. Now pensions may have become a labor cost to avoid.

Implications of the Corporate Use of Pension Funds

The increasing use of pension tactics by corporations has created a number of aggrieved parties. These parties include the U.S. Treasury, which has suffered a tax loss by exempting pension contributions and returns from tax only to see them recouped in terminations and reversions and workers, who have lost inflation protection, projected benefits, and the security of well-padded funds in the event of a healthy termination. Workers have gained something from the PBGC insurance of terminated underfunded funds, but early retirement benefits generally are not covered; healthy firms increasingly have had to pay higher premiums to the PBGC in order to pay for problems that are located mainly in the steel industry. Workers lose some benefits when interest-free loans are made to the company sponsor-plan fiduciary's brother-in-law. The loss is assured if it involves a defined-contribution plan.

Most analysts agree that workers lose when their well-funded pension plan is terminated. The law does not recognize the loss and this lack of recognition is a bona fide loophole. Total pension liabilities can be divided into five parts: the present value of vested liabilities for terminated workers and retirees and dependents, the present value of unvested benefits, the cost of the pension based on the service of workers not yet vested, and the liability caused by current participants' increases in future earnings and future service. The FASB requires firms to report these liabilities to the financial community. The IRS and the Department of Labor do not require these liabilities to be paid to workers.

The intricate relationship between the government's insurance of pensions and industry and corporate financial decisions is made clear in the case of the steel industry. The fortunes of that industry have been inextricably tied to the actions of the PBGC. Unwittingly, the U.S. government, through its pension insurance, is engaging in pseudo-industrial policy when it bails out and negotiates with the steel industry on the condition of its pensions. The PBGC also has played a minor role in the restructuring of the airlines, through its dealings with bankrupt companies such as Braniff.

When sufficiently funded pension plans terminate, the law requires the employer to pay off only the vested benefits. Five other tangible and intangible elements of the plan are lost: the unvested benefits, a funding cushion for unanticipated poor economic performance, the yield loss on future service and salary increases, and the ability to pay ad hoc cost-of-living increases to retirees. And when termination liabilities are paid off, pensions are frozen at the current salary, not the salary at the time the worker retires; even at modest rates of inflation this creates a large loss. Richard Ippolito has shown in various studies how much workers lose when this happens (Ippolito 1986c).

Younger workers lose most (as percentage of their salary), but older workers lose more in dollar amounts. He compares the difference between the value of a benefit in an ongoing plan and the value in a terminated identical plan for an identical worker. A fifty-five-year-old with twenty years of service loses 63 percent of her or his benefit, while a forty-five-year-old with ten years of service would lose 86 percent of her or his benefit. Even if the plan is replaced with an equivalently generous plan—over 30 percent of healthy terminated plans are not replaced at all—only very young workers with few years of service recoup their losses.

Many firms also used a funding surplus to pay for cost-of-living increases for their retirees. Inflation has ravaging effects on the real value of a fixed pension. Buying power can fall by one-half in fourteen-and-a-half years at just a 5 percent rate of inflation; at 10 percent it takes just nine years. Before investor Charles A. Hurwitz bought Pacific Lumber in 1985, the company boosted retiree pensions about every two years. After the takeover, Hurwitz terminated the plan, used the surplus assets to pay off his debts, and bought annuities from Executive Life, a now bankrupt insurance company. Some workers have filed suit against Hurwitz, seeking a guarantee for their annuities—a pension benefit they assess as being much less secure than it would have been under the old owners.

Analysts have concluded that a majority of plan terminations are motivated by takeover and merger activity and are not schemes to lower worker compensation. Motives might matter for the moralist, but the workers still lose compensation when a healthy pension plan is terminated. Unions reduce the probability of termination of an overfunded plan, most likely because they have provisions against it in their contracts (Ippolito 1986a).

Outcomes and Contradictions: Challenges to Corporate Use

Unions, the Department of Labor, the Pension Benefit Guaranty Corporation, and the Internal Revenue Service have challenged the corporate terminations and manipulations, but their protest has been fragmented—fought case by case—and usually only the most blatant cases are pursued. The efforts to curb terminations suffer from the pro-termination environment created by the Reagan administration.

The number of pension plan terminations peaked in 1985, greatly aided by the 1983 IRS ruling (Congressional Research Service 1988). Workers lost pension coverage in over 50 percent of the large pension terminations between 1986 and 1989, because their plans were not replaced or were replaced by an inferior plan. The Treasury Department balked, worried about loss in revenue due to the usurpation of tax-free corporate income, and in 1986 Congress imposed a 10 percent levy on reversions and in 1988 raised the levy to 15 percent. The Treasury regained some losses due to terminations, but so far legislation designed to alleviate workers' losses has failed in the Senate and House.

Since 1983 Senator Howard Metzenbaum (D, Ohio) has introduced some types of legislation limiting reversions. The only success chalked up was a year-long moratorium on terminations, which ended on May 1, 1989. Apparently, the parties interested in termination legislation have been split up, weakening the momentum against a ban on terminations. The Treasury Department got its tax levy on reverted assets and on funds that exceeded 150 percent of current liabilities. The Pension Benefits Guaranty Corporation, concerned that terminations increased its exposure, received a premium increase in 1986. Limitations of actuarial assumption maneuvers were put in place in 1987. Firms must now choose an interest-rate assumption within a narrower band than corporate financial interests dictated. In 1989, the Committee for Retirement Income Security (CRIS), a coalition of Fortune 500 firms who have organized around pension issues, devised a strategy to deflect the narrower band. In a clever move they sought legislation that would move surpluses into retiree health insurance.

In late 1986, when pension benefits of LTV and Wheeling-Pittsburgh steelworkers were threatened by corporate bankruptcies, legislators (Metzenbaum and others) offered legislation to aid workers in these particular cases and a comprehensive approach toward pension reform was dropped.

The Bush administration, continuing Reagan administration proposals, wants to amend ERISA to make it easier for corporations to borrow from their employees' pension funds, so that termination would not be necessary. The irony of this solution, correcting an abuse by making the abuse legal, is not peculiar to Bush-Reagan politics. The irony stems from the contradiction within the U.S. policy toward social insurance. The proposal for borrowing from funds rather than prohibiting terminations has an intellectual basis. Ippolito (1986a) shows that although workers lost benefits when overfunded plans were terminated, the firm's intention was to borrow from, not "dupe," workers. He was concerned with the tax subsidy the employers got by borrowing from tax-exempt funds and called for a surcharge on reverted assets. Advocates for pension termination legislation also call for a surcharge, but for different reasons.

In seemingly unrelated legislative initiatives, former Senator Proxmire and the Senate Committee on Banking investigated ways to regulate insider trading on the stock market and scrutinize speculators, investment banks, and so-called corporate raiders in the wake of the 1988-1989 indictments on Wall Street. Because parties are responsible for proving their assets were misused, a compilation of which investors gained or lost because of the insider trading is not available. If such an assessment was made, it seems likely that funds from institutional investors (workers' pension funds make up a large proportion of institutional investors' funds) were active in these takeover deals and that much of the capital used by firms to defend themselves came from their own workers' pension funds. Private pensions own 25 percent of junk bonds compared to 27 percent of all bonds (Turner and Beller 1989: 20). Because over 30 percent of new capital in the stock market comes from pension plans it is likely that much of the insider trading was fueled by worker pensions.

Organized labor turned its focus on pension interests from termination legislation to an initiative by Representative Peter Visclosky (D, Indiana) designed to thwart the leveraged buyout trends in corporate acquisitions and mergers by putting pension participants on pension administration boards. The connection between curbing speculative corporate financing behavior and pension rights is not direct. It depends on a thin string between pension funds and the financing of leveraged buyouts (LBOs). The string is weak because LBOs do not hang from pension financing (Congressional Research Service 1988; Ippolito and James 1990).

The Visclosky legislation, however, may be fought for on more solid ground as pension reform. In 1970, the legislation might have been successful as a workers' rights issue, but in the 1980s it may be sold as a device to improve pension-fund administration and labor management relations. For example, the college professors pension-fund, the Teachers Insurance and Annuity Administration-College Retirement Equity Fund (TIAA-CREF), has always had worker representatives. In the 1980s, these representatives led the way toward allowing participants choices in investment vehicles; the plan now offers a money market fund. Without the input of participants it is unlikely that the plan would have been so responsive to participant demands.

There are other examples (found in chapter 6) of innovations in pension investments and structure that have come about because of representatives on the pension trusts. The Visclosky initiative may also appeal to firms who are making forays into many different kinds of joint labor management projects under the assumption that "jointness," as the initiatives are called at GM and in the UAW, makes labor more connected and sensitive to industry needs.

As more firms discover the advantages of managing corporate pension funds as an extension of their business, I expect more challenges of pension-fund managers. Amendments to ERISA that would require that the accrued and projected liabilities are paid and any excess funds from terminated plans be distributed to the participants may also be on the horizon.

Pension Funds and
Financial Democracy

The possibility that pension funds can harbor and transform economic power predictably enters the consciousness of public debate like a comet. In 1959, Robert Tilove, in a report for the Fund for the Republic, a liberal and influential committee of educators and intellectuals, described the tremendous growth in corporate-sponsored pension trusts and addressed the concern that corporate managers would gain undue and threatening economic power through the investments and voting rights of corporate pension funds. Tilove (1959; 86) concluded his short report with a sentiment that would not be out of date today:

In a way it is strange that self-insured pension funds have aroused interest as a potential source of concentrated economic control. The problem is by no means new and is certainly not limited to pension funds. Perhaps the reason is that their rate of growth has been dramatic.... It is startling to realize that pension funds may accommodate sufficient assets to be able to buy a significant part in the ownership of corporations.

In the same year, another liberal think tank, the Twentieth Century Fund, published a book by Paul Harbrecht that explored Tilove's issue, that pension-fund ownership could control corporations, but Harbrecht approached the issue from the point of view of organized labor. He addressed whether workers, through their pension funds, were becoming owners of the means of production; in other words, if the broadening of equity and debt holdings meant that the major decisions affecting economic activity were therefore subject to more scrutiny, input, and democracy.

Recently, enthusiastic proponents of pension and profit sharing funds have been hailing them as instruments for creating a "people's capitalism.".... But it should be obvious ... that the typical beneficiary is, in his present situation, neither a proprietor nor an owner ... he enjoys none of the prerogatives of management and direction that usually pertain to ownership or proprietorship. (Harbrecht 1959; 266)

Harbrecht analyzed the possibilities that the seven-year-old labor federation, the AFL-CIO, could strategically use pension plans. He recognized that labor demands and successes in bargaining for employer-funded pensions—money invested for the member of organized labor—could result in a new source of power for labor.

In the late 1960s, the UMWA recognized this new source of influence when their pension funds bought stock in the utility companies, which needed to be convinced to buy union coal. The courts deemed the activity to be out of bounds for legal behavior of trustees.

Over ten years later, in 1976, Peter Drucker, an American management pundit for the thinking and wry corporate executive, declared in a small polemical book that socialism had come to the United States because American workers owned a substantial and increasing portion of the means of production through their pension funds. For a decade afterward, a pension-industry publication, *Pension and Investments Age*, regularly advertised itself, quoting Drucker's book, alongside a page-sized portrait of Karl Marx, with the caption: "Socialism Has Come to America."

More recently, Randy Barber and Jeremy Rifkin (1978) answered Drucker and repoliticized the nation's pension plans. Like Harbrecht, their audience was organized labor. They repeated the question U.S. labor periodically faces: When is economic influence, such as strike power, less effective than shared control of investment or marketing decisions? Barber and Rifkin recast the question and reargued Tilove's point, that labor union's corporate equity and debt ownership do not automatically bring on intended economic outcomes without attaining simultaneously some of the prerogatives of management. They documented provoking examples of how the separation of pension-fund ownership from pension-fund control undermines union strength. Pension funds own substantial equity in firms that violate labor law, provide capital to nonunion companies, and finance plant closings and capital flight.

Economic Power

The AFL-CIO responded enthusiastically to Barber and Rifkin's challenge by instituting procedures whereby affiliates could obtain technical and legal advice on pension-fund strategies. As a result, since 1978, nonconventional pension-fund tactics by unions have bolstered conventional union bargaining power, despite the practical problems of obtaining current information on pension-fund holdings, as well as more fundamental problems such as competition for control of pension funds from investment houses, state and local governments, and companies themselves.

In the 1980s, new constituencies for control of pension funds emerged. Unions, churches, state and local governments, consumer groups, environmentalists, and even the concerned individual, make up what can almost be called a populist movement, the "corporate control movement." The activists in this movement are not entirely the common folk, but the call to action has a populist root. The movement for corporate control is a movement for owners to assert their "rights" and gain control of the corporation whose shares they own. These emboldened owners range from corporate raiders to proponents of South African divestment.

Among the most vivid champions of the corporate control movement were corporate raiders, the vilified and sometimes criminal financial actors who challenged established corporate management by threatening to dump management personnel after buying the company in a hostile takeover. Sometimes the threats were sincere efforts to improve the efficiency of the company; at other times it was an effective way to have shares purchased at inflated prices by nervous or clever management. Whatever the motive, these challenges to so-called entrenched management enriched the shareholders and even the managers who owned inflating shares of a target company. If, in order to maintain control of a company, managers borrowed in a leveraged buy-out, they could still win by paying off the debt by stripping subsidiaries, terminating cash-rich pension plans, or cutting back on activities with deferred returns, such as research and development departments. Investment bankers also gained from the corporate control movement. They garnered high fees for stewarding mergers and acquisitions and speculated in junk bonds, which were issued to fund a corporate takeover and whose expected rate of return depended on the resale value of the rearranged company. Target companies, however, were rarely made more efficient (Scherer 1988). In fact, management defensive tactics and efforts to pay off the buy-out debt often made the firm less attractive, mostly by stripping it of valuable assets, demoralizing workers and managers, and cutting back on long-range plans.

Despite the riches amassed in hostile takeovers by already wealthy individuals, the activity is supported by American ideology. In academia, the school of free market economics expresses the buttressing ideology most simply. The neoclassical argument is that a group of shareholders can be an effective force to shake up entrenched management (Jensen and Ruback 1983). By asserting their voting rights, an almost sacred endowment in any aspect of American life, shareholders can insist on more profits from the firms they own. This activity has, in theory, a salubrious effect on the economy.

Where are pension funds in these matters? "Passively sitting by," complains almost everyone. Pension funds are major players in terms of size in financial markets, but have much less influence in the major restructuring of those markets than investors with assets a fraction of their size. Some pension-fund managers want to change this state of affairs. Representatives, mostly from state and local pension funds, organize to promote pension-fund strategies to influence corporate behavior. Raiders have wooed unions, and vice versa, to direct pension funds into deals that would help all parties—the United Airlines (UAL) buy-out is a good example. Portfolio managers and brokers ushered in a new product—socially concerned, politically correct, investment vehicles. Unions contribute to the developing range of pension tactics through boycotts and corporate campaigns. Civil rights activists have used capital strikes and investment boycotts for decades to add muscle to demands that companies divest their holdings in South Africa.

Pension funds for the United States may be called "the largest lump of money in the world," but it is a lump that is unlike the assets of a few Japanese banks. The money is not centralized, its trustees are diverse, and the hopes for and demands on the money are many.

Pension funds have a political dimension that is not exhibited by trust funds or savings accounts. These realizations should inhibit analysts, economists, companies, and workers from describing pensions as deferred wages. Pension plans have become hoped-for vehicles for massive social change and corporate profit and flexibility.

This may be what Tilove feared. Competing interests in American society were bound to turn to the nation's collectivized savings to stake a claim on the pension plans' growing trusts and seek more influence, power, and control.

Here I focus mainly on organized labor's efforts to strategically control pension funds and show that expectations of leftist thinkers have not been, and are not likely to be, met. Leftists hoped that Peter Drucker's assertions would come true, that labor would control investment and production decisions by stewarding the misnamed "largest lump of money in the world." Unions have encountered four types of limitations, some that are fatal.

The first area of limitation is that unions operating within the U.S. system of industrial relations function primarily as service agencies for workers. An inadequate Social Security system creates a service need for unions to negotiate employer pensions. Therefore, a union's pension-benefit goals may conflict and circumscribe goals of pension-fund activism.

The second reason the employer pension system may remain a key capital accumulation device under terms unfavorable to labor is that the Taft-Hartley Act bars plans from being solely trusteed by unions, and ERISA's fiduciary requirements, along with the distance between the pension management industry and unions, limit labor's influence over pension-fund investments.

Third, pension ownership—union locals, churches, state and local governments—is decentralized and the "owners" are often in conflict over pension fund uses. The lack of a coordinating agent (and conflict of interests) creates an institutional barrier to the collective use of pension clout. Moreover, the ambiguity of pension-fund-ownership designation weakens unions' legal claims to pension-fund control.

Fourth, if unions gain significant control over investment funds they will, theoretically, be constrained by the performance requirements for capital in a capitalist economy.

Many proponents of "alternative" investments had hoped unions would use pension funds offensively—to launch a campaign to bypass the market and replace market rate-of-returns with a new definition of "value"—a strategy that would take into account the value of creating jobs and stabilizing communities. It was hoped that union control of pension funds would incorporate social-needs criteria into investment decisions and steer finance capital away from speculation toward productive investments. Yet, the labor movement primarily has used pension funds defensively, as a tactic in traditional strategies to garner bargaining power and to organize new members. Even when unions bypass capital markets to fund housing projects, the motivation is the loss of union construction and not the dire social consequences of housing shortages, although social concerns do complement and embolden labors' tactics.

As discussed in chapter 3, employer pensions originated in the 1920s as personnel devices to control worker mobility between firms and sometimes to fight unions and a federal retirement program (Brandes 1976: 103–112). Despite these origins, the reconstituted industrial and craft unions in the immediate post-war period conducted a record number of strikes for the right to bargain all aspects of pay, hours, and working conditions, especially employers' discretionary pension plans. The 1949 Supreme Court ruling that pensions are a mandatory subject of bargaining under the National Labor Relations Act is considered a hard-won union victory (*Inland Steel Company vs. the NLRB*, 170 F 2d 247, 7th Cir. 1948).

In 1952, the newly formed AFL-CIO issued a ten-point pension bargaining agenda for its affiliates that gave equal importance to bargaining for joint (management and labor) investment boards and bargaining for noncontributory (the employer pays all pension expenses) pension plans. In 1958, the UAW made formal proposals to the Ford Motor Company for joint trusteeship of the Ford pension fund. Ford and other employers resisted joint-control demands so much that, over time, unions relinquished their demand for joint control of pension assets in favor of bargaining solely over benefits.

For over thirty years, unions and management have considered pensions helpful negotiating devices because the ambiguity over the true value of a pension promise provides bargaining flexibility (Ghilarducci 1990). For example, a 10 percent pay increase can be computed accurately and must be paid for immediately. On the other hand, depending on the funding method used and the assumptions made about future liability and performance of the fund, a 10 percent increase in pension promises can vary in cost by a factor of ten.

Moreover, placing pensions on the bargaining agenda helps solidify the central authority of the national leadership, relative to the rank and file. The experts at the national union and AFL-CIO level can better negotiate pensions than members on the shop floor (Ulman 1961). In addition, employers gain advantages from the fact employer-based social insurance, such as pensions, can create an "industrial feudalism," by increasing the worker's attachment to the firm.[1]

Employer-based social insurance helps a business union thrive. In organizing, unions can offer prospective members services—grievance procedures, pension and health plans, vacations, and so on. The lack of an adequate national pension plan, as well as due process rights for workers and nationalized health insurance, increases a union's appeal as a bargaining agent. However, the value of an employer pension plan to the workers requires close scrutiny. As discussed in chapter 3, the distribution of employer pensions is regressive (higher-income workers have higher pensions benefits and are more likely to receive a pension) and most households with heads over the age of sixty-five receive the significant portion of their "retirement" from earnings and Social Security.

U.S. Financial Markets

The importance of the benefit side of employer pensions has certainly not kept up with the growing presence of pension funds in U.S. financial markets. Pension-fund assets now equal $1.7 trillion, and, before the October 1987 stock market crash, they had grown by more than 15 percent (in nominal terms) per year since the late 1970s (U.S. Bureau of National Affairs 1986c, 1988b) (see table 6.1). Pension funds own almost 39 percent of all outstanding equity in American firms and 50 percent of corporate bonds. In 1950, pension funds owned a fraction of outstanding corporate equity and 13 percent of corporate debt (see table 6.2).

Labor's potential control over pension assets is determined by the current structure of pension-fund management and the labor movement's traditional and prospective pension objectives.

Labor's Access to Pension Fund Management

Barber and Rifkin (1978) responded to Peter Drucker's (1976) claim that pension-fund growth had brought socialism to the United States, because through their pension plans workers own an increasingly large portion of corporate America. Drucker claimed that this emergence of "workers' capitalism" disproves Marx's prediction that socialism—workers owning the means of production—would come about only through the demise of capitalism. Rifkin and Barber highlighted the fact that ownership does not imply control. The structure of pension fund control and the potential influence unions have in controlling their members' pension fund assets is important to understand in order to follow Barber and Rifkin's argument. Private sector unions can influence their pension funds through collective bargaining under the National Labor Relations Act. Public sector unions, under certain public labor laws, can bargain over pension plan investments. Public employees also can be elected to any elected investment boards, or politicize the investments through collective voter action. Public sector funds constitute one-third of total pension-fund assets.

Over 75 percent of people covered by private pension plans are in defined benefit plans (Kotlikoff and Smith 1983). In such plans, participants' benefits are considered liabilities and are financed and administered in one of three major ways. First, employers contribute to a single-employer controlled "trust" fund (a pension fund) that is owned, but not controlled, by the workers covered by the plan. Second, contributions to an insurance company pay for future annuities. And third, contributions are made to a trust fund that has union members as joint trustees.

A majority of participants in defined-benefit plans are covered by collective bargaining contracts; so, in theory, the funding practices, composition of the board, and the designation of manager are subject to

Table 6.1
Pension assets in billions of dollars, percent changes (in 1987 dollars): 1950–1987

Year	Total pension assets	Total private pension assets	Total real pension assets (1987 dollars)	Percent change of real pension assets
1950	16.8	11.9	79.3	—
1951	19.4	13.8	84.9	7.1
1952	22.9	16.3	98.1	15.5
1953	27.3	19.3	116.0	18.3
1954	32.1	22.6	137.7	17.0
1955	39.2	28.4	166.4	22.6
1956	44.4	32.3	185.7	11.6
1957	49.8	36.0	201.1	8.3
1958	58.8	43.2	231.1	14.9
1959	67.2	49.6	262.0	13.4
1960	74.6	54.9	286.3	9.3
1961	86.7	64.4	329.4	15.1
1962	91.7	67.2	344.5	4.6
1963	104.0	76.6	386.1	12.1
1964	118.5	87.9	434.2	12.5
1965	134.0	99.9	482.7	11.2
1966	142.0	103.9	497.3	3.0
1967	162.9	120.3	554.5	11.5
1968	183.2	135.2	598.5	7.9
1969	192.0	138.8	595.2	−0.6
1970	209.8	149.5	614.1	3.2
1971	243.8	174.8	684.2	11.4
1972	294.4	213.8	799.8	16.9
1973	297.6	212.9	761.1	−4.8
1974	300.1	212.1	691.6	−9.1
1975	394.4	289.6	832.8	20.4
1976	451.9	331.5	902.2	8.3
1977	495.9	363.4	930.1	3.1
1978	588.0	434.1	1,024.3	10.1
1979	683.1	513.4	1,069.6	4.4
1980	819.9	621.8	1,130.9	5.7
1981	883.4	659.2	1,103.9	−2.4
1982	1,044.1	781.6	1,229.4	11.4
1983	1,234.4	923.2	1,408.1	14.5
1984	1,350.7	994.1	1,477.9	5.0
1985	1,590.7	1,186.0	1,680.6	13.7
1986	1,809.0	1,339.6	1,875.1	11.6
1987	1,956.1	1,436.1	1,956.1	4.3

Source: Turner and Beller 1980: 104, 105.

Table 6.2
Share of total financial assets, corporate and foreign bonds and equities owned by all private pension funds and individual households, 1950–1987

Year	Private pension share of total financial assets (percent)[1]	Total pension share (percent)		Private pension share (percent)		Total household (percent)[2]	
		Bonds	Equities	Bonds	Equities	Bonds	Equities
1950	3.1	13.0	0.9	11.6	0.9	16.4	91.3
1955	4.6	24.1	2.2	19.8	2.1	11.1	90.0
1960	6.4	33.0	4.1	25.2	4.0	12.0	87.2
1965	7.8	41.6	6.3	27.4	5.9	7.4	84.1
1970	9.2	38.9	9.6	21.6	8.4	17.6	79.4
1975	12.7	39.0	17.0	20.2	14.1	20.5	70.5
1980	15.0	47.0	18.6	28.0	15.8	12.0	70.7
1985	17.0	45.6	21.6	29.8	16.9	5.9	65.2
1987	17.5	39.3	24.0	27.3	18.0	7.2	59.0

1. Total financial assets is the sum of amounts from two different accounts in the flow of funds: total credit market debt owed by domestic nonfinancial sectors, and corporate equities.
2. Includes bank-administered personal trust funds, as these are held on behalf of individuals.
Source: Beller and Turner 1980: 106, 108, 110, Tables 6.3, 6.5, 6.7.

bargaining. The barrier is a lack of bargaining power. And, if the fund is administered by an insurance company, then control of the investments is made even more remote, because pension contributions are comingled with other insurance company revenues.

Most multiemployer plans are trusteed by equal numbers of employer and union representatives. Multiemployer plans primarily exist in cases where one union represents all workers in an industry. Most building trades funds, the Teamsters funds, and the United Mine Workers funds, are examples of jointly trusteed funds.

Ownership rights are less ambiguous in the defined-contribution case than in the defined-benefit case. Workers are considered sole owners of the assets in defined-contribution cases, because the contributions are a certain amount and the employee bears the risk of the funds performance. In the defined-benefit case—with the exception of one recent court decision (Gillipsie 1986)—the corporate sponsor is assigned property rights, because, presumably, the company bears the performance risk, as the benefit promise must be paid regardless of the fund's earnings.

When the AFL-CIO investigated the potential for union control of pension funds, it estimated, based on 1979 data, that two-thirds of all private plans were subject to collective bargaining and that more than one-third of these plans had union trustees. Insurance companies manage one-third of all pension assets and probably that same proportion of collectively bargained plans. Insurance companies comingle their funds, making strategic investment almost impossible.

Union-affiliated funds pay approximately $500 million in fees to financial institutions each year. The AFL-CIO's Committee on Union Pension Fund Investments is considering ways to turn this fact into "consumer" (union) leverage. The Committee proposes to identify portfolio managers and brokerage houses that will accede to a union-sanctioned list of boycotted investments and principles of investing (McDonald 1987).

Pension management performance has been poor. The tendency of pension-fund managers to hold bonds of the Fortune 500 firms and to engage in a higher-than-average number of transactions explains why Standard & Poor's index and other measures of mutual fund rate of returns were higher than the average risk-adjusted rate of return on pension funds between 1968 and 1985 (McCarthy and Turner 1989). Pension funds are subsidized by their tax-favored status and function as a low-cost pool of capital for U.S. firms. The system also enriches the growing pension-fund management industry. So far, capital has been accumulating into pension funds on terms favorable to corporations and flows to retirees on terms favorable only to the highest-income elderly.

Competition for the Control of Capital

In addition to the structural barriers and bargaining power problems faced by unions, the conflicts of interest among groups vying for control of pension funds, as well as technical barriers to collective action (among groups who share goals), create more problems. The following is a descriptive analysis of these groups, beginning with the factions in the labor movement.

The AFL-CIO and the Industrial Union Department (IUD)

The AFL-CIO began to tackle the technical problems of decentralized information by collecting data on the holdings of public sector pension funds and large multiemployer plans in 1980. In 1981, the IUD began publishing a newsletter, *Labor and Investments*, and in 1984 the department began collecting portfolios to construct a data set on the holdings of large single-employer funds. The portfolios are collected through the IUD's coordinated bargaining structure. Notably, the AFL-CIO did not include control over investments and finance capital in its 1985 self-critical planning document as a tactic or goal to revitalize the labor movement (AFL-CIO 1985). Coordinated corporate campaigns were listed as a "new method of advancing the interests of workers." Subsequently, the IUD has begun to advise unions to mount corporate campaigns that include pension-fund tactics; for instance, initiating shareholder resolutions, using proxy voting, and sending information to shareholders (Uehlein 1985). Pooling and updating portfolio information requires cooperation from the thousands of union locals that jointly trustee pension funds. The daunting task will test both the AFL-CIO's technical resources and test the relationships between the AFL-CIO and its affiliates. The AFL-CIO and the IUD are motivated to use pension funds defensively, to regain strength in collective bargaining, and not to transform the relationship between workers and financial institutions.

Public Employee Department of the AFL-CIO

In an effort to coordinate and encourage pension investment activities of affiliate unions representing state and local employees, the Public Employee Department (PED) of the AFL-CIO (AFL-CIO 1986) issued guidelines to portfolio managers and investment staffs of public sector retirement systems. The guidelines are designed to "promote economically beneficial activities" and discourage economic "unequitable" growth and violations of "human rights." The "Code of Fair Community Practices" directs managers, first, to rank companies and projects according to their achievements in promoting desirable and discouraging undesirable activity, and, second, to construct a portfolio from the top-ranking vehicles that yields a risk-adjusted rate of return that is no worse than a portfolio constructed without regard to the "Code of Fair Community Practices." The guidelines should be acceptable to most unions, as well as attractive to some state and local politicians and administrations.

The PED's activities may initiate long-lasting changes in how public employee unions can cooperate with public sector governments to achieve goals in broad, non-labor-relations areas. The strategy ensures that public employee pension money does not aid and abet undesirable activity, but this boycott strategy will not alter corporate practices, or the flow of capital, without tremendous cooperation by like-minded pension-owning groups. In addition, the rate-of-return criteria will mean that many worthy, but only slightly profitable projects needing credit—child care centers, low-income housing, small business—would not be funded under this strategy.

National Unions

National unions have used pension funds defensively, in corporate campaigns, union organizing campaigns, boycotts, and proxy fights with varying degrees of success. The Amalgamated Clothing Textile Workers Union of America's (ACTWU) campaign against the J. P. Stevens Company is a well-known case of combining union ownership of pension funds with a defensive corporate campaign (Barter and Rifkin 1978).

The ACTWU recently used pension clout in a fresh and innovative way in the first half of 1986. The union enlisted the help of a UAW local in its efforts to organize the North Carolina firm of Reeves Brothers, Inc. In conjunction with its organizing campaign, the ACTWU investigated the history and financial structure of Reeves and discovered that the Bell Helicopter Union Pension Fund owned 2 percent of its shares. The ACTWU organizer contacted the Texas UAW local that had a trustee on the Bell Helicopter Union Pension Fund. The trustee, writing as a union member and part owner of the firm they worked for, sent a letter to every Reeves employee asking her or him to vote for ACTWU. Marc Streep, a UAW vice president, also wrote the employees, disputing the company's claims that auto manufacturers would drop their contracts if Reeves Bros., Inc., unionized. This was a corporate campaign with a savvy twist; labor uses its position as capital owner to dispute claims by traditional capital owners, as an appeal to workers in an ordinary organizing campaign.

The United Auto Workers, United Mine Workers (AFL-CIO affiliate in 1989), and the American Federation of State County and Municipal Employees are key unions in a seventy-member coalition in the Royal Dutch-Shell corporate campaign initiated in 1986. In addition to organizing a consumer boycott of Shell products, the coalition organized unions, religious organizations, and state and local governments to instruct investment managers—hired by the trustees of union and church pension and other trusts—to divest of Shell stock, or, barring that, to use the rights associated with owning Shell stock to petition Royal Dutch-Shell for a special shareholders' meeting on divestment in South Africa (National Labor Boycott Shell Committee 1987).

The Shell boycott is one example where unions found common interests among shareholders and managers. Some of labor's success in corporate campaigns may, in part, be caused by the "shock" effect of union involvement in financial matters. Managers are seeking ways to fend off raiders and complainers by instituting differential voting rights and other protective strategies. Shareholder activism works only if ownership implies control.

National unions also, with less frequency, have used pension funds offensively. In 1979, the UAW achieved one of the AFL-CIO's recommendations in its historic agreement with the Chrysler Corporation. The parties agreed that 10 percent of all new pension contributions will be invested in health maintenance organizations, worker housing, retiree centers, and other socially desirable projects. In 1984, the UAW reached an agreement with GM that 5 percent of new pension contributions would be invested in "socially desirable" investments defined by an annual list provided by the union. In exchange, GM can move more of its assets to in-house management. Randy Barber consulted with the Machinists' union at Eastern Airlines and won a similar union investment participatory role for the Machinists (but this agreement fell apart after the Frank Lorenzo–Texas Airlines buyout). Despite these precedents, most unions will not likely have the bargaining power to win participation in investment decisions for single-employer pension plans.

The strategic use of Employee Stock Ownership Plans (ESOPs) is also increasing. The employee ownership strategy is not new to the labor movement. Cooperatives sponsored by the Knights of Labor, religious groups, or utopians often did not survive because large companies retaliated and financial institutions failed to extend credit to such ventures. Recently, unions have taken advantage of the burgeoning use of employee stock ownership plans to gain leverage vis-à-vis an employer. In 1983, in Weirton, West Virginia, the non-AFL-CIO affiliated union at the National Steel Company, Weirton Steel Works, used pension liabilities as a bargaining tool to negotiate an employee buy-out of the firm in lieu of its closure (Marshall 1987). In 1986, the Teamster members and employee owners of Transcon Corp. rebuffed corporate takeover magnate Harold Simmons's efforts to have Transcon buy another Simmons acquired company and take over its liabilities.

The Service Employees International Union (SEIU) is collecting its own data base of portfolios of pension funds it can potentially influence. The SEIU also has issued social investment guidelines for its own staff pension funds.

Building Trades

The building and construction trades have made the most direct gains in using pension funds offensively. Funds from building trades union pensions formed three labor banks in Colorado, New Mexico, and Arizona.[2] The building trades have also channeled funds into union-built construction. Over eleven projects across the country with varying arrangements and goals have pooled money from regional pension funds. One notable example is the Bricklayers and Laborers Non-Profit Housing Company, Inc. The Bricklayer Union and Laborer Union pension fund buys federally insured certificates of deposit (with small subsidies from participating unions) from the U.S. Trust Bank in Boston, which, in turn, finances construction loans for union-built, low-price housing for South Boston residents.

Other building trade investment projects operate like the Union Labor Life Insurance Company (ULLICO) "J for Jobs" project, which invests union pension funds in an open-ended trust that invests in union-built construction. The Housing Investment Trust (HIT) has, since 1964, financed union-only housing construction projects with union pension money. In 1987, the AFL-CIO has expanded the HIT scope and established the Building Investment Trust (BIT), which will finance commercial and industrial real estate investments. In May 1988, the Bakery and Confectionery Pension Plan and the Bricklayers National Pension Fund committed $15 million to the BIT; its first project was a $5.8 million hotel complex in Taos, New Mexico. BIT's advantages to pension funds are its relatively low administrative costs and the assurance that union labor will be used in the construction and maintenance of the project.

The Sheet Metal Workers are using their national pension funds in a fashion that could be interpreted as a type of industrial policy. They seek to increase the demand for their members by closing gaps in financial markets and in the surety industry. In order to help contractors in the asbestos removal industry obtain bonds with lower premiums, the union bought a bonding company. The union pension fund already owns a stake in an asbestos removal contractor (U.S. Bureau of National Affairs 1988c). Edward Carlough, President of the Sheet Metal Workers, calls pension funds the labor movement's "Star Wars Weapon" (U.S. Bureau of National Affairs 1988c). Approximately $500 million has been directed into real estate projects by building trades investment financing foundations (Westerbeck 1985).

The building trades have come closest to systematically challenging the appropriateness of using only the market rate of return in assessing the quality of an investment. Instead, they use a Keynesian multiplier argument and argue that pension funds, unlike other trust funds where all the income comes from financial investments, have two sources of income—employer and employee contributions and investment earnings—and the rates of return from both sources, not just from the more visible financial markets, must be considered. The multiplier argument is primary rhetorical and has not been quantified.

Most of the DOL challenges to building trade investment projects have failed because ERISA's prudent expert rule allows each investment vehicle to be evaluated within the context of the portfolio and the interests of the participants Leibeg 1980). The unsuccessful 1981 DOL challenge of the Florida Operating Engineers low-interest mortgage program (for plan participants) showed that legal pension-fund investments must have a reasonable rate of return and must serve the needs of the participants (U.S. Bureau of National Affairs 1986a, 1986c). The Reagan administration had sent mixed signals about these union initiatives. The DOL continues to issue warnings about union social investment projects, but then President Reagan, speaking to a building trades meeting in 1982, applauded the unions' efforts in setting an example for local initiatives (Smith 1984). In fact, the building trades' activities have not threatened the traditional control of capital.

Each project has different effects in terms of reallocating capital. Some projects clearly correct a market failure, or barrier, by providing funds to projects that would have otherwise faced a credit problem. The Boston Bricklayer and Laborer project is an example of reallocating capital. Other projects can be viewed as substitutes for organizing new members. The enemy in the building trades is not always perceived as the nonunion worker or the aggressive employer; and in periods of high unemployment the nonunion contractor is not blamed as much as insufficient demand. The building trades have sidestepped organization in favor of using pension-fund monies as a primary way to increase the market share of unionized construction (U.S. Bureau of National Affairs 1985; Freeman 1985).

State and Local Governments

State and local social investing, practiced by public funds in about twelve states, is confined to mortgages or loans to small businesses. The main purpose is to increase employment in the relevant region by filling a capital gap and not by providing loans below "market rates." The state of Michigan's project to coordinate investments of private and public funds to provide small business loans and the Pennsylvania MILRITE project are just two examples of the many affirmative investment strategies of governments. These trends can be tracked through the BNA's *Pension Reporter, Labor and Investments,* and other pension-industry publications.

From a distance, these programs look like models of socially responsible investment because the government, endowed with the duty to maximize social goals, invests. Only some projects reallocate capital to worthy projects that otherwise would have faced a credit shortage. Other projects involve granting some privilege to the private sector and usually do not involve the public sector labor unions. Moreover, I have not found cases where state and local governments have opted for owner control; they have not operated the projects they finance through pension funds. Another, more political, state and local use of pension plans is represented by the efforts of the late California State Treasurer, Jesse Unruh, who, at the end of 1984, organized the Council of Institutional Investors (CII), which now has representatives from twenty-two state and local pension funds, six multiemployer funds, and one single-employer plan administrator (*Pensions and Investment Age* 1989). The CII seeks to monitor and influence corporate policies that affect its state and local pension-fund investments, such as green mail, golden parachutes, and poison pills, because these practices threaten dividend income. CII was very vocal in its criticism of GM management's buyout of its largest individual shareholder, H. Ross Perot. Despite GM's assertion that a $720 million price tag on $350 million worth of shares represented a good investment, CII, as well as most of the financial press, cited H. Ross Perot's increasingly shrill criticism of GM management, for example, his public questions, such as, "Why does it take longer to design a GM car than it did to fight World War II?" as a leading motive for the buyout (Kraw 1989). CII forced a meeting with senior members of GM management. A few years later, in January 1990, two CII members, the New York and California state funds, in reportedly uncoordinated efforts wrote to GM asking for a say in the replacement of Roger Smith as GM chief. Most of the CII's tools are public embarrassment, shareholder resolutions, proxy votes, and capital boycotts. CII actions often seek to protect shareholders from entrenched management resisting a takeover. In many cases, labor would be directly opposed to the interests of the shareholders and in agreement with managements' efforts to save the plant from a hostile takeover and possible plant closing.

Under criticism from Edward V. Regan, New York State comptroller and sole trustee of the $44 billion New York State and Local Retirement Fund, Governor Mario Cuomo's Commission on "The New York State Pension Investment Task Force" recommended that pension funds obtain guarantees from federal agencies to invest in projects to improve the state's infrastructure. Regan argued against the Commission's report and financier Felix Rohatyn's similar suggestions that the federal government was overburdened by guarantees and the first and foremost duty of the fund was to earn the highest return.

This sort of reasoning was further displayed in 1990 when several state and local pension funds threatened to divest themselves of the stock of all Pennsylvania-based companies to protest Pennsylvania's restrictions on hostile takeovers. The pension funds' position is that hostile takeovers bid up the price of the stock and any restriction on hostile bids constrains the potential profit from holding that equity. Lawmakers in Pennsylvania want to halt hostile takeovers in order to stabilize communities and the business environment. What the Pennsylvania pension plans do will reveal how sharp the horns of the dilemma actually are when it comes to defining socially responsible pension-fund strategies.

Churches, Wealthy Individuals, and Endowments

The Interfaith Center for Corporate Responsibility and the Investor Responsibility Research Council are research and advocacy institutes with strong church connections. Their publications provide advice on shareholder rights and strategies. Most of the alternative investments of university endowments have been in South African divestment and clean fund investments. In addition to specific actions and research functions, the financial industry has responded to the concern of churches, unions, endowments, and wealthy individuals who fear their investments are encouraging antisocial activities by the offering of "clean funds" (Domini and Kinder 1984). Currently, in the U.S., eight mutual funds and three money market funds advertise holdings that are screened according to various criteria. Two Canadian funds, the Summa Fund and the Ethical Growth Fund, and one British fund, The Stewardship Unit Trust, use social screening criteria in selecting investments. Each fund seems specifically tailored to one or more groups. For instance, the PAX World fund does not contain "sin" stocks, such as holdings in tobacco or liquor companies or defense contractors. The performance of these socially screened funds beats the market average. As a 1986 *Wall Street Journal* headline noted,

"Investors Can Do All Right By Doing Good." So do the brokerage houses and money managers who have developed this market niche.

From the point of view of labor and churches, however, the structure of capital markets limits the effectiveness of the clean fund strategy. Multinationals and conglomerates issue debt and equity. Targeting money into a particular region, or to a particular subsidiary of a conglomerate, is not possible, because capital allocation decisions are made internally. Managers make investment decisions. Unions face the same problems as shareholders if they attempt to transform companies through the ownership of corporate equity. The advantage the labor movement has over most shareholders —its national presence—can either create enormous clout, or unresolvable conflicts of interest among unions. (How successful would the Shell boycott have been if the Oil, Chemical and Atomic Workers Union represented Shell employees?)[3]

But, trustees of funds of many corporations and entities with trust funds are asking the same question Harbrecht (1959) and Barber and Rifkin (1978) exhorted labor unions themselves to ask. In the words of a pension attorney, "What is it that says trustees of the American Cancer Society can't say (its pension fund) won't invest in tobacco stocks" (Gerald Feder, quoted in *Pensions and Investment Ages* 1989).

Corporations

Corporations have discovered in the 1980s that their pension funds can be convenient sources of cash and can serve other corporate needs. A combination of legal, political, and economic factors explains why single-employer pension funds are now used as a corporate financing tool.

The interpretation, and Reagan administration's enforcement of ERISA, all but encouraged corporations to put their funds to innovative and, indeed, alternative uses. To fend off hostile takeovers, or to court "white knights," a corporation can often obtain DOL permission to direct its employee pension fund to buy the company's stock (as long as it is not "overpriced"). A corporation can terminate a plan that happens to have more assets than legal liabilities, pay the liabilities, and use the extra cash. The corporation can also manipulate the rate of return the fund is assumed to earn in order to alter the cash contributions required to fund the liability. Raising the assumed rate assumes the fund will earn more and, therefore, require less from the firm.

Between 1980 and 1987 about $19 billion had been recaptured by corporations in defined-benefit pension plan terminations (VanDerhei and

Harrington 1989: 189). Such practices prompted passage of the Pension Protection Act of 1987. The Act raises the penalties for this activity and changes funding requirements to help shore up underfunded plans, but the practices essentially remain legal (U.S. Bureau of National Affairs 1988a). Corporate executives are also using their pension funds to engage in their own brand of shareholder activism. The Financial Executive Institute (FEI) composed of corporate executives is alarmed by the corporate practices of the companies whose shares the FEI owns and is operating to stop them much like the CII. These corporate executives and the CII's goals may conflict with union goals. These groups want share values to rise, even if it means hostile takeovers and the spinning off of assets. These activities may cause corporate indebtedness and layoffs. Except for a few instances (the United Airline pilots, for one), unions have not found a way to manipulate stock takeovers to meet union objectives.

Pension-fund strategies will continue to confront and challenge the conflict-of-interest problems created by the variety of groups who want pension-fund control. Unions also face problems from remote and anti-union money managers, investment bankers, and other institutional managers who handle pensions funds. As the labor movement takes on more financial sophistication via pension-fund activity, pro-union clean fund architects will enter the U.S. finance sector and bid for labor's business.

Prospects for Worker Capitalism

In Keynesian and radical political economics, the amount of investment funds available is presumed to be determined by business confidence and the result of a struggle over income shares: wages and profits. Neoclassical economists would emphasize the role of personal savings decisions (Marglin 1984). The institutional facts complicate the theoretical description. Deferred wages in the form of forced-group savings (employer pension funds), and not individual savings accounts or profits, are the main source of accumulation and are controlled by money managers at the largest financial institutions in the nation. Pension funds help U.S. corporations avoid banks and avoid relying solely on profits for investment.

During the last ten years, the labor movement's severe loss in bargaining power has been accompanied by its increasing strategic use of pension funds. During the same period the stewards of capital—labor's capital —used pension funds in speculative investment activity, which closed plants and strangled communities. Labor's pension-fund tactics have not significantly altered or challenged the criteria by which investment decisions are made. Yet, despite the fact that labor has not become a key player in financial markets and that pension strategies have not altered economic investment criteria, labor's pension strategies have made political breakthroughs.

Successful union targeting of pension-fund investments helps erode union member suspicion (a residue from the Teamster pension scandals) that union leaders cannot be trusted with pension funds. The facts that corporate-managed funds underperformed in the market during the period from 1968 to 1983 and that union-built and -financed construction helped correct market failures by funding otherwise unfunded worthy projects, help further erode beliefs that corporations and money managers are the only legitimate pension-fund managers.

These political and ideological changes are tempered by the fact that unions must satisfy a group of voluntary members, most of whom want a service union. Therefore, a union pension strategy, as well as other policies, must advance traditional union goals: surviving, organizing, and bargaining. Using precious bargaining power to obtain pension control will be a rare phenomenon; workers want and need supplements to Social Security. Abandoning employer pensions for an expanded Social Security system would benefit most workers but would cause unions to lose the institutional advantages associated with negotiating over pensions. Although the conflict-of-interest problems, the ideological problems, and the legal hurdles are many, if they are surmounted labor still will not likely realize the remarkable amount of political and economic potential pension strategies can provide. The continuing barriers will be the fact that the labor movement, in developing its pension strategies, has eagerly embraced two economic concepts—market rates of return and property rights—that work against its interest.

This explains the odd development that despite the potential for conflict between the financial and pension management industry and workers, social investment schemes have, so far, generated little opposition and politicization. One piece of evidence for the lack of politicization is found by observing that both Ronald Reagan and Jesse Jackson (in his 1988 campaign) have endorsed the alternative use of pension funds. Much of the potential conflict over ownership and control has been blunted, because most alternative investments have not entailed a sacrifice of a risk-adjusted "market" rate of return. In addition, corporate "alternative uses" (terminations and so on) that benefit corporations and shareholder activism (South Africa divestment strategies) do not threaten the pension management industry. Thus, the battle that labor fought earlier (Moody 1989) has never been confronted, that market rates of return do not measure social rates of return. Because the flaws, biases, and limitations of using rates of return to allocate capital have not been seriously challenged, the legal criterion, ERISA's "prudent expert" rule, has not become a serious barrier to most so-called alternative investments.

Moreover, unions have placed too much emphasis on the claim that pension-fund "ownership" endows them with the "right" to control pension-fund investments. Unions have made property rights the focal point of the legal issues and moral issues in the debate over who should control the investments of the workers' group savings. There are a number of problems with this focus. First, labor has lost most legal battles over ownership "rights." Although workers are the economic *source* of pension funds they are not the designated *owner*. Corporations have consistently won the right to terminate plans and revert "excess" assets to their own use. The second problem is ideological. In using the ownership and control argument, labor becomes a defender of property rights. Property is a legal concept and the ownership of the employer pensions cannot be traced to any single party, because pensions are a product of the evolution of U.S. industrial relations and specific policies of the state concerning the Social Security system and the appropriate mechanism for capital accumulation. The source of the funds can be traced to workers, but fighting over ownership rights avoids the real contest over just how pension funds should be used.

Outcomes and Contradictions: Ownership and Strategies

During the last ten years, the labor movement has developed creative and successful pension-fund strategies. Labor has used pensions defensively in corporate campaigns and offensively in construction financing. The most important gains made by these pension strategies may, however, be political, rather than economic. Labor's pension activism helps create a hospitable climate for regulating and directing financial markets; these tactics do lay bare the central fact that labor creates capital (not only from the sweat of workers' brows, but, as noted earlier, through deductions from their pay) and that capital is not always invested to advance worker interests.

The economic effectiveness of labor's pension tactics is limited by the U.S. labor movement's waning bargaining strength and by the union's consequential role in U.S. industrial relations. In addition, labor's emphasis on property rights and the noncritical use of market rate-of-return criteria may further hamper union efforts to redirect the flow of financial funds. Yet it is difficult to imagine how, alone, the labor movement could be more successful by abandoning the rights-based arguments away from the resonant property rights arguments toward rights for stable communities and good jobs. Labor needs a coalition to demand socialized capital investments within a coherent industrial policy framework so that owner-ship-based rights claims do not result in competition with other pension-fund "owners."

Unions use pension funds tactically and are careful to meet their current legal obligations by seeking the maximum market rates of return on the pension investments they do control. This careful portfolio management can mean employment-endangering speculation and short-term profit considerations that often yield high profit rates but jeopardize the achievement of other union objectives. Labor would have to work collectively in order to confront this contradiction and adopt alternative criteria for worthy pension investments, those that secure jobs, communi-ties, and retirement income.

A public board investing union pension funds and a nationalized universal pension plan could create such criteria by providing adequate pensions and by incorporating employment and community effects when calculating the rate of return of a particular investment. The pension benefit logic of President Carter's mandatory universal pension system can be concatenated to the industrial policy logic of creating a collectivized pool of social capital, or community investment funds. Property rights and the legitimacy of market rates of return are the foundations of a capitalist economy. If the pension fund system, the system of capital accumulation by means of workers' forced savings, continues to be governed by these rules, the system will function on terms favorable to the most powerful interests in the economy.

7

What Makes a Good Private Pension System?

The 1964 Studebaker Corporation's closing and abrupt cutoff of actual and promised pensions to retirees and workers has been identified as the instigator of activist government regulation of private pensions.[1] The Studebaker closing also is cited frequently as the emotional and political impetus behind the passage of ERISA. But the private pension system was, at every step of its development, shaped by various structures and actions—and the lack of action—of the federal government. These structures and actions include the lack of a Social Security system, a tax policy directly encouraging private pensions, the battles surrounding developing labor law, and excess wartime profit taxes and wage caps applied during World War II and the Korean War.

Eastern Bloc nations are undergoing a transition from socialism to capitalism and are looking to the United States for examples of social insurance programs that cushion the risks of capitalism. In light of their investigations, we must assess our own system of public, quasi-public, and private social insurance.

The appropriate criteria to judge employer-based private pension systems come from both utopian and politically feasible notions about what a private pension system should do. Judging the system also requires examining its consistency with other national goals for tax, retirement, and employment policy and capital accumulation. The third area of judgment concerns the private pension system's real costs and opportunity costs weighed against its benefits. Taxpayer costs of a privatized system are tax expenditures and regulation costs. Other costs are intangible. These include opportunity costs in terms of the equity and efficiency the nation might be losing, because the existence of a privatized system stymies the expansion of a federal system. On the other hand, support for Social Security might not be so strong and widespread, if the federal government had not given tax favoritism to the private system.

Ideally, an employer-specific pension system subsidized by federal tax policy and voluntarily constructed should meet the following economic and political criteria. The criteria address what makes the system good, as well as what will enable it to survive: (1) adequacy in terms of retirement income, (2) flexibility in terms of meeting the different needs of workers in different occupations, (3) security, that the pension promise is certain, reliable, and backed by sufficient assets, and (4) the legitimacy of an institution, or system, that depends upon what people expect, aligned with their actual entitlements. Legitimacy, defined here as the equivalent of, and harmony among, expectations and entitlement, requires more than financial security and stability. To be legitimate, the system must involve participants so that changes are anticipated and decisionmaking is not autocratic.

There are signs that the private pension system is slipping in all four areas, that the system is becoming less worthy of tax favoritism or support. The suspicions are rooted in recent failures and special cases, but also in the inherent structure of private and voluntary social insurance. This underlying weakening of confidence occasionally surfaces in the popular press. A 1990 *New York Times* article headlined "Company-Financed Pensions Failing to Fulfill Promise" (Uchitelle 1990: 1) concludes an analysis of the effects of inflation and the decline in the popularity of defined-benefit plans on pension benefits with this judgment: "The upshot is that many workers risk being left short of retirement income." A 1989 *Chicago Tribune* series documented fraud, bankruptcy, and shrinking lack of coverage for workers. The first article in the series began: "The expectation held by Americans for merely two generations—that a lifetime of work and loyalty would lead to a guaranteed pension and comfort in retirement—is melting away" (Tackett 1989: 3).

The Department of Labor is increasingly seeking criminal prosecutions for firms mismanaging pension assets and during the Reagan administration pension reforms were passed almost every year to deal with terminations, reversions, and other corporate actions seen as eroding the system. Republican Senator Nancy Kassebaum and Secretary of the Treasury Nicholas Brady intended to punish pension fund managers who engage in short-term investment activity by imposing an excise tax on pension fund earnings made from the sale of assets held less than six months (U.S. Bureau of National Affairs 1990b).

Peoples' expectations about their employer pensions are lower than their expectations for Social Security. Over 2,000 people in 1981 were surveyed by the PCPP and were asked to assess whether their employment-based pension, from the employer or union, would be an important source of income. People were much more confident that Social Security would be an important source of their retirement income than their union or employer pensions. And, surprisingly, since the vast majority of the elderly poor are women, women were much more likely to express confidence in the adequacy of their prospective retirement income, and in Social Security in particular. They were, explicably, less sanguine about the importance of their expected employer pensions (Ghilarducci 1984).

What analysts view as goals of a national system of private pensions also reflects their economic ideology. Neoclassical economists such as Cornell professors Olivia Mitchell and Gary Fields, and University of Chicago professor Edward Lazear (1983) generally support the voluntary nature of the system and minimum regulation, because, in their view, the system represents optimal contracts made between workers and firms (Fields and Mitchell 1984). The efficient contract view sees pensions as helping to preserve on-the-job skills and prevent slacking off as workers become older; in other words, to allow a firm and its work force to agree to a payment system that gets the most pay and production. Institutionalists such as Merton Bernstein (1964) and W. Andrew Achenbaum (1989) would see the system as reflecting particular bargains and power relations made among the relevant parties at any one point in time. A Marxist analysis, such as that of Laura Katz Olson (1982), would view the system as a state-corporate agreement to increase the rate of surplus value from workers and make lower-paid workers subsidize the higher-paid and managerial class.

Requirements for an Optimum Pension System

Bert Seidman, former head of the AFL-CIO Social Security Division, and long-standing practitioner and expert on social insurance, puts the requirements on government policy succinctly. He joked that the person who comes up with an adequate and flexible national retirement income security policy should win an award.[2]

In addition to Seidman's two principles of a good private pension system—adequacy and flexibility—I append "security" and "legitimacy." A national policy on retirement income security must be integrated with the private sector. There are too many interests—employers, unions, labor, the pension industry—and too little commitment by government to provide only a government system, to expect the Social Security system, as it is devised, to provide all retirement income. Although no other system relies solely on the public sector, the United States relies on private pensions more than Japan, Australia, New Zealand, or any European nation.

Pensions should be tied to occupational idiosyncrasies, and private pensions are one way to do this. Private pensions are also important for capital accumulation. The vast amounts of savings gathered in pension plans probably would not be saved for retirement without an institution, a group plan, that is tax-favored and coercive.

Given the developments in the last twenty years, an ideal pension system does require more government intervention, chiefly in promoting honest administration of plans, accumulating financial capital, and regulating the investment of pension funds. Government policy will also have to deal with the fact that people who have relatively shorter tenure on the job receive considerably less pensions—the so-called portability issue. The Bush administration attempted to address this issue by making it easier for larger firms to adopt Simplified Employee Pensions (SEPs; see chapter 4). Moreover, a majority of female workers, and barely half of male workers, are covered by any employer pension. This coverage rate has not increased in ten years. Policymakers will also have to deal with the disparities in income between single elderly women and elderly couples. A persistent, vexing problem is inflation's effect on the buying power of a fixed pension. In just eighteen years at a modest 4 percent inflation rate the buying power of a fixed-pension annuity decreases by half. Moreover, an employee who earns a vested benefit and at age forty-five loses that job, then moves to a job without a pension plan, the value of his or her employer pension could decrease by one-half at the time of retirement at the modest rate of inflation of 4 percent a year.

The private pension system has diminished in all areas that constitute a good pension system: adequacy, flexibility, security, and legitimacy. Mild to radical ideas for pension reform that would improve the private pension system in these four areas need to be examined. The proposals range from preventing lump-sum disbursements of pension benefits, to adding worker trustees to pension boards, to mandating an advance-funded mandatory pension system. This is discussed in chapter 8.

Adequacy and Equity

The adequacy of a pension benefit is determined by three factors: the corporate sponsor's willingness and ability to pay, the workers' or union's bargaining or economic leverage, and, not so obviously, the administrative structure of the pension plan. The effect of the administration structure and pension plan benefit formulas on eventual pension benefits is critical. The forestalled IRS Section 89 sought to promote fair distribution of benefits between high- and low-income workers in tax-preferred fringe benefit plans, mainly because gross inequities occur in single-employer pension plans. Approximately 73 percent of all plans are proportional or regressive, meaning high-income earners receive disproportionate shares of pension benefits (Kotlikoff and Smith 1983). Fourteen percent of plans are progressive—low-income workers have a higher percentage of preretirement earnings replaced than higher-income workers. Collectively bargained plans—those derived from a type of labor-management cooperation—are more likely to be equitably distributed and in keeping with long-standing public-policy principles against discrimination in tax-preferred plans. A major reason union plans are more progressive than nonunion plans is that they do not include management and salary workers and thereby cover persons with a relatively small wage spread. Nonunion plans, those that cover all employees, are likely to be regressive, most often because of Social Security integration.

ERISA allows workers to take a tax-free "roll-over"—a transfer of a lump-sum pension benefit received when workers leave a pension plan before retirement—into an individual retirement account (IRA) if done within sixty days. Employers prefer to pay the vested benefit in a lump sum, rather than maintain the obligation. Moreover, the lump sum is determined using an interest rate assumption that is often larger than actual returns on an IRA; a lump sum is cheaper for the employer.

Most employees with lump sums do not, however, save them for retirement (Employee Benefit Research Institute, 1986). Shortsightedness alone does not cause this behavior. The worker may realize that the annuity the lump sum could buy would not be significant at the time of retirement, especially during inflationary times. Moreover, the nearly stagnant rate of wage earnings growth between 1973 and 1988 caused households to decrease personal savings rates in order to maintain their standard of living (Pollin 1987). Although the lack of coverage, intermittent work histories, the bias of pension plans toward long stayers, and the fact that after an employee leaves or retires pensions are not indexed for inflation are the primary reasons for inadequate pensions, not lump-sum dispersals (Andrews 1990). The larger problems of inadequate coverage, benefits, and lack of inflation indexing will likely not be tackled by the Department of Labor under Bush.

Political awareness and mobilization around the differences in pension benefits between women and men will grow. Women's private pensions are 51 percent of men's—a gap that is larger than the wage gap--and are even lower in the same industry for the same years of service (see chapter

4). Women are also less likely to be entitled to pensions than men. In 1984, 25 percent of women workers between the ages of twenty-five and sixty-four were entitled to a pension (66 percent were covered) whereas 41 percent of men were entitled (72 percent of men were covered by a pension plan) (Andrews 1988). Cynthia Fryer Cohen (1983) simulated women's employment experiences to predict the effect of certain changes in pension rules on the eventual pension income of retired women workers. She controlled for the particular earnings profiles, employment patterns, occupations, and industries common to women, and found that proposals for universal coverage, like the mandatory universal pension system (MUPS) proposed by President Carter's 1981 Commission on Pension Policy, would substantially increase pension income to women. The proposal would require all employers to contribute 3 percent of a worker's income to an account such as an IRA. She found that lowering vesting to five years (as the 1986 Omnibus Act did) would have little effect on women's pensions. In fact, more men may have benefited from the Retirement Equity Act's (REACT) participation liberalization because more men are employed by firms that offer pensions. REACT's requirement that a spouse must approve in writing any waiver of the survivor benefit, which lowers the monthly pension benefit in exchange for a lifetime benefit to a surviving spouse, certainly helped more wives than husbands.

Inflation is a major reason private pensions have not grown as a percentage of retirement income in the late 1970s and 1980s. Pensioners who retired as production workers in firms with more than 5,000 employees in manufacturing, mining, or transportation were more likely to receive a post-retirement pension adjustment in the early 1980s. In general, however, private pension recipients were more likely to receive inflation adjustments in the 1970s than in the 1980s. Between 1973 and 1978, 45 percent of all plans, containing 51 percent of all participants, increased pension benefits in recognition of the decline in buying power. But between 1983 and 1987, the percentage of retirees with at least one cost-of-living increase for their private pension fell to 26 percent.

Social Security, the major source of retirement income, had, in the meantime, been automatically indexed to inflation (in 1983, legislation was passed that required Social Security COLA increases to be triggered by an inflation rate of more than 3 percent). Tables 7.1 and 7.2 show that Social Security benefits beat inflation, but private pensions did not. Table 7.1 shows the level and rate of changes in the consumer price index, Social Security benefits for men and women, and private pensions for men and women. Table 7.2 converts the 1986 pensions into 1976 dollars and we see

Table 7.1
Levels and rates of change in prices, median Social Security, and private pensions for recipients sixty-five years of age or older, by sex

Year	Consumer price index (1967 = 100)	Social Security (median)		Private pensions (median)	
		Men	Women	Men	Woman
1976	170.5	$248	197	171	112
1986	328.4	549	420	316	162
Percent change 1976–1986	93	121	113	84	45

Sources: U.S. Department of Commerce 1988: 450, Table 738; Turner and Beller 1989: 398, Appendix, Table D7.

Table 7.2
Change in the buying power of Social Security and private pensions for recipients sixty-five years of age or older, by sex, in 1986

	Men	Women	Men	Women
1986 pension in 1976 dollars	$285	218	164	83
Percent change in buying power	12	96	−4.1	−29

Sources: U.S. Department of Commerce 1988: 450, Table 738; Turner and Beller 1989: Appendix, Table D7.

that women—as a group who receive private pensions—have lost the most between 1976 and 1986. Their real benefit fell by 29 percent, while men's real buying power fell by only 4.1 percent. Social Security benefits for women, on the other hand, increased by 9.6 percent and men's real Social Security benefit increased by 13 percent.

A study of Canadian firms and reported cases in the United States (as discussed in chapter 4) shows that healthy pension funds, those with assets greater than liabilities, are more likely to give ad hoc benefit increases to retirees than underfunded plans. Some unions, for instance the miners' and autoworkers', often include pension COLAs in their bargaining demands. Members of these unions are often linked to retirees by familial ties, ties that bind them to the pensioners' welfare. U.S. firms also had ties that bound them to their pensioners' welfare in the 1970s, but those ties were loosening in the 1980s. Corporate restructuring as well as U.S. corporations' global expansion in the 1980s most likely helped the decline in ad hoc benefit increases.

The fact that defined-benefit pension contributions have fallen, COLAs have diminished, women have lost relatively more, fund asset cushions have shrunk (when projected benefits are added), and healthy-fund terminations skyrocketed in the 1980s suggests that structural changes in the nature of the pension fund contract have occurred. These changes have made pensions relatively less important as a source of retirement income and have fostered waning confidence and growing suspicion about the adequacy of private pensions.

Flexibility

Flexibility in a pension system refers to the ability of a system to adjust to the unique retirement needs of particular occupations, industries, and even firms within the same industry and same occupation. The Social Security system provides a uniform floor of support, but the diversity of occupations and industries requires more finely tuned systems to satisfy worker retirement needs. One of the defensible schemes for government-subsidized, but none-the-less private, pension systems is intended to provide this flexibility. For example, university professors may effectively and pleasurably teach and research until the ends of their lives; on the other hand, coal miners need to retire earlier in order to save their lives.

Plans differ greatly by deductions, or rewards, given for early retirement or working past age sixty-five. Using models of how individuals make trade-offs between working and leisure and a detailed analysis of ten pension plans, Fields and Mitchell (1984) found that differences in retirement age across plans can be explained by differences in worker preferences for retirement and by different rewards for retirement in individual pension plans.

From a perspective that is not so individual-centric, one that views employer concerns as important determinants of retirement benefits, my study found great differences in the benefit structures among retirement plans in the same industry for the same occupation (Ghilarducci 1991). The big three auto firms—Ford, GM and Chrysler—offer larger benefits for early retirees. The Japanese transplant companies have much less generous early retirement formulas; in fact, they have less generous pensions overall. The differences appear to be caused by the fact that employment in the big three is falling, while it is increasing in the Japanese plants. Worker tastes are not considered to be the determining factor explaining the differences. What the Fields and Mitchell study and my work show is that private plans do exhibit flexibility, although for different reasons. The policy questions are, how can the system deliver more and what costs are there to flexibility?

Obviously, ERISA and subsequent legislation have traded flexibility for equity, adequacy, and security. ERISA requires minimum vesting and participation. Some flexibility was preserved when ERISA did not mandate benefit levels. But funding flexibility has steadily been reduced by funding standards and limitations on actuarial assumptions. How can flexibility be enhanced without exacerbating inequity, inadequacy, and insecurity?

If flexibility is defined as the accommodation of worker interests—the antithesis of rigidity, nonresponsiveness, and uniformity—then worker input, either through collective bargaining, or worker trustees, would help promote flexibility through improved communication. Employers only know imperfectly what workers need and want in retirement and even complain that workers do not understand or appreciate the pension plans the firms provide. If an employer's benefit menu is not fine-tuned to the employees' needs (because it is a copycat program either recommended by consultants or observed), the lack of communication could deprive the employer of the opportunity to provide a plan that fits both employer and worker needs.

Worker representatives could also reduce the cost of employee communications at the same time the effectiveness of the pension plans increases, because workers have a voice in the design of pension plans. Management can better know the value workers place on, say, an increase in pensions versus a reduction in vesting. Early retirement may be a subjectively more valuable offer to workers than another, more costly, pension improvement. Worker representation educates management as well as workers themselves. Another area of flexibility is on the investment side. Jointly trusteed plans across the nation have been leaders in safe, innovative, socially beneficial, and highly profitable investment projects, as discussed earlier. The AFL-CIO Housing Investment Trust and the Building Investment Trust directs union pension fund money into worthy construction projects, sometimes helping to revitalize our nation's inner cities. The Bricklayers and the Laborers housing venture in Boston is a well-known example of these efforts. The long history of the garment unions' successes in providing credit, insurance, and housing to low-income workers in New York State also demonstrates that investments can do well by doing good.

Interviews with trustees of jointly managed plans about their investment strategies reveal two things: a history of conservatism and a second-nature, sophisticated sensitivity to the two-sided consequences of investment strategies—(1) that bold investment strategies can adversely affect the risk and size of workers' pensions, (2) that bold investment strategies can likely affect workers' jobs and standards of living.

The business community's objections to worker representatives, which surfaced again over the Visclosky legislation, paint workers as being both too reckless and too conservative. The objections stem from resistance to worker representation and a prejudgment of workers' investment philosophies and feelings about risk. For example, an administrator for a major pension plan told me that unions would object on political grounds to foreign investments that would otherwise yield high return. There is, however, no evidence of such anti-foreign investment bias on behalf of the jointly trusteed funds. The working class in this nation has deep attachments to Eastern Europe and probably will, as enthusiastically as Western financiers, direct labor's capital there.

Moreover, comparing the rate of return of joint funds and single funds might suggest that joint funds forewent profitable investments that single-employer pensions snapped up. This is not true. Multiemployer plans did earn a lesser rate of return than single-employer plans in the 1980s, because corporate sponsors could handle more variability in earnings as corporate treasuries could cover pension expenses, while multiemployer plans only had the fund as a reserve (Congressional Research Service 1990). The multiemployer plans had greater proportions of their portfolio in bonds and real estate whereas corporate funds were held in more risky equities and junk bonds (Congressional Research Service 1990). Flexibility must be viewed from the benefits and the investment side.

Security

U.S. workers are among the more uncertain about what their pension benefits will be, when compared to workers in other industrialized nations. Not only is there more purposeful asymmetry of information in the U.S. system (the advantages of ambiguity about what pension plans will deliver is explained in chapter 3), but there are more contingencies on which pensions are based. For instance, most U.S. workers are also less certain of their final pension, because U.S. pensions are more sensitive to investment and funding strategies of firms. The percentage of retirement income that comes from a state pension (the most reliable source) in the United States is 50 percent, which is the lowest percentage except for Switzerland and Canada (Turner and Beller 1989: 328). In no other industrialized nation, including Canada and Switzerland, are pensions less portable and rights to employment less secure. Each factor alone makes the estimate of one's pension more variable.

Another aspect of pension security is the exposure taxpayers have to bailing out underfunded plans. Jointly trusteed pension plans help promote certainty, because multiemployer funds are better funded than single-employer plans. The Pension Benefit Guaranty Corporation reports that although jointly trusteed pension plans only charge a $2.60 premium, compared to the single-employer plans' premium of $16 and $50, the single-employer fund is $1.5 billion in deficit, whereas the jointly trusteed pension fund has a $90 million surplus.

In addition, the termination rate for multiemployer, jointly trusteed pensions plans is smaller than that for single-employer plans. This makes the pension contract from a jointly trusteed pension plan more secure and trustworthy.

Terminations of single-employer healthy pension funds make pension confidence more insecure. As reported in chapter 4, over 12,000 defined-benefit plans have terminated in the thirteen-year period between 1975 and 1989, which is more than the number terminated in the twenty-four year period between 1950 and 1974. The largest number of terminations occurred in 1985 and the largest amounts reverted to their corporate sponsors in the following year.

PBGC research director Richard Ippolito (1986b) estimated that workers lose, on average, over 50 percent of their pension when funds terminate, because the inflation protection workers have in healthy ongoing plans disappears when funds terminate. A final-salary pension provides some cost-of-living protection, but when a plan terminates pensions are calculated at current salary. Moreover, in the past, firms with pension asset cushions often paid a cost-of-living increase to retirees.

In the regulatory environment of the 1980s, however, firms do not have to terminate a pension plan to get access to the cash. Corporate sponsors of single-employer corporate funds enjoyed a great deal of funding flexibility in the 1980s. Actuarial assumptions fluctuated and corporate contributions fell. Corporate finances may have been stabilized by this pension flexibility (Ghilarducci and Wolfson 1991). But corporate stability may have been bought at the expense of pension income security. The fact that funding levels are down means the level of asset cushions that may be needed in a bull stock market and inflationary period is flattened. This is the case where flexibility in all the wrong places can cause insecurity about future pension wealth. This insecurity, as well as the stagnant pension coverage and waning importance of pension income as a source of retirement income, has adversely affected legitimacy, the fourth criterion for a decent pension system.

Legitimacy

The legitimacy of any system can be measured by the difference between what people expect from the system and what people are entitled from it. Single-employer plans have created gaps between expectations and entitlement. Another source of legitimacy in a system is the difference between what is promised and what is paid for. Generous pension promises can only be realized if they are funded. Single-employer plans do not fully fund promised benefits. Government funding standards and monitoring, as well as worker representation, help bring expectations and entitlement in line. One way worker representation helps legitimacy is through the conveyance of reliable information about the plan to workers. As described in chapter 5, workers often overestimate what their pensions will pay. Union members were, however, less likely to exaggerate in their own minds the value of the pension. This is attributed to union members' relatively large involvement with overseeing and negotiating their pension plans.

The case of the steel industry shows that even when the news is bad—that corporate pensions are in desperate shape—improved communication with the union could have maintained some legitimacy surrounding the pension. The LTV situation demonstrates this point: Even when there is a union, a worker pension trustee might have lessened a crisis by aligning expectations with entitlement. As described in chapter 4, the IRS allowed LTV to legally underfund its plans below the ERISA minimums. This added to the erosion caused by the IRS's 1982 decision to allow LTV to substitute two million shares of LTV preferred stock (soon to decrease in value) for cash as 25 percent of LTV's pension contributions that year. In 1983, one of the largest steelworkers' locals in the nation contacted me regarding the consequences of this move. I was asked to confirm or allay their suspicions that these moves jeopardized their promised benefits, especially their early retirement benefits. I confirmed that local's fears, but I have since pondered whether the crisis that followed could have been softened if LTV had deliberated with workers about the pension risk taken in its efforts to save the company. Worker trustees probably would have agreed to LTV's actions. Instead, the majority of LTV workers were continually promised their pension benefits and were crushed when the bankruptcy and termination occurred. Such events shake the legitimacy-foundation of the system.

The older problem of underfunded plans, coupled with the phenomenon of healthy terminations, haunts the private pension system. When a so-called overfunded plan terminates, the "good risks" in the pool of insured participants are reduced. Recent studies also show that the pension system may not be as secure as commonly believed (cited in chapter 4). Mark Warshawsky (1988), from the Federal Reserve Board of Governors, showed that although the Congressional Budget Office reports that 80 percent of plans are overfunded, overfunding as determined by each plan's accounting practices. The study pointed out that the common accounting method used in reporting the status of pension funds overstates the health of the pension funds. If pension funds from 1981 through 1985 used the FASB 87 accounting rules (which require calculating projected liabilities rather than termination liabilities) and accounted for a COLA that yields only a 50 percent cost-of-living increase, the percentage of so-called overfunded plans would fall from 79 percent (in 1985) to 36 percent. Legal, but misleading, reporting increases the gap between expectations and entitlement, further confusing workers and eroding confidence.

Terminations, underfunding, and sponsor-stock contributions are not technically illegal, although the Office of the Inspector General of the Department of Labor claims illegal activity is on the rise. But these manipulations have the same effect on perception as malfeasance: they threaten the legitimacy of the system.

ERISA and the creation of the PBGC were prompted by the Studebaker Corporation's financial problems, which shut off pension promises. Now, the loss of tax revenue and pensions stems from the terminations of "overfunded" plans and pension manipulations by restructuring corporations—events ERISA clearly did not foresee. In addition to the insecurity caused by the terminations and funding manipulations of the pension plans, there is concern that pension annuities bought by firms from insurance companies for retirees may be unstable. The April 1991 seizure of the Executive Life Insurance Company by the California Insurance Commissioner may mean that annuity holders will receive only 70 percent of their benefits. Executive Life held 64 percent of its assets in junk bonds. Some members of Congress are attempting to persuade the PBGC to reconsider its position that it does not insure insurance company annuities that are not paid from an ongoing defined benefit plan. Forty-seven states have some insurance for failed insurance companies but the funds are small in comparison to the potential losses if more insurance companies fail (*Wyatt Insider* 1991: 1).

Straightforward and quasi-criminal activity, malfeasance, embezzlement, and fraud also plague the system. The Office of the Inspector General (OIG) of the Department of Labor, in testimony and in its semi-annual report of 1989, made the nation aware of illegal dealings in single-employer pension plans. Over one-half of the plans audited were not in keeping with ERISA requirements. Moreover, only 1 percent of the 870,000 pension plans are audited and joint-trusteed plans are more scrutinized than single-employer plans. The inspector general's report made a case for increased staff and the ability to impose criminal sanctions of ERISA violators. The report does support the principle of joint trustees for the nation's pension plans.

The OIG report also cited the Department of Labor's inability to "conceptualize and monitor a strong and integrated enforcement strategy" as being the cause of a "window of opportunity for those who would steal and embezzle from plan participants." The Bush administration responded by introducing legislation in 1989 that provides incentives for participants to bring private litigation against their plan sponsor by allowing attorney fees and expert witnesses to be compensated by an award in favor of a plaintiff, as well as award a bounty to the plaintiff if penalties are assessed. Other proposals include requiring plan fiduciaries to issue more reports and disclose records. David Ball, assistant secretary of labor, notably cited such initiatives as having a democratic component, in that they require fiduciaries to notify participants how they voted on proxies, "As a matter of economic democracy ... it's important that proxies not be squandered." (Ball quoted in U.S. Bureau of National Affairs 1991: 899).

During the 1980s, any nation-state and institution that slouched toward democratic procedures could claim moral excellence, high rank, and valor. The Visclosky proposal for joint trustees and the Bush administration Department of Labor initiatives differ in opinion over the definition of democracy.

Democracy can have a use value beyond itself. Joint trusteeship can chill illegal and unethical behavior, thus narrowing the population of malfeasance incidents for the Department of Labor. Democracy, in the form of joint trustees, could make enforcement cheaper. Assistant Secretary of Labor David Ball argues that democracy is having "rights" to information, but apparently only some information, since the Bush administration opposes the Visclosky bill.

The waning legitimacy of the private pension system could hinder efforts to improve U.S. productivity by establishing trust between employers and workers. A 1990 *Newsweek* cover story reported that white-collar professionals and managers felt less loyal to their firms because of their own experience with, or their witnessing of, the deleterious employment consequences of corporate restructuring in the 1980s. This development could seriously affect U.S. productivity, not only because worker effort is important for productivity, but so too is job stability.

Pension reform will become part of a new industrial and labor relations accord. There are now two avenues of pension reform whose points of origin are different, but whose ends may converge. One avenue is legislation or unionization that increases worker participation in designing and managing pension trusts. The other is a trend toward defined-contribution plans. In these plans individuals decide the level of contributions and employers match the contribution to some extent; together they determine a level of retirement income security. Many defined-contribution plans allow individuals to choose among many investment vehicles: mutual funds, socially responsible funds, equities, bonds, real estate vehicles, and so on. This individual approach can be viewed as a form of worker input, and as the ultimate form of democracy. But do defined-contribution plans make for decent retirement income security? Do these employee-centric savings plans help establish trust and long-term attachments to the firm?

Pensions have, throughout the modern post-war period, helped create business-labor coalitions. Ironically, one of the most effective business-labor coalitions has not been providing improved bus service or making substantially better cars, but has successfully resisted taxation of employee fringe benefits. Advocates for taxing employee pensions will be a tougher foe for a business-labor coalition in the 1990s and may vanquish even this small form of labor-management cooperation. The federal deficit is not the only motivation for the sentiment to tax fringe benefits. The private pension system has lost credibility and legitimacy because of corporate behavior and the regressivity of benefits. The growth of the lucrative pension management industry, pension fund financing of leveraged buyouts with dubious socially redeeming value, and the billions of dollars recouped from plans in terminations and reversions, have led analysts and thinking people to question the desirability of huge tax expenditures some say are needed to maintain and encourage the existence of private pensions.

To restore legitimacy in the system, pension reform will have to deal with the contradiction in the law. ERISA mandates that pensions should be managed solely for the interests of the participants, yet the courts, the Treasury, the IRS, and the DOL have continually allowed corporations to administer the pension fund in concert with their own needs. For example, the LTV case shows that public policy recognizes, despite the language in ERISA, that the pension fund is inextricably tied to the fate of the company; the sponsor is not required, in practice, to steward a trust for the sole benefit of the participants. Regulators have always allowed firms to consider the corporate sponsor's health when managing the corporate pension.

This contradiction underlies the crisis of legitimacy and joint trustees can meet this contradiction head on. The contradiction in the law exhibits the vexing, but true nature of a private social-insurance system. The pension trust cannot be separated from the life of the entity and the firm (and union) that feeds it. The state of labor relations and the firm's economic strategies all determine the health of the pension promise—its adequacy, flexibility, security, and legitimacy. This will govern pension reform in the 1990s.

Another source of legitimacy concerns the relationship between the private pension system and the taxpayers. The largest tax break in the federal budget is for company pensions. This taxpayer expense establishes expectations that the system will supplement Social Security.

Is the Pension System Consistent with Government Goals?

ERISA, the major piece of pension reform, and previous and subsequent legislation, shaped the pension system. Did these reforms align themselves with national goals in areas that are affected by pensions?

The structure of the Social Security system is one indication of government policy toward retirement income security. Unlike Social Security, however, the private pension system is skewed toward high-income workers. Higher-income elderly are more likely to receive private pensions, because workers in "primary" sectors are more likely to be covered, and because, internally, pensions are skewed toward the well-paid members of a work group. The lowest-paid retiring worker could expect Social Security to replace about 40 percent of preretirement earnings while the highest-income workers would have replaced only 23 percent. The private pension system differs significantly from the goals of the federal system. Two alternative meanings can be attached to this reality: that the private system is out of rhythm with government goals, or that the very differences between the two systems are part of the federal design, a part of a deliberately mixed pension system.

The difference in the two systems of retirement income support, the public and private pension systems, represents another possibility: that government policy has been haphazard, because policymakers are ambivalent about what direction reform is to take. The ambivalence is caused by policymakers having to adhere to two very strong and opposing characteristics of a voluntary social insurance program: to encourage companies to adopt them and to restrict them when they do. Insurance company and corporate representatives threaten to abandon plans in the face of more regulation, and have, in fact, slowed the growth of defined-benefit plans in response to the costs involved in adhering to ERISA's regulations (Clark 1987). Moreover, legislative changes designed to curb the moral hazard when companies terminate healthy pension plans have added to firms' inducement to reduce the cushion in their defined-benefit plans. The 1987 Omnibus Budget Reconciliation Act, by taxing (otherwise tax-exempt) excess contributions—contributions defined as those that tip plan assets over 187 percent of liabilities (Warshawsky 1989)—seeks to prevent firms from terminating overfunded plans but it may have negative consequences. Plans with smaller cushions may be less able to deliver promised benefits when economic growth slows. Policy attempts to protect workers from corporate self-interested manipulation of pension assets may, in fact, make the pension promises more risky.

There is evidence that equity is a national goal for retirement income security and that the private pension system has a difficult time delivering it. The IRS's efforts to deny tax breaks to firms who favor high-income workers began in 1926. Recently, stricter antidiscrimination rules were passed, but Congress, under pressure from business, backed off and did not implement Section 89 of the IRS code. A main cause of defined-benefit plans bias against low-income workers is Social Security integration. Although merely banning integrated formulas would be administratively simple, employer opposition succeeded in forestalling that move. The problem with banning integrated formulas, some feel, is that the wide disparity in earnings in U.S. companies between high-and low-paid workers would mean that companies that provide proportional benefits, in addition to Social Security, would sometimes provide lower-paid workers with a much greater proportion of preretirement earnings than higher-paid workers—even more than 100 percent—while still leaving high-income workers without sufficient pensions relative to their preretirement earnings.

Another national goal affected by retirement income security programs is employment security. When the soldiers came back from World War II and defense production stopped, national policymakers feared high levels of unemployment. The rise in corporate pension plans and increases in Social Security during this time were not entirely motivated by some national policy to curb unemployment, but unemployment was used as an argument for expanding any scheme that got old workers to retire: pensions, mandatory retirement, and the practice of not crediting service past a certain age. The 1988 amendments to the Age Discrimination in Employment Act, which eliminated mandatory retirement and the Omnibus Budget Reconciliation Act of 1986 (OBRA), that requires pension accrual past the age of sixty-five, were designed to protect the older worker from being discriminated against in employment and wages on the basis of age.

The Age Discrimination Act is also seen as serving the goal of encouraging older workers to remain in the labor force and for employers to hire and maintain them. Demographic changes that are causing the aging of the population diminish the supply of younger, cheaper workers—teenagers. A good example of the economy's awareness and adaptation to the age shift is the McDonald's Corporation employment advertisement campaign that target older workers. Employment protection for the aged has a much larger and stronger constituency than do calls for protection on the basis of sex or race. Perhaps it is because everyone changes his or her age, but not sex and race, and hence is a potential victim of age discrimination. Moreover, the 1983 alterations to the Social Security Act gradually have extended normal retirement age under Social Security from sixty-five to sixty-seven, thus encouraging the employment of older workers. National policy toward retirement policy goes both ways. In certain times and in certain industries, retirement is seen as a way to relieve unemployment. In order to meet other concerns—equity and labor shortages—older workers are protected and encouraged to stay in the labor force.

National employment policy hopes for pension plans and a Social Security policy program that allow retirement decisions to be voluntary, but also to encourage retirement when labor supply is high and discourage it when low. Therefore, a retirement system aimed at encouraging productive and scarce workers to stay working and unproductive and surplus workers to leave with generous pensions will look "schizophrenic" (Munnell 1984). However, the structure is not irrational (or psychotic); protection of older workers and tax subsidies for retirement plans can be better described as coping mechanisms to deal with conflicting goals. On the whole, workers, especially men, have not slowed their trend to retire early and often. Social Security increases and the availability of private pension income have allowed more nonworking time at older ages. This suggests that older workers will be those forced to work because of the lack of income, which would violate, in spirit at least, the concern that the system be voluntary.

The other national employment goal affected by company pensions in conflicting ways is labor mobility. In times of labor shortages mobility is seen as undesirable in terms of lost specific skills (and indeed, during these times, mobility might ratchet up wages that would be vexing to employers). Neoclassical economists were suspicious of pensions (and union-negotiated, seniority-based compensation), because they abhor the idea that workers would have incentives not to move to firms that could use them in more productive ways (in the model there is no other reason why firms would be luring or workers lured). University of Chicago professor Lazear has, in numerous studies (1980, 1983), helped neoclassical economists restore their confidence that employers are engaged in productivity-enhancing activities. He has argued that pensions are important in ensuring that older workers maintain a high level of effort, since, presumably, workers shirk—try to minimize work effort—every day. Pensions also help employers utilize expensive training by inducing the worker to stay with the firm, using skills the company paid for, and to maintain high levels of effort.

Do private pensions help accumulate capital? In 1984, the answer would have been, yes certainly. Before then, the growth in pension funds had been rapid, 786 percent since 1970, or, in dollars, $60.4 billion. Pensions as a share of household savings also increased from 7.6 percent, to over 14 percent, from 1974 to the late 1970s. That share has declined slightly during the 1980s. Between 1980 and 1987 assets grew by only $8 billion (see table 7.3). In the 1970s, funds grew because contributions grew, but in the 1980s funds grew because the stock market grew while the rate of contribution growth fell (see table 7.4).

What these trends show is that tax-exempt pension funds have remained about the same as a percentage of household savings throughout the late 1970s and 1980s, which does not confirm any great effect of pensions on the composition of savings, nor on increasing total savings, since household savings as a percentage of income have fallen in the last decade, reaching a low of 3.7 percent in 1987. The decline in the growth of contributions reflects not only the fact that larger absolute amounts represent smaller rates of growth, but also a trend, documented by Board of Governors economist Mark Warshawsky (1988), and Alicia Munnell (1987), that contributions slow, and actually fall per capita, when stock market

Table 7.3
Growth in private pensions funds, 1970–1987

Period	Rate of growth (percent)	Assets at beginning of period (billions of dollars)	Share of household saving (percent)[1]
1970–1974	243	8.8	7.6
1975–1979	130	45.0	14.8
1980–1984	110	62.4	14.7
1985–1987	− 12	80.5	14.2
1970–1987	800		

1. Average share in subperiod.
Source: Turner and Beller 1989: 365, Table A12.

Table 7.4
Growth in contributions to single-employer plans, 1975–1987

Period	Rate of growth (percent)	Contributions beginning of period (billions of dollars)
1975–1979	64	32.9
1980–1984	38	58.7
1985–1987	8	82.9
1975–1987	172	

Source: Turner and Beller 1989: 365, Table A12.

earnings are good. This suggests that a target amount of pension trusts exists and the tendency to accumulate capital is constrained by these targets.

In addition to capital accumulation, pension policy has an unwitting effect on industrial development and is part of the system of U.S. de facto industrial policy. For instance, issues concerning underfunded pension funds almost entirely deal with conditions facing the steel industry. A decision to bail out these funds is a decision about subsidizing the steel industry, steelworkers, and their communities. Industries with defined-benefit plans, mature workers, and a commitment to loyal workers will be more influenced by pension changes than companies with a younger work force and defined-contribution plans. Moreover, the fixed costs of private social insurance put us at a competitive disadvantage with nations who spread the coverage and costs to a larger group—the residents of the nation and not the workers of a particular firm. This affects industrial development and U.S. "competitiveness." The UAW research department cites internal research showing that the cost of private health care in the United States adds $400 to a car price in the United States compared to the identical car produced in Canada, where a national health care system exists.

Federal Pension Law: 1920–1989

Despite the broad scope of ERISA and the commonplace designation of 1974 as the birth year of federal regulation, government policy toward pensions has remained about the same since the 1920s. The policy has been one, primarily, of tax favoritism: deductibility of employer and employee contributions and tax exemption of pension trust earnings. In exchange, the government has some control over the structure, content, and conduct of company pensions. Over time, the federal government has fine-tuned these regulations. What has changed is employers' assertions that pensions are revokable gifts. Firms agree and ERISA makes explicit that promises must be funded and the chance (through vesting, participation, and coverage rules) for workers to earn a nonrevocable pension benefit must exist.

The oldest examples of pension regulations are those aimed at influencing the structure of pensions: the nondiscrimination rules that have evolved since 1926. Most of the restrictions on benefit design, though, have been implemented since the passage of the 1974 ERISA legislation. These restrictions include minimum vesting, participation, and crediting requirements. ERISA mandated that employees with ten years of service be fully vested, which was in keeping with the standard practice of large firms at the time. (ERISA did allow gradual vesting from five to fifteen years, but less than 20 percent of the plans adopted this option). Twelve years later, the Omnibus Budget Reconciliation Act of 1986 (OBRA 1986) cut in half that vesting period. Participation requirements have been tightened, as have nondiscrimination rules, especially around Social Security integration.

The 1980s witnessed almost annual changes in funding standards; making corporations' use of pension funds both easier and more difficult. Corporate use of pension funds became easier as the Reagan administration relaxed standards for terminations and reversions. The vexing budget deficit and blatant usurpation of pension funds for sometimes dubious corporate use nudged Congress into levying excise taxes on the amount of reversions. Limitations of tax deductibility for very "overfunded" plans were imposed, making sure that renegade firms did not unduly shelter corporate earnings from taxation. These changes represented defeats for advocacy groups, the AFL-CIO, the Pension Rights Center, and the American Association of Retired Persons (AARP), which sought to orient pension reform toward the interest of workers and retirees, not the budget deficit.

The following is a chronology and brief description of changes in pension law in the twentieth century (Hoopes et al. 1989; American Council of Life Insurance 1985).

1921–1926

The Revenue Act of 1921 made employer contributions to profit-sharing trusts tax-deferred. These provisions were expanded to pension trusts in 1926. Tax qualification relied on meeting anti-discrimination criteria. This act encouraged plan formation and equity in benefit structure.

1934–1937

The Railroad Retirement Act (RRA) and the Social Security Act were adopted in recognition that company pensions covered far too few workers, were too sensitive to the vagaries of business conditions, and offered little to lower-income workers and survivors and dependents of workers. Politically, the RRA and the Social Security Act were passed in the context of railroad workers organizing and the formation of the "Grey Lobby"—the growing popularity of utopian plans for the elderly. Huey P. Long's "Share the Wealth" plan, Upton Sinclair's California plan, and the national Townsend movement also contributed (Achenbaum 1989: 118). Social Security expanded coverage throughout the 1940s and 1950s. Medicare was adopted in 1965 and supplemental security income benefits to persons sixty-five and older who were poor were implemented in 1972. In 1977, benefits were indexed to inflation and in 1983 benefits were cut (Bernstein and Bernstein 1988).

1949

The U.S. Supreme Court ruled that pensions were a mandatory subject of collective bargaining and the Steel Industry Fact-Finding Board held that steelmakers had a "social obligation" to provide pensions and other forms of social insurance (Sass 1989). Unions were able to force management to bargain over pensions; it is not clear that the incidence of plans increased, but this labor relations policy development helped affect the adequacy, equity, security, and legitimacy of company pensions. Unions bargain for strict funding standards (although it is the unionized industries that suffer more from underfunded plans), higher benefits, and more progressive structures. Worker participation in the schemes improves the legitimacy of the system.

1958

The Federal Welfare and Pension Plans Disclosure Act provided for detailed reporting to the federal agencies concerning pension and welfare trusts. This aided in enforcement, which added to security and legitimacy of the expanding private pension system. Most of this law was replaced in 1974 by stricter reporting and fiduciary liabilities defined in ERISA.

1959

The Life Insurance Company Income Tax Act excluded investment income of insured pension reserves from tax. This further expanded the company pension plans because it aided the industry.

1962

The Self-Employed Individual Retirement Act (Keogh Act) was passed, allowing tax-favored retirement savings plans to unincorporated small business and the self-employed. This expanded tax-subsidized retirement income to an emerging class of service professionals: doctors, lawyers, and so on.

1965

The President's Committee on Corporate Pension Funds and Other Retirement and Welfare Programs issued a report that helped frame the ERISA legislation by emphasizing vesting, coverage, and fund security issues.

1974

The Employment Retirement Income Security Act provided minimum vesting, participation rules, and funding standards. ERISA also established the Pension Benefit Guaranty Corporation and information and disclosure rights for participants. This act made what were implicit pension promises more explicit and verifiable, thus reducing the moral hazard and improving the legitimacy of the system.

1978

The Age Discrimination in Employment Act (ADEA) raised the mandatory retirement age from sixty-five to seventy for all workers except federal employees (where it was eliminated altogether). This act did not delay retirement (retirement age is determined most by income availability), but probably added incentives for firms to provide more generous early retirement benefits.

1981

The Economic Recovery Tax Act (ERTA) liberalized individual retirement accounts (IRAs) and Keogh (H.R. 10) plans by raising contribution limits and extending IRA coverage to those workers already in an employer pension plan. This tended to shift tax expenditures toward higher-income workers but did not induce more savings.

1982

The Tax Equity and Fiscal Responsibility Act (TEFRA) restricted top-heavy plans—those in which 60 percent of the benefits, or contributions, go to the officers or owners. TEFRA affected mostly medium and small employers and was in response to egregious violations of the spirit of the law, but allowed any scheme that got old workers to retire: pensions, mandatory retirement, and the practice of not crediting service past a certain age. However, the 1988 amendments to the Age Discrimination in Employment Act, which eliminated mandatory retirement, and the Omnibus Budget Reconciliation Act of 1986 (OBRA), which requires pension accrual past the age of 65, were designed to protect the older worker from being discriminated against in employment and wages on the basis of age.

Alterations to the Social Security Act gradually extended normal retirement age under Social Security from sixty-five to sixty-seven, thus encouraging the employment of older workers. Revisions effectively limited the maximum funding limitation for defined pension plans to 150 percent of termination liability, by changing the full funding limitation for deductible contributions. Reversions received after 1985 are subject to a 10 percent excise tax.

1987

The Pension Protection Act (PPA) restricted funding flexibility by restricting funding waivers, shortening funding amortization periods, restricting corporate sponsor stock investments, requiring more frequent contributions, and penalizing underfunded plans with higher PBGC premiums and increased exposure liabilities. Seriously underfunded plans must notify participants and shareholders. Terminations and reversions are allowed only if provisions were in effect for at least five years. A year-long moratorium on healthy pension fund terminations and reversions was passed, ending May 1, 1989. The peak of reversions appears to have been in 1985. The moratorium may have had no economic or political effect, except to denigrate the practice.

Financial Accounting Standards Board (FASB)

In addition to federal regulations, the Financial Accounting Standards Board rules affect the funding flexibility enjoyed by single-employer pension plans. The intent of the FASB disclosure standards is to provide investors with accurate information about equity and bond-issuing firms. The availability of information should improve the legitimacy of the system, but the effects on adequacy, flexibility, and security of the pension are uncertain.

FASB 36 rule, issued in 1980, mandated that the accrued pension liabilities and the market value of plan assets appear in a footnote to the corporate balance sheet. This, however, omitted liabilities due to future salary and benefit increases and allowed a wide range of valuation methods (Warshawsky 1989: 157).

FASB Statements 87 and 88 (issued in 1985 and implemented in 1989) require that the unfunded liability appear as a liability on the corporate balance sheet and that a more standardized interest rate assumption be used.

So far, Congress has avoided taking on the Reagan administration's sanctioning of the corporate use of pension funds, which redefined and further checked the effectiveness of ERISA. Pension legislation after 1974 fine-tuned tax laws and liberalized vesting and participation standards.

Efforts to designate workers as owners of their property and therefore endowed with proprietary prerogatives were persistently rebuffed.

The 1983 IRS ruling that allowed assets to be set aside for projected benefit increases, COLAS, and early retirement schemes eroded the protection of ERISA. As it has developed, ERISA confers to workers the "rights" to paternalism, not property or proprietary rights. Presumably, acquiring a firm, defending against a hostile takeover, and improving cash flow are actions that justify corporate uses of pension funds.

Most of the Costs and Some of the Benefits of Private Pensions

The major cost to government of the private pension system is tax expenditures, or "revenue losses attributable to provisions of the Federal tax law which allow special exclusion, exemption, or deduction from gross income or which provide a special credit, preferential rate of tax, or a deferral of liability." (U.S. Department of Commerce 1989: 296, Table 475). Indeed, this is the cost the federal government bears in order to induce the formation and maintenance of private pensions and to regulate them in ways that conform to public policy goals.

By 1980, the tax expenditures for private pensions exceeded all others. The tax expenditures for employer pension plans equal the taxes not collected from corporations (and shareholders) on the pension fund earnings and contributions. Retirees pay income tax on pensions received, but, presumably, at a much lower tax rate than on earnings. This offset is not included in the tax expenditure figures. Every year these expenditures have grown and are estimated to equal $53 billion in tax revenue by 1991.[3] In 1975 exclusion of pension contributions and earnings was the fifth largest tax expenditure. In 1980 it took first place and has held it since (see table 7.5).

This tax favoritism for company pension plans is not consistent with national goals for tax equity, states Boston Federal Reserve Bank vice president Alicia Munnell (1988). She has argued that the tax favoritism toward pensions should be eliminated, because pensions are skewed toward high-income earners. The Congressional Budget Office (1987b) notes that the "projected gains" of tax advantages for retirement plans are "strongly related to income." "The gain among the poorest quartile of elderly couples is 14 percent compared with 24 percent among the richest quartile. The poorer half of single persons, with incomes below or near the poverty level, gains almost nothing from the tax advantages. This population consists almost entirely of women with limited work histories (Congres-

Table 7.5
Tax expenditure ranked by size, 1975–1987

	1975	1980	1985	1986	1987[1]
1. Deductibility of nonfederal taxes (other than mortgages)	1	5	5	5	6
2. Investment credit	2	2	4	7	7
3. Capital gains	3	3	3	3	4
4. Mortgage interest deductions	4	4	2	4	3
5. Exclusion of pension contributions and earnings	5	1	1	1	1

1. The second largest tax expenditure in 1987 was accelerated depreciation.
Source: U.S. Department of Commerce 1989: 296, Table 475.

sional Budget Office 1987b). The Tax Reform Act of 1986 restricted some of this bias and, ironically, eliminated some portion of the tax advantages enjoyed by high-income earners by lowering the top tax rate to 28 percent! Congress will pay increasing attention to the equity issue, if only because of desires to reduce the budget deficit.

Outcomes and Contradictions: The Costs of Volunteerism

In the 1980s pension reform was directed toward containing the tax expenditures for the system—the excise tax of reversions and restricting top-heavy plans. Little has been done to address the following problems:

1. the lack of inflation protection,

2. stagnating coverage at 46 percent of the work force,

3. lack of portability,

4. unequal coverage of women and low-income workers,

5. termination of pension funds and PBGC difficulties, and

6. lack of worker participation in the construction and investment of the pension plans and funds.

The fact that the employer pension system is unresponsive to the retirement needs of the diverse U.S. work force makes sense only when one realizes the system must be responsive to the needs of business conditions and firm profitability. The problems of voluntary social insurance, of moral hazard, and of incomplete coverage, identified at the turn of the century, have not been solved after nearly a hundred years of legislation. Still, there is no significant political call for a mandatory employer pension system. The Bush administration revived the MUPS proposal by offering its plan in opposition to it. Under-secretary David Ball told a group of pension experts in February 1990 that a plan for portability should be seen as a substitute for a MUPS-inspired plan. Indeed, in 1991, the administration presented a plan that would allow firms with over 100 employees to use a Simplified Employer Pension (SEP). That plan (discussed in chapter 4) is portable as long as a worker's employer decides to have a pension plan.

The fact that a voluntary private pension system is enormously expensive for taxpayers is contradictory: If a system is private why does it involve so much public support? The taxpayer's largesse warrants a reevaluation of the private pension system's merit.

8   Directions for Private
Pension Reform

Pension reformers cannot ignore the fact that the private pension system heightens income inequality among the aged and will continue to contribute to a dualistic income structure for households with heads over age sixty-five. In addition, the division of workers may increase as labor markets become more segmented, divided unequally into those who do have private social insurance and those who do not.

Rights (a say in the direction of pension investments and over the size and structure of benefits) are also distributed unequally. They are granted to some union members and wealthy individuals and not to others. Access to retirement and leisure at the end of one's working life may also be more unequal as pension reformers seek to encourage people to work past age sixty-five.

Pension reform must also face the financial side of pensions. Pensions are paid to individuals, but pension funds are collected on behalf of a group. This peculiar structure keeps alive the decades-long debate over what the privileges of ownership are and to whom finance managers are responsible. Demands for "democratizing" pension fund investments will undoubtedly continue as assets grow, individual capital becomes more global and less predictable, and the needs for employment-generating investment increase.

Outlook for Employer Pension Policies in the 1990s

Defined-Contribution versus Defined-Benefit Plans

From a policy point of view many of the problems of defined-benefit plans—terminations, underfunding, moral hazard—could be solved by replacing defined-benefit plans with defined-contribution plans. This would follow the trend in pension growth. Between 1981 and 1985, 57 percent of primary pension plan growth was in defined-contribution plans, compared to 52 percent between 1975 and 1979 and 23 percent from 1966 to 1970 (Lawrence 1989: 72).

Interpretations of the trend range over a passive shift of employment from traditional, defined-benefit employers toward traditional, defined-contribution employers to an analysis that employers are terminating their defined-benefit plans in favor of defined-contribution plans. Indeed, there has been a contraction of industries that traditionally had defined-benefit plans (and unions); over one-half of defined-benefit assets and participants are in manufacturing (Ippolito and Kolodrebutz 1985: 28–29). There also has been a relative increase in employment in smaller firms, which prefer defined-contribution plans. But defined-benefit plans have been replaced with defined-contribution plans. In the 1980s, about one-third of companies terminating large defined-benefit plans adopted defined-contribution plans. All interpretations, taken together, explain the trend (Ippolito 1990).

Can the popularity of defined-contribution plans be explained by the (presumably) superior features of defined-contribution plans prevailing over an increasingly costly and overregulated defined-benefit system? And is this a positive change from a policy perspective? Or are inferior defined-contribution plans driving out generous defined-benefit plans—what can be thought of as a Gresham's Law phenomenon, where bad labor standards drive out good ones.

There are numerous acknowledged advantages of defined-contribution plans: employees know exactly how much is in their individualized savings accounts. Workers can also "take" their account when changing jobs. Most young people, upon transferring jobs, do not transfer their retirement accounts into another retirement savings vehicle. The cash is withdrawn, extra tax is paid, and the balance is spent, for consumption, home ownership, or education (Employee Benefit Research Institute 1986).

Moreover, an advantage to workers that also works to the advantage of an employer is that workers drive the cost and generosity of the plan. Most defined-contribution plans are matched plans—employers will match a worker's contribution up to a specified maximum in so-called 401-K plans (also known as profit-sharing, thrift, or stock bonus plans.) This delivers the message that workers have control over their choices between consumption now and consumption later: and if employees have little motive for savings, the matching share can be small indeed. Another advantage is the clarity of the defined-contribution plan—a savings account balance is easier to understand than a future defined-benefit promise. The contribution rate is clearly defined, the relationship between the fund's earnings and expected benefits is in plain view. "In a defined contribution plan ... what you see is what you get" (Schwartz 1990).

Defined-contribution plans commonly feature participant-directed accounts. This also enhances the worker's sense of control, or participation, which is one aspect of financial democracy. Every worker has a "portfolio" and can choose between social investment funds, high yield–high risk stock funds, mutual funds, bonds, and government securities—every worker a finance mogul. Firms also may succeed in defining economic democracy as individual control—no matter how powerless—instead of collective action, and may confuse political support for initiatives like the Visclosky proposal for joint trusteeship or a modified MUPS—a government-managed, advance-funded Social Security. Instead of pension funds becoming labor's capital, directed by worker representatives, pension funds can be turned into individual accounts, bank accounts that are directed by professional money managers.

An additional reason why employers like defined-contribution plans is that they are comparatively simpler and cheaper to administer. Some of the cost advantages of defined-contribution plans, relative to defined-benefit plans, are in terms of up-front fixed costs: administration and insurance costs. For instance, employers with defined-contribution plans do not have to insure with the PBGC—insurance costs for a defined-benefit plan can be as high as $18 per employee per year—nor do they have to hire actuaries to do complex accounting.

There is evidence that ERISA and other federal regulations in regard to defined-benefit plans have influenced, but not primarily caused, the move toward defined-contribution primary pension plans (Clark 1987). In the 1980s firms were eligible for massive tax breaks when they adopted Employee Stock Ownership Plans, so that the relative advantages stemming from government actions that favor defined contribution plans may have contributed to their relative growth.

A firm's motives to move toward defined-contribution plans may go beyond avoiding the increased costs of defined-benefit plans. Defined-contribution plans may signify a "shortening" of the labor contract, because contribution plans do not reward long service as generously, and as obviously, as defined-benefit plans. This may be desirable from the neoclassical point of view (that labor mobility aids economic development), because workers can quickly transfer to growing industries away from twilight ones. The flip side of the flexibility argument is not as cheery. The decline in the popularity of the defined-benefit pension plan may merely reflect the larger changes in the structure of U.S. corporations. Instead of encouraging worker loyalty to the firm, the shift in pension plans reflects increasing capital mobility and a decrease in corporate attachment to workers, communities, and even products.

Moreover, defined-contribution plans are generally regressive (a "matching" plan requires that workers initiate the savings rate and higher-income workers save more than low-income workers) and provide lower benefits to nonmanagerial workers. The defined-contribution trend could indicate a worsening of labor standards. Defined-contribution plans are cheaper and have the potential to favor higher-income workers. The bias harkens back to the firm's initial motive to provide pensions for management and other select employees.

Another, less direct source of cost savings, but one that can result in substantial long-term savings, is that defined-contribution plans eliminate the pressure to index benefits for retirees—especially in a unionized situation. An employer can avoid, for example, the big three auto firms' confrontations with vociferous retiree groups who, every contract year, appeal to the company's sense of moral obligation to maintain pension benefits by demanding cost-of-living increases. In defined-contribution plans the economic and moral ties with the company are neatly severed: When a worker leaves, the moral and economic obligations disappear when he or she cashes out of the defined-contribution account. Moreover, because these relationships are severed at retirement the pressure for retiree health plans, a huge projected liability for U.S. companies, may be less because the institutional relationship between firm and retired worker does not exist.

Unions and other advocacy groups, such as the Pension Rights Center, argue that workers prefer defined-benefit plans because, unlike a defined-contribution plan, they know exactly what their pension will be when they retire. In addition, some defined-benefit pension formulas are based on final salary, which automatically helps index the pension to inflation. Even those workers who do not expect to stay with a firm for a long period of time approve of schemes that reward service with a pension. Defined-benefit plans do favor longer-service workers over shorter-service workers, not just because of the usual vesting period (most likely five years), but because final benefits are often tied to final earnings. Defined-contribution plans have immediate vesting, but most likely provide lower benefits for the longer-service workers (because leavers are not generally subsidizing stayers) and the relatively low-paid participant, because contribution rates are driven by the worker and savings rates fall with income level. There are no current, reliable data on average benefits for defined contribution plans by wage level of workers.

Corporate Internalization of Funds

Another reason firms may abandon defined-benefit plans is that the corporate "internalization of pension funds"—the link between corporations' financial strategies and their pension funding and termination decisions—went too far. The very allure of flexible funding in defined-benefit plans may be their downfall. As long as the tax law required that pension trusts must be managed solely for the benefit of plan participants and firms *funded* and *paid* benefits as promised, firms could, in fact, manage the plans for their own benefit. For about five years after ERISA passed (1974), firms were careful to meet funding obligations and maintain the pension fund as a real trust.

But, in the 1980s, corporate restructuring and the Reagan administration's accommodations increased corporate predilections to utilize the pension funds for financial purposes (see chapter 5). Corporations break the implicit contract between workers and firms when they manipulate pension funding. The internalization of pension funds is not much different from employers' abandonment of plans during depressions and the sheltering of profits in pension funds during expansions over the last hundred years. Recent corporate use of pensions is not an aberration: It is in keeping with the long-run history of corporate sponsorship of pension funds and an inherent danger in voluntary social insurance funds.

Brazen corporate encroachment on sponsored pension funds also represents a structural change in firms' commitments to workers. Indeed, firms' time-horizons have shortened in many areas: ownership and management change frequently and product design and production are undergoing speedup. The only elements of production that have inexorably grown longer are workers' lives and the expectation of retirement.

Workers' retirement security is not the only issue involved with the stagnation of pension coverage. Financial market stability may also be affected by corporate use of pensions. The comforting view that for the sake of financial flexibility firms should be able to resort to pension funds when cash-flow problems arise is drawn from studies that examine only one or two years and assume that firms' financial difficulties are not related, that ups and downs even themselves out. Such sanguine conclusions are disturbed when the last decade is viewed in the context of recurring financial crises. If the trend continues away from healthy, well-funded, defined-benefit plans, then firms will face new problems in future recessions. Well-funded pension plans will not be there to soften the expected credit crises and, consequently, the financial decline could be much worse than that of the 1980s. Far from destabilizing credit markets in the October 1987 stock market crash, pension funds may have provided a soft landing, not in the stock market, but at the source of the funds, the corporate balance sheet. Corporations' ability to fall back on the pension funds for credit and cash will be diminished in the 1990s (Ghilarducci and Wolfson 1991).

In sum, numerous trends (and consequent implications) should emerge in the 1990s. Firms likely will cut back on all forms of private social insurance. Health care insurance should experience the most immediate reductions, but pension changes also represent subtle reformulations of the firms' commitments to workers, as well as a lessening of the generosity of the plans. The move toward defined-contribution plans and the decrease in cost-of-living adjustments in defined-benefit pensions (covered in chapter 7) could be in the interest of flexibility, a move prompted by firms lessening commitment to their current workers, or, alternatively, firms choosing workers (young workers) who can be expected to have a weaker commitment to the firm.

These trends in benefit structure should affect a corporation's ability to "internalize" the pension fund. For a number of reasons firms with ongoing defined-benefit plans may find it more difficult to strategically use their pension funds. First, tighter tax rules and FASB changes will make funding less flexible. Moreover, the conditions of the 1980s that allowed pension liabilities to appear small and allowed funds to greatly appreciate—low interest rates and a booming stock market—are not likely to persist in the 1990s. This loss in corporate financing flexibility may also spill over into all financial markets. Pension funds were a cheap source of credit in the 1980s. The waning of this source may increase competition for funds and make competing corporations even more concerned with short-term performance.

The Likely Direction of Government Policies

The federal budget problems of the 1980s will shape the pension reform proposal responses in the 1990s. Hungry for tax revenue without new taxes, legislators may opt to cut tax favoritism for pensions, punishing the system for moving toward more regressive benefit structures (influenced in part by the growth in defined-contribution plans) and pension raiding. Portability legislation will seek to strengthen the pension aspect of defined-contribution plans by restricting the payment of benefits in lump sums. Reforms to strengthen the PBGC may also continue, but Congress forestalled a financial crises of the PBGC by raising premiums in 1987. The stagnant growth in private pension coverage, especially among the groups that need Social Security supplements the most, the effect of inflation on real benefits, the powerful influence pensions have on capital markets, and the potential effect on corporate governance, likely will not be addressed. This lack of policy response will exacerbate divisions among the elderly in terms of income and control of their income, the quantity of their income, and leisure.

Pension Insurance: The PBGC

In the next ten years policy probably will be directed at the pension insurance system and the problems of pension-fund deficits in distressed industries. These are the oldest problems facing a private social insurance scheme in a capitalist economy. The "insurance" is only as good as the business cycle. The PBGC was set up to cushion the effects of bankruptcies on participants, not on industries. Yet, increased competition as well as corporate restructuring, especially in the steel, automobile, and transportation industries, help create underfunded defined-benefit plans and increased exposure for the PBGC (Hoffman 1989: 149–150). Because a major recession will hit hardest the very industries with the highest percentage of pension coverage, the PBGC will have few other employers over which to spread the risks of bankruptcies. Some losses will then have to fall back on the government, or on workers.

The PBGC collects premiums from companies based on the number of participants. From the inception of the insurance scheme in 1974, the PBGC had actuarial liabilities that exceeded assets. Assets are derived from (1) annual premiums per participant—underfunded plans paid higher premiums after the Pension Protection Act of 1987, (2) assets from terminated plans, (3) investment income, and (4) employer liability payments. Projected liabilities are simply measured; they are the total amount of underfunding among the universe of insured plans.

The PBGC's exposure was lessened considerably by the June 18, 1990, Supreme Court decision that prevented LTV (and the steelworkers) from negotiating a new pension agreement after LTV filed for bankruptcy and dumped the $2 billion in unfunded liabilities incurred for LTV's retirees. The PBGC will continue to push for legislation (some was passed in the 1980s) that minimizes the moral hazard in pensions by restricting funding waivers, underfunding, and the latitude in making pension assumptions. The PBGC did win variable rated premium increases in 1986 and 1987. The PBGC situation is not like the Savings and Loans bailout—the PBGC does not have the regulatory capability that the FSLIC and FDIC had, and has, over banks, and the PBGC has a limited credit line (for total liabilities) with the Treasury. Congress could reduce the amount of pension insurance, or set higher funding standards. Moreover, unlike the full insurance of bank deposits of $100,000, the PBGC does not cover COLAS, early retirement benefits, insurance annuities bought by firms on behalf of their workers, as Executive Life annuants know too well (*Wyatt Insider* 1991: 1), or benefits over a certain amount. Worker pensions are not fully insured and a serious recession might force Congress to reduce the amount of insurance.

Portability

Portability will be presented as an adequacy issue (recognizing that peripatetic workers do not have adequate pension coverage), but not one of major significance. The most likely policy change, with regard to "portability," will be to make lump-sum pension payments more costly to spend on purposes other than old-age income. Thus, a person leaving a job with a pension will have a "portable pension," in the sense that the law will force the lump-sum pension disbursement to be transferred to a type of individual retirement account where monies cannot be withdrawn before the age of 59.5 without a tax penalty.

The movement to tax private pension contributions, and all or part of fund earnings, should resurface in the next decade. The clamor is coming from many directions: from those who argue that tax expenditures are too large for schemes that favor well-heeled workers from those who argue pension funds are biased against long-term investment and cause volatility in financial markets. The system's favored tax position will remain under a shadow as long as the deficit looms large.

Fairness and Tax Breaks

The Congressional Budget Office (CBO) concerned itself with the fairness of the benefit side of the private pension system. It concluded a report on the inequity of tax expenditures by recommending that further restrictions on contributions to tax-favored schemes be increased and that tax rates on disbursements for retirees in the upper half of the income distribution be increased. The CBO also recommended that monies gained by decreasing the tax advantages to the higher-income elderly be used to expand Social Security or Supplemental Income payments to those elderly. This would help out the poorest aged households (Congressional Budget Office 1987b).

On the taxation side, there is considerable concern over raising federal tax revenues. The most remunerative would be a 5 percent tax on pension funds and earnings. This move would considerably change the direction of pension policy set in motion since the 1920s, and it would also reduce the tax expenditures for company pension plans by about 15 percent. The CBO estimates a $37 billion tax gain from a 5 percent tax over the five-year period from 1988 to 1993 (Congressional Budget Office 1987b).

Another proposal to limit the tax favoritism toward pension funds is a Treasury proposal to eliminate the double taxation of dividends. This would reduce the tax advantages to pension funds. The Treasury Department's tax integration proposal—known as "eliminating the double taxation of dividends"—would equate the tax treatment of dividends and interest income, thereby lessening the attraction of tax-exempt entities, such as pension funds, by making all investments nontaxable (Congressional Budget Office 1987b).

Republican senators Nancy Kassebaum and Robert Dole's jointly sponsored bill (S 1654) opens the way for a radical change in tax policy toward pensions, for reasons other than benefit inequities and increasing tax revenue. It proposes that pension fund earnings derived from assets held less than six months be taxed. Their goal is to alter the pattern of corporate investments by penalizing markets for rewarding short-term gains in equity prices, but the reasoning is controversial. Japan, for instance, has rapid stock turnover and is still an economy that rewards long-term investment; stock turnover and long-term planning horizons are not necessarily correlated.

Rights

The other area of pension reform may be on the "rights" of pension fund owners, most likely in the area of joint trusteeship of defined-benefit plans—the Visclosky bill—and clarification of the responsibilities of pension fund administrators to vote corporate proxies. Both the Visclosky bill and the Republican proposals come from the same spirit of corporate management distrust. Furthermore, the proposed Visclosky legislation is the result of a new rights movement that sprang up in the 1980s. It is a peculiar rights movement, in that it seeks to empower a traditional elite by asserting and expanding property rights. In addition to identifying an untraditional oppressed group, the new rights movement represents an odd coalition. It includes capitalist shareholders who engage in hostile takeovers and workers who engage in pension-fund politics. Both groups asserted property rights and challenged corporate management in the 1980s.

An example of how the issues of ownership and the prerogatives of ownership are discussed arose out of the 1990 hearings on the Visclosky bill. A question put to all the witnesses by the House Subcommittee on Labor-Management during hearings for the Visclosky legislation was, "Who owns the pension assets?" Labor representatives answered, "Workers do," because pensions are a deferred wage. Business witnesses agreed; they did not dispute that workers owned the funds. But they defended management's sole control over the pension funds on the basis that it is the firms that bear the risk of poor performance in defined-benefit plans. The argument that risk-bearing justifies a corporation's sole control over investments adds a dimension to the notion of property rights. In this context, business argues that prerogatives from risk-accepting supersede prerogatives derived from ownership.

The Democratic position is actually a milder attack on corporate management of pension funds and would have less monetary ramifications than the Bush administration's proposals and initiatives. Though the politicking around the Visclosky bill has, so far, been partisan, Democrats and the Bush administration—through the Kassebaum-Dole-Brady initiatives to tax some pension-fund earnings and the Office of the Inspector General of the Department of Labor's increased vigilance for pension fraud and malfeasance—are calling for much the same thing: oversight and control over corporate behavior.

Rights Dualism among the Aged

The employer pension system divides workers in terms of access to control or influence in capital markets. Union workers, especially those in jointly trusteed pension plans that, for instance, engage in offensive investment strategies in real estate, have a source of efficacy other workers do not. The range of their collective action is larger than workers who have no input with regard to their own pension investments. Soon-to-be retired bricklayers, for example, could benefit from their union's pension fund management by supporting economic development financing, or, more directly, mortgages and residential construction. Public sector workers are in a unique position to influence the investment of their pension funds. Public sector workers can affect their pension funds through their roles as workers and by virtue of their membership in unions and can exercise their rights as citizens to influence the investment of funds that are already in the public domain (Barber 1987).

Worker input, with regard to one's pension fund, can be regarded as a stand-alone goal toward a furthering of rights, or democracy. But that argument would not go far with many constituents, even workers. What constitutes property rights—what is conferred through ownership—is always contended, except in the pure theory of capitalism. Workers want good investments and good returns, and would sacrifice control for a better pension. A more compelling argument for worker input—for the democratization of finance capital—is that the autocratic stewards of capital under the rules of capitalism are not doing their job well. Rates of return on pension funds are sometimes smaller than the stock market average, management fees are high, and there is no evidence that pension funds are more likely to invest in productive activity and eschew speculative activity.

The division, in terms of worker input and participation in pension fund investments, is just one form of dualism created and enhanced by the private pension system.

The Dualism of Income and Access to Leisure among the Aged

Higher unemployment and the relative growth in service sector jobs, the stagnation of private pension plan coverage, and political attacks and economic pressure on Social Security will likely increase income and leisure inequities among the elderly in the next century. These inequalities have been somewhat compressed by increases in Social Security benefits and the expansion of union pension plans from the 1950s through the 1970s. Social Security increases especially helped male middle- and working-class workers to retire. But the social contract between employers and workers and the government to retirees has changed in the last decade.

The elderly are tracked along two major dimensions: income and access to leisure, that is, the elderly who can retire and those who cannot afford to retire.

In the early 1980s, two things happened that rekindled public debate on what workers deserve in old age. Ronald Reagan was elected president of the United States and the Social Security Retirement Fund—the Old Age Insurance (OI) fund—had a projected short-term and long-term deficit. President Reagan mused early on in his administration whether or not Social Security could be made voluntary. His proposed cuts created the first successful organized political opposition to a Reagan initiative and, in 1981, the president, in order to quell the political firestorm, appointed a bipartisan commission, chaired by Alan Greenspan, to devise solutions to the projected Social Security shortfall. Many of the proposals were incorporated into the 1983 Social Security Amendments, which cut Social Security benefits, raised payroll taxes, and built in a trust fund surplus to help pay for the baby-boom generation's retirement.

Social Security's cost-of-living increases were delayed by six months (this was the source of most of the cost savings); student benefits were cut (black college students were more likely to depend on Social Security benefits for school financing than whites [Ghilarducci 1981]); up to half of benefits were made taxable for higher-income elderly, and although the early retirement age was kept at age sixty-two a phased-in reduction from 80 percent to 70 percent of the full benefit received at that age was implemented. By 2010, the normal retirement age will be sixty-seven and not sixty-five. There will be increased incentives to work beyond retirement, because, beginning in 2009, workers will only lose $.33 of Social Security benefits for every dollar earned working instead of the $.50 now lost (Bernstein and Bernstein 1988). This means less leisure to the aged who, without the reduction in benefits, would have been able to afford to retire earlier (Doeringer 1990: 25–26).

As discussed in chapter 4, private pensions increase the inequality of retirement income because of the structure of the private pension system. Emily Andrews and Deborah Chollet (1988: 71–96) argue that the baby-boom generation will have more of its preretirement income replaced by employer pensions and less from earnings and Social Security than retirees in the 1980s. Shoven and Hurd (1982) showed that wealth disparity among the aged in 1969 was widened by private pensions and compressed by Social Security. The wealthiest tenth of the aged population of households received 9.7 percent of its income from pensions and the lowest tenth received 3 percent. The ratio of the mean value of assets received by the persons in the lowest decile to the value held by the wealthiest was 1.6 percent, $364 compared to $23,027. This means that the lowest decile received about 1 percent of the pension wealth received by the top decile. Compared to Social Security, where the lowest decile received 18 percent of what the wealthiest owned, only stocks and physical assets were more skewed. When these two trends are combined—private pensions create more disparity and private pensions becoming relatively more important to the baby-boom retirees—then the income disparity among the aged will grow.

There are signs that private pension income will become even more unequal than the trends Shoven and Hurd (1982) picked up, as wages themselves grow more divergent, coverage rates stagnate, unions weaken, and defined-benefit plans are replaced by defined-contribution plans (Bluestone and Harrison 1988). Most pensions are tied to earnings and earnings inequality has grown. Increasing labor market segmentation has caused lower-paid employees to be less likely to be covered by a plan. Retirement income disparity between women and men may fall, however, as women get more access to pensions of divorced spouses and come to rely increasingly on their own earnings and pensions. Mandated vesting after five years will increase that rate of pension recipiency among women, but benefits will not be large enough to reduce the forecast that 40 percent of baby-boom single women will be in poverty in old age (Andrews and Chollet 1988).

The other endowment the aged vie for is leisure. Recent changes in Social Security may skew access to leisure toward high-income elderly, even though the benefit structure is skewed toward the low-paid worker. Retirees with lower career earnings will receive a larger percentage of preretirement earnings than higher-income workers. The increase in Social Security's normal retirement age, which is the equivalent of a decrease in benefits, may increase income and social inequality among the aged. The conventional wisdom among economists is that the most important factor in the decision for white men to retire is income, rather than occupation or health status (Quinn 1977). Those workers with less savings and earnings will work longer when Social Security is reduced. The new elderly work force will likely be tapped by the retail and service industry, which has grown accustomed to depending on youth labor.

In addition, the move toward defined-contribution plans and declining unionization will probably diminish early retirement provisions for middle-income, nonmanagement workers. These developments are not only meant to divide the elderly, in terms of income, but also along the lines of who gets leisure after their working lives.

Democratizing the Social Security Trust Fund

The Greenspan Commission wisely, from an economist's point of view, planned for a build-up in the trust funds so that the payroll taxes, 8 percent for both employer and employee up until 2035, can remain constant when the baby-boomers retire and dependency ratios—the ratio of workers to beneficiaries—falls from three to one to two to one. In 1989, Senator

Daniel Patrick Moynihan, a former member of the Greenspan Commission and long-time supporter of the Social Security system, proposed to cut payroll taxes and eliminate the trust fund buildup. The proposal exposed the Republicans' attempt to contrive the perception that the Reagan-Bush administration cut taxes, unveiled the regressiveness of the payroll tax, and drew attention to the deficit that is masked substantially by the inclusion of the Social Security budget in the total budget. In the end, the proposal had no hope. Increases in the more progressive incomes to replace proposed decreases in the regressive payroll tax were never seriously considered and cutting taxes without cutting spending was untenable. Henry Aaron and Charles Schultze, (1990: A18) economists at the Brookings Institution, wrote, "The best hope is that Senator Moynihan's proposal will provoke a review of the nation's currently absurd budgetary proposals. The worst fear is that it would be enacted." It looks like the Social Security budget will be computed off-budget, which makes the deficit look bigger (which was why, ironically, President Johnson put Social Security on-budget in the first place; it masked the cost of the Vietnam War.) To expose the Republicans the Democrats attempted to undo a Democratic initiative.

Bush's economic advisor, Michael Boskin, wrote positively about the projected surplus in the trust fund. He argued that it would increase savings and allow the baby-boomers to retire without increasing the tax rate on their children. But he warned that this was only possible if government and private deficit spending did not persist (Boskin 1988: 111–114). As discussed earlier, the MUPS proposal from President Carter's Commission on Pension Policy recommended an advance-funded Social Security system as well. The mandatory universal pension system can be viewed as a payroll tax of 3 percent to be used to finance workers' retirement. The current Social Security surplus is invested in special government treasury bills. Yet, the nature of the original MUPS investments was not specified. Both the trust funds and the MUPS proposal introduce intriguing possibilities for improving the adequacy and security of the retirement system and obtaining goals for increasing savings and targeting investment.

Democratizing the investment of pension funds can mean many, not necessarily exclusive, options. The first policy choice is the status quo. Pension regulation can remain one that monitors and regulates pension-fund managers and sponsors; second, laws could aid the pension strategies of unions and other populist democratic groups (one example is the proposed legislation in the United States that would mandate worker trustees for single-employer plans); and third, employers and pension-fund managers may continue to hand over investment choices to individuals, as is the case in many defined contribution plans. Last, pension funds can be included in a government or quasi-government industrial policy scheme; in short, the government can accumulate and strategically invest collectivized savings in the form of pension funds, encourage "financial" democracy by broadening the representation of pension-fund managers, or it can continue its role as pension police.

What I am proposing is the means to finance a national industrial policy. The financing would be from collective forms of retirement savings and could be democratically administered. Political economist Barry Bluestone and his colleagues proposed in 1990 a specific use of the Social Security trust funds—student loans (Bluestone et al. 1990). They proposed a "generational alliance" in which all citizens, regardless of income, could borrow money for college and pay over a twenty-five-year period through payroll deductions. The capitalization would come from the Social Security trust funds. Bluestone's plan essentially directs the Social Security trust funds toward a specific investment, one that increases the productivity of the economy. Increased productivity underlies any pay-as-you-go social insurance system. Today's workers could invest in the earnings ability of the next generation, which would strengthen the Social Security system by having a stronger economy. Banks would lose profitable student loan guarantees but default rates would plummet because the IRS would collect the repayments.

The plan could worsen class divisions, because most workers contribute to Social Security but not all workers' children go to college. Moreover, it is possible that many of the children who receive the benefit would come from families that garner income through ownership, not labor. Strategic use of the Social Security trust funds should benefit a wider base.

In his book on worker trustees in the United Kingdom, Thomas Schuller makes a distinction between financial participation, worker cooperatives, and economic democracy, and links the latter with pension funds (Schuller 1986: 55–80). Financial democracy refers to participation of workers in corporate decisions. This may involve some, often marginal, transfer of stock ownership—as is the case of Employee Stock Ownership plans in the United States. These shares are held on an individual basis and limit the possibilities for meaningful collective use of ownership rights. Worker cooperatives are also limited in their ability to elicit democracy in a capitalist economy, since the workers' say and democratic ownership is limited to an enterprise. Yet, "since capital is not constrained by organization, industrial or even national boundaries" (Schuller 1986: 57), that participation in pension-fund management is the only structure, the only institution, that can achieve the most wide-reaching form of economic democracy.

For three reasons Schuller argues that Swedish "wage-earner funds" are the most promising model for true economic democracy. Philosophically, the system entitles workers to a portion of the economic surplus they create and structurally the system directs the surplus toward investments aimed at increasing the Swedish worker's living standard. And, moreover, the proceeds from the investments go to retirees.

Wage-earner funds were first proposed by Swedish union economist Rudolf Meidner in 1976 and were implemented on a nationwide basis in 1983. Five regional funds, directed by representatives from business, labor, and government receive contributions, a tax of profits over a certain level, from capitalist enterprises. The investment of the funds is limited to firms operating in Sweden and the proceeds go to the Pension Insurance System. The system aims to close the circle connecting the surplus that workers create, from new investments to working class consumption.

Resolving the Private Pension Contradictions

There are some practical policy directions that can be pursued that would both initiate a contest over how capital should be allocated in the United States and would aid in improving retirement income levels and distribution. I recommend a gradual democratization and replacement of the voluntary private pension system.

On the investment side, and for the short run, the Visclosky recommendations should be adopted. In addition, federal or state legislation that required all pension funds to allocate 10 percent of their funds into a "redevelopment" fund would begin the process of amassing capital designated for "socially" productive activity. In 1981, the AFL-CIO had urged its affiliates to bargain for a small percentage of their pension funds to be invested in the aforementioned ULLICO and HIT. The pension-fund investment industry—banks, insurance companies, and money managers— would not necessarily lose its clients and the funds' performance would hardly be affected if only 10 percent were invested in the "social capital" redevelopment fund. This fund, like the thousands of community redevelopment funds and federal demonstration projects, would easily find and fund productive investments that were missed by traditional capital markets. A board directing the funds would represent a cross section of society, perhaps reflecting the same principles in Swedish wage-earner funds. Precedents have been established for such a public representative board, such as the National Cooperative Bank and the Federal Reserve regional boards. There are European examples of public-sector directed capital investment and prepaid retirement plans in France, Sweden, Finland, and proposals in England. Such a plan would shift emphasis away from property rights—as the reason pension funds should be controlled differently—to a social-needs criteria. In summary (and in the short run), the fund should

1. require all single-employer funds to have worker trustees as investment advisors; and

2. create a national strategic fund, composed of 10 percent of all private pension funds, that guarantees a fixed rate of return and is invested in projects that demonstrate the ability to enhance and stabilize the national economy.

In the medium run, the employer-based pension system, as well as the employer-based health insurance system, could gradually be eliminated for a nationalized and universal advance-funded scheme. Tax exemptions for employer-sponsored pension contributions could gradually be eliminated and replaced by a new tax structure that would support an advance-funded Social Security system.

Under a nationalized pension scheme, such as Social Security, pension credits are portable and benefits are based on a worker's entire work history rather than service with one employer—some pension plans are portable within an industry, TIAA-CREF (for university professors) and union multiemployer plans. An advance-funded Social Security system would substitute the tens of thousands of employers' (tax-exempt) funds for national or regional Social Security funds. The Social Security system's small surplus could be invested in public ventures instead of government bonds. Unions may balk at this proposal because they would lose the advantages of negotiated employer-based pensions (as discussed in chapter 3)—that pensions serve as a fudge factor in bargaining and as a leverage in organizing. Employers would lose all the benefits of a voluntary system—the personnel tool and the source of internal funds. The pension fund management industry would not survive in its current form. The losses are as apparent as the current benefits. However, the gains overall, compared to the current system, are considerable. In summary I recommend, in the medium run,

1. tax contributions to employer pension funds,

2. mandated 3 percent contributions to each worker's pension fund,

3. creation of a public board of trustees to invest the funds strategically.

Large employers, now competing internationally, may welcome the benefits of not being an exception in the world community by having to pay a third of labor costs in private social insurance. A MUPS may help lessen the problems of aged income dualism created by a pension system that exacerbates the inequalities in a segmented labor market. A public capital fund could help correct the most unproductive tendencies of capitalism by steering capital away from outrageously speculative investments and toward employment-generating activities. Finally (in the long run), an advance-funded Social Security system could reinforce the very foundation of our nation by adding economic democracy to our system of political democracy.

Notes

Chapter 3

1. Interview with Meredith Miller, Social Security Department, AFL-CIO, September 1988.

2. Interviews with Harvey Sigalman, president of the Amalgamated Insurance Company, August 1, 1988, and Theodore Bernstein, pension administrator for the International Ladies Garment Workers Union, August 2, 1988. Both interviews were held in New York City.

3. The Proceedings of the AFL-CIO, 43d Annual Convention, p. 327, quoted in Ilse 1954: 337.

4. Jacoby (1989) describes the strengths of a company union that is based in part on charismatic leadership, employee involvement programs, employee surveys, and worker loyalty. National union threat effects are also a main determinant of "good" employee relations at the nonunionized Thompson plants.

5. Interview with Theodore Bernstein, August 2, 1988.

6. These arguments and controversies are contained in the vast literature on segmented markets and dualistic production systems (see Edwards et al. 1982; Kerr 1954; Doeringer and Piore 1971; Piore and Berger 1982; Rosenberg 1987).

Chapter 4

1. There are numerous neoclassical views of the pension role in labor contracts. A significant portion of the literature highlights pensions as personnel devices that attract stable workers and that encourage those with waning productivity to leave (Lazear 1983; Diamond and Mirrlees 1985). Union-related pension models view pensions as the product of a union catering to a median voter, or exerting monopoly power (Freeman 1981; Gustman and Steinmeier 1986).

2. Deductibles and limitations on coverage all protect the insurer against the insuree's ability to influence the probability the insured event occurs by shifting some of the cost of the event onto the insuree. Insurance against bicycle theft,

accidents, and poor health all have limitations on coverage and deductibles because the insuree has substantial influence over whether the event occurs. The insurance literature discusses moral hazard emanating from insurees but never discusses that originating from insurers.

3. Telephone interview with Charlotte Von Salis, Pension Rights Center, June 21, 1989.

4. Calculated from Grad (1988: 16, Table 49 and Table 8) by taking the estimated average income of the third and fourth quartile and multiplying it by the share of private pension income. This amount was divided by the number of persons receiving pension income in the quartile to calculate the average level of pension benefit in that quartile.

5. Telephone conversation with David McCarthy, Office of Policy Research, Office of Pension and Welfare Benefit Programs, Department of Labor, June 1, 1989.

6. An example of internal factors is the following: An autoworker covered by a UAW-GM contract would receive a pension of about $1,000 a month after thirty years of service, whereas former GM president Roger Smith receives $104,000 per month for forty-one years of service (Levin 1990). Two electricians with the same years of service may have widely different pensions depending on the industry (such as construction) or utility in which they work.

7. In the Social Security step-rate formula the pension plan promises to pay a percentage of the earnings base (defined by the plan as the average of the last few years of work or a career average) up to a specified ceiling, and another percentage (usually higher) for earnings above the ceiling. The Social Security offset formula deducts a worker's Social Security benefit (primary insurance amount) from the defined promise. Proportional formulas are unit formulas that are based on earnings. The proportional formula yields a pension equal to a certain percentage of earnings for every year of sevice. A unit formula based only on earnings pays a pension that is a certain percentage of the earnings base regardless of service (Kotlikoff and Smith 1983: 210).

8. The compensating wage differential theory suggests that workers give up wages for fringe benefits and other pleasant aspects of work and get paid for hazards or other unpleasant conditions of work. The theory says that equal access to information and market power means workers give up just the right amount of wages for the pensions they want. The view of pensions as a compensating wage differential is expressed in Fields and Mitchell (1984).

9. Pesando (1984) found that funds with "excess" assets—those that exceed minimum liability—were likely to pay ad hoc benefit inflation adjustments to their retirees.

10. The argument is that wage increases are approximately equal to price inflation so that pensions in final-salary defined-benefit plans are similar to Social Security benefits. Both pension plans and Social Security, the argument goes, improve imperfect capital markets that do not allow workers to borrow on their hefty amount of human capital at the beginning of their careers. Therefore, a "portfolio

imbalance" between human and physical capital among retirees and workers is corrected (Bodie et al. 1988).

Chapter 5

1. Meeting with Karen Ferguson, August 22, 1989, Washington, D.C.

2. Interview with former Crown employee, who wishes to remain anonymous, July 1990.

3. Although Ippolito (1986a) rejects the conclusion that each firm's decision to terminate an overfunded plan is related to the size of the workers' capital losses, which is generally what workers lose by not receiving a pension annuity based on final salary—an inflation-adjusted pension. Yet, the decision to terminate is positively related to the size of the potential reversion or the fund's surplus.

4. Recent popular treatment of this phenomenon can be found in Geoghegan's study (1991) of the Wisconsin Steel Company pension case.

5. Bowers and Moore (1989) conclude there is no unpaid gold mine for bidders when a firm acquires another with overfunded pensions. Bidding firms must pay target shareholders for the wealth implicit in the overfunded pension. But bidders get some gains. From a sample with 131 pairs of targets and bidders they found that for every $1.00 of net pension assets there is a gain of $1.84 for the target and 22 ¢ for the bidder. An offer increases by 12 ¢ for every dollar of pension surplus.

6. Jeremy Bulow and Myron Scholes, prominent mainstream economists, argued in 1983 that participants clearly owned defined-benefit pension assets. Richard Ippolito (1986b) uses the same argument about the nature of labor contracts to argue that participants own the assets needed to pay for projected pension benefits.

7. Stein (1986) argues that actuarial methods can create false overfunding because actuaries must base funding on a projected base. Advocates will accede to some notion of erroneous calculations but they will use a narrower definition than just the existence of surplus. Actuaries may make mistakes in projecting earnings. For example, firms can lower benefits to create a surplus (this was ruled illegal in *Van Orman vs. American Insurance Co. no. 75–20007*) or there may be a sudden change in the mortality, age, or sex composition in a participant group plan (women will cost less, younger workers will cost less).

8. Interview with John Sheehan, United Steel Workers of America, September 1987, Washington D.C.

Chapter 6

1. Arthur Ross (1950) makes this point as does Francis Green (1981). Before the 1974 Employee Retirement Income Security Act (ERISA), U.S. workers, like British workers, could lose all their pension accrual by quitting or striking. ERISA mitigated that loss somewhat, but firm-specific pensions do foster worker attachments to a firm.

2. These banks are reminiscent of the labor banks developed in the 1920s. Unions and union members owned shares in these banks, which provided then-innovative services such as installment credit, personal loans (without collateral), and loans to strikers. The number of labor banks peaked at thirty-six in 1925 and at least two survived the 1930s depression (Boeckel 1923). Perhaps the recent interest in labor banks harkens back to this other period when labor turned to its role as financial agent when traditional strength from its role as worker waned.

3. For instance, the LTV-AM General plant in South Bend, Indiana, lost a major Pentagon project in 1988 because its project bid was higher than others. Management blames the overgenerous UAW contract and wants major wage cuts; the UAW blames management greed. If, at a likely bargaining impasse, the UAW called for a labor-movement wide boycott of LTV stock, the Steelworkers would object because they finally settled a difficult pension-underfunding problem with LTV in 1987. Moreover, a boycott of LTV credit may only erode the LTV's steel division and not affect decisions by management in South Bend.

Chapter 7

1. The Pension Restoration Act of 1991 (S 351), which was added to an amendment to the Older Americans Act Reauthorization (S 243), would have paid some pensions to those who lost vested pension rights before ERISA insured these claims (the bulk of so-called pension losers are former Studebaker workers). After twenty-eight years of lobbying, the measure had gone further in Congress than ever before (the bill increasingly became cheaper because claimants die every year). But in September of 1991, the PBGC maintained that the bill was too expensive. The PBGC's opposition may have been politically motivated because at the same time it wanted new legislation protecting the PBGC's status in bankruptcy law. A perceived PBGC financial crisis might have helped that lobbying effort.

2. Interview with Bert Seidman, South Bend, Indiana, June 1, 1989.

3. The data is from "Estimates of Tax Expenditures," prepared by the staff of the Joint Committee on Taxation (Turner and Beller 1989: 423, Appendix, Table F1).

Bibliography

Aaron, Henry, and Charles Schultze. 1990. "Moynihan's Right, But..." *New York Times*, Jan. 18:A18.

Abraham, Katherine, and Henry Farber. 1987. "Job Duration, Seniority and Earnings." *American Economic Review* 77:278–297.

Achenbaum, W. Andrew. 1989. "Public Pensions as Intergenerational Transfers in the United States." *Workers and Pensions: Intergenerational Justice in an Aging World*, edited by Paul Johnson, Christoph Conrad, and David Thompson, pp. 113–136. Manchester: Manchester University Press.

AFL-CIO. 1979. Committee on the Investment of Union Pension Funds. *Investment of Union Pension Funds.* Washington, D.C.: AFL-CIO.

————. 1985. Executive Committee. *The Changing Situation of Workers and Their Unions.* Washington, D.C.: AFL-CIO.

————. 1986. Public Employees Department. "Public Pension Investment Policy." Washington, D.C.: AFL-CIO.

Alchian, Armen Albert and Demsetz, Harold. 1972. "Production, Information Costs and Economic Organization." *American Economic Review* 52:777–795.

Allen, Donna. 1964. *Fringe Benefits: Wages or Social Obligations?* Ithaca: Cornell University.

Altman, Nancy. 1987. "Rethinking Retirement Income Policy: Nondiscrimination, Integration, and the Quest for Worker Security." *Tax Law Review* 42:443.

Ambachtsheer, Keith. 1986. *Pension Funds and the Bottom Line: Managing the Corporate Pension Fund as a Financial Business.* Homewood Ill.: Dow-Jones-Irwin.

American Council of Life Insurance. 1985. *Pension Facts 1984–1985.* Washington, D.C.: American Council of Life Insurance.

Andrews, Emily. 1985. *Changing Profile of Pensions in America.* Washington, D.C.: Employee Benefit Research Institute.

Andrews, Emily. 1988. *Changing Profile of Pensions in America.* 1985, quoted in "Fact Sheet: Why Women Do Not Receive Pension Benefits," National Senior Citizens Law Center, for the Pension Equity Forum, Washington, D.C., Mar. 7.

Andrews, Emily. 1990. Remarks before a Labor Department conference on International Pensions, Washington, D.C., Feb. 18.

Andrews, Emily, and Deborah Chollet. 1988. "Future Sources of Retirement Income: Whether the Baby Boom" in *Social Security and Private Pensions*, edited by Susan M. Wachter, pp. 71–96. Lexington, Mass.: Lexington Books.

Babson, Stanley M. 1925. *Fringe Benefits—the Depreciation, Obsolescence, and Transience of Man Costs, Strategies, and Trends for Financial Managers, Personnel Directors, and General Management.* New York: Wiley.

Ball, Robert. 1949. "Pension Plans under Collective Bargaining: An Evaluation of Their Social Utility." *Industrial Relations Research Association, Proceedings of the Second Annual Meeting, New York.* Madison: Industrial Relations Research Association. Dec.

Barber, Randy. 1987. "Public Employee Retirement System: Issues of Investment and Administration." Manuscript. Washington, D.C.: The Center for Economic Organizing.

Barber, Randy, and Jeremy Rifkin. 1978. *The North Will Rise Again.* Boston: Beacon Press.

Barnard, John. 1983. *Walter Reuther and the Rise of the Auto Workers.* The Library of American Biography, edited by Oscar Handlin. Boston: Little, Brown.

Becker, Harry. 1949. "Labor Approaches the Retirement Program." *Industrial Relations Research Association, Proceedings of the Second Annual Meeting, New York.* Madison: Industrial Relations Research Association. Dec.

Beller, Daniel. 1986. "Coverage and Vesting Status in Private Pension Plans, 1972–1983." In *The Handbook of Pension Statistics, 1985*, edited by Richard Ippolito and Walter Kolodrubetz, pp. 56–118. Chicago: Commerce Clearing House.

Beman, Lamar T. 1927. *Selected Articles on Old Age Pensions.* New York: H. W. Wilson.

Bergmann, Barbara. 1986. *The Economic Emergence of Women.* New York: Basic Books.

Bernstein, Merton. 1964. *The Future of Private Pensions.* London: The Free Press of Glencoe.

Bernstein, Merton, and Joan Blaug Bernstein. 1988. *Social Security.* New York: Basic Books.

Black, Fischer. 1980. "The Tax Consequences of Long-Run Pension Policy." *Financial Analysts Journal* 36(4):21–28.

Bluestone, Barry, Alan Clayton-Matthews, John Havens, and Howard Young. 1990. "Financing Opportunity for Post-Secondary Education in the U.S.: The Equity Investment in America Program." Economic Policy Institute Briefing Papers Series, Washington, D.C.: Economic Policy Institute.

Bluestone, Barry, and Bennett Harrison. 1988. *The Great U-Turn.* New York: Basic Books.

Bodie, Zvi, Jay O. Light, Randall Morck, and Robert Taggart. 1987. "Funding and Asset Allocation in Corporate Pension Plans: An Empirical Investigation." In *Issues in Pension Economics*, edited by Zvi Bodie, John Shoven, and David A. Wise, pp. 15–48. Chicago: University of Chicago Press.

Bodie, Zvi, Alan J. Marcus, and Robert C. Merton. 1988. "Defined Benefit versus Defined Contribution Plans." In *Pensions in the U.S. Economy*, edited by Zvi Bodie, John Shoven, and David A. Wise, pp. 139–160. Chicago: University of Chicago Press.

Bodie, Zvi, and John Shoven. 1983. *Financial Aspects of the United States Pension System*. Chicago: University of Chicago Press.

Boeckel, Richard. 1923. *Labor's Money*. New York: Harcourt, Brace.

Boskin, Michael. 1988. "Future Social Security Financing Alternatives and National Savings." In *Social Security and Private Pensions*, edited by Susan Wachter, pp. 111–145. Lexington: Lexington Books.

Bowers, Helen, and Norman Moore. 1989. "Abnormal Returns for Merging Firms and the Presence of Excess Pension Assets." Working paper. University of Notre Dame, Notre Dame.

Bowles, Samuel. 1985. "The Production Process in Competitive Economies: Walsarian, Neo-Hobbsian, and Marxist Models." *American Economic Review* 75(1):16–36.

Brandes, Stuart D. 1976. *American Welfare Capitalism, 1880–1940*. Chicago: University of Chicago Press.

Browne, William P., and Laura Katz Olson, editors. 1983. *Aging and Public Policy: The Politics of Growing Old in America*. Westport: Greenwood Press.

Buchholz, Gregogy. 1989. "Discrimination in Pension Plans." Unpublished paper. University of Notre Dame, Notre Dame.

Bulow, Jeremy, and Scholes, Myron. 1983. "Who Owns the Assets in a Defined Benefit Pension Plan?" In *Financial Aspects of the United States Pension System*, edited by Zvi Bodie and John B. Shoven, pp. 17–36. Chicago: University of Chicago Press.

Burr, Barry. 1984. "Contribution Cut in the Works." *Pensions and Investment Age* (Dec. 10):20.

———. 1990. "Accounting Wizardry Helps Shore up Profits and GM, Ford." *Automotive News* (May 21):43.

Business Roundtable. 1979. *Pensions, Social Security Benefits: Levels, Costs and Issues*. New York: Business Roundtable.

Carter, Susan. 1988. "The Changing Importance of Lifetime Jobs, 1892–1978." *Industrial Relations* 27:287–300.

Chemoff, Joel. 1984. "Steelmakers Seek to Tap Fund Again." *Pensions and Investment Age* (Nov. 12):1.

Clark, Gordon L. 1990a. "Location, Management Strategy and Workers' Pensions." *Environment and Planning Administration* 22:17–37.

————. 1990b. "Restructuring Worker Pension Rights and the Law." *Environment and Planning Administration* 22:147–168.

Clark, Robert L. 1987. "Increasing Use of Defined Contribution Pension Plans." Unpublished paper. Washington, D.C.: Department of Labor.

Clark, Robert L., Steven Allen, and Ann McDermed. 1987. "Pensions and Lifetime Jobs: The New Industrial Feudalism Revisited." Unpublished paper. Raliegh, N.C.: North Carolina State University.

Clark, Robert L., Stephen Allen, and Daniel A. Sumner. 1990 "Inflation and Pension Benefits." Final Report for the Department of Labor Contract J-9-P-1-0074. Washington, D.C.

Cobble, Dorothy Sue. 1991. "Organizing the Postindustrial Work Force: Lessons from the History of Waitress Unions." *Industrial Relations and Research Review* 44:419–436.

Cohen, Cynthia Fryer. 1983. "The Impact on Women of the Proposed Changes in the Private Pension System: A Simulation." *Industrial and Labor Relations Review* 36:258–270.

Conant, Luther, Jr. 1922. *Critical Analysis of Industrial Pension Systems.* New York: Macmillan.

Congressional Budget Office. 1987a. *Federal Insurance of Private Pension Benefits.* Washington, D.C.: U.S. Government Printing Office.

————. 1987b. *Tax Policy for Pensions and Other Retirement Saving.* Washington, D.C.: U.S. Government Printing Office.

Congressional Research Service. 1988. *Junk Bonds: 1988 Status Report.* Washington, D.C.: U.S. Government Printing Office.

————. 1990. "Joint Pension Trusteeship: An Analysis of the Visclosky Proposal." Hearings before the Subcommittee of Labor-Management on H.R. 2664, Feb. 21–28, 1990, Washington, D.C.

Council of Economic Advisors. 1990. *Economic Report of the President.* Washington, D.C.: U.S. Government Printing Office.

Council of Economic Advisers. 1991. *Economic Report of the President.* Washington, D.C.: Government Printing Office.

Dearing, Charles. 1954. *Industrial Pensions.* Washington, D.C.: Brookings Institution.

Deaton, Richard Lee. 1989. *Political Economy of Pensions: Power, Politics and Social Change in Canada, Britain and the United States.* Vancouver: University of British Columbia Press.

Derthick, Martha. 1982. *Policy-Making and Social Security.* Washington, D.C.: Brookings Institution.

Diamond, Peter A., and James A. Mirrlees. 1985. "Insurance Aspects of Pensions." In *Pensions, Labor and Individual Choice*, edited by David Wise, pp. 317–343 Chicago: University of Chicago Press.

Dionne, George. 1982. "Moral Hazard and State-Dependent Utility Functions." *Journal of Risk and Insurance* 49:405–422.

Doeringer, Peter B., editor. 1990. *Bridges to Retirement: Older Workers in a Changing Labor Market*. Ithaca: ILR Press.

Doeringer, Peter, and Michael Piore. 1971. *Internal Labor Markets*. Lexington, Mass.: D.C. Heath, Lexington Books.

Dolan, Thomas G. 1986. "Gold-Plated Steel Parachutes." *Barron's* (Dec. 1):11.

Domini, Amy, and Peter Kinder. 1984. *Ethical Investing*. Reading, Penn.: Addison-Wesley.

Drucker, Peter Ferdinand. 1976. *The Unseen Revolution: How Pension Fund Socialism Came to America*. New York: Harper & Row.

Edwards, Richard. 1979. *Contested Terrain: The Transformation of Work in the Twentieth Century*. New York: Basic Books.

Edwards, Richard, Michael Reich, and David Gordon. 1982. *Segmented Work, Divided Workers: The Historical Transformation of Labor in the United States*. Cambridge, Cambridge University Press.

Employee Benefit Research Institute. 1985. *The Changing Profile of Pensions in America*. Washington, D.C.: Employee Benefit Research Institute.

————. 1986. *Spend It or Save It? Pension Lump-Sum Distributions and Tax Reform*. Washington, D.C.: Employee Benefit Research Institute,

Epstein, Abraham. 1926. *Problems of Old Age Pensions*, Harrisburg: Pennsylvania Old Age Pension Commission.

Epstein, Abraham. 1972. *Facing Old Age: A Study of Old Age Dependency and Old Age Pensions*. New York: Arno Press.

Estrella, Arturo. 1987. "Corporate Uses of Pension Funds." In *Contemporary Developments in Financial Institutions and Markets*. 2d ed., edited by Thomas Havrilesky and Robert Schweitzer, pp. 259–276. Arlington Heights: Harlan Davidson.

Feder, Gerald. 1989. Quoted in "War of Conscience Tugging at Pension Funds." *Pensions and Investment Age* (Nov 1989):(3).

Feldstein, Martin, and Stephanie Seligman. 1980. "Pension Funding, Share Prices, and National Savings." National Bureau of Economic Research, Working Paper no. 509. Cambridge, Mass.

Ferguson, Karen. 1989. Statement to the Employment and Housing Subcommittee of the Committee in Government Operations, Washington, D.C. Aug. 2.

Fields, Gary, and Olivia S. Mitchell. 1984. *Retirement, Pensions and Social Security*. Cambridge, Mass.: MIT Press.

Freeman, Richard. 1978. "The Effect of Trade Unionism on Fringe Benefits." Working paper series. Cambridge, Mass.: National Bureau of Economic Research.

————. 1981. "The Effects of Unionism on Fringe Benefits." *Industrial Labor Relations Review* 489–509.

————. 1985. "Unions, Pensions, and Union Pension Funds." *Pensions, Labor and Individual Choice,* edited by David A. Wise, pp. 89–118. Chicago: National Bureau of Economic Research.

Friedman, Benjamin. 1983. "Pension Funding, Pension Asset Allocation and Corporate Finance." In *Financial Aspects of the United States Pension System,* edited by Zvi Bodie and John B. Shoven, pp. 107–152. Chicago: University of Chicago Press.

Gabrielli, Gilberto, and Daniele Fano, editors. 1986. *The Challenge of Private Pension Funds: Present Trends and Future Prospects in Industrialized Countries.* London: Economist Publications.

Geoghegan, Thomas. 1991. *Which Side Are You On? How to Be for Labor When It's Flat on Its Back.* New York: Farrar, Straus & Giroux.

Gersovitz, Mark. 1980. "Economic Consequences of Unfunded Vested Benefits." Chicago: National Bureau of Economic Research, Working Paper no. 480.

Ghilarducci, Teresa. 1981. "Reagan's Social Security Cuts." *Labor Center Reporter.* No. 32. University of California, Berkely: Institute of Industrial Relations.

————. 1984. "Pensions and Collective Bargaining." Unpublished doctoral dissertation. University of California, Berkeley.

————. 1990. "Uses of Ignorance in Pensions by Unions and Firms." *Journal of Labor Research* 11 (2):203–216.

————. 1991. "Pension Costs and Changing Pension Norms: The Case of Japanese Auto Transplants and Unionized Auto Firms." Paper presented to the Fourth Labor Market Segmentation Conference, University of Notre Dame, 1991.

Ghilarducci, Teresa, and Martin Wolfson. 1991. "Pension Funds and the Financial System." Unpublished working paper. University of Notre Dame.

Gillipsie, Richard. 1986. "Employees Awarded Surplus Assets." *Pensions and Investment Age* 27(Oct.):1.

Government Finance Research Center. 1983. *Public Pension Investment Targeting: A Survey of Practices.* Washington, D.C.: Government Finance Research Center.

Grad, Susan. 1988. *Income of the Population of Those Aged 65 or Older, 1986.* Office of Policy, Office of Research and Statistics. Washington, D.C.: U.S. Department of Health and Human Services, Social Security Administration.

Gray, Hillel. 1983. *New Directions in the Investment and Control of Pension Funds.* Washington, D.C.: Investor Responsibility Research Center.

Green, Francis. 1981. "Occupational Pension Schemes and British Capitalism." *Cambridge Journal of Economics* 6(5):267–283.

Greenstone, David. 1969. *Labor in American Politics*. New York: Knopf.

Grossman, Sanford, and Joseph Stiglitz. 1976. "Information and the Competitive Price System." *American Economic Review* 66(2):246–253.

Gustman, Alan L., and Thomas Steinmeier. 1986. "Pensions, Unions and Implicit Contracts." Working Paper no. 2036. National Bureau of Economic Research. Cambridge, Mass.

Gustman, Alan L. and Thomas L. Steinmeier. 1989a. "Evaluating Pension Policies in a Model with Endogenous Contributions." Working Paper; no. 3085. Cambridge, Mass.: National Bureau of Economic Research.

————. 1989b. *The Stampede toward Defined Contribution Pension Plans: Fact or Fiction?* Working Paper no. 3086. Cambridge, Mass.: National Bureau of Economic Research.

Harbrecht, Paul. 1959. *Pension Funds and Economic Power*. New York: The Twentieth Century Fund.

Hart, Robert. 1984. *The Economics of Non-Wage Labor Costs*. London: George Unwin.

Harvard Business Review. 1980. *Pension Management*. Harvard Business Review Reprint Series, no. 21470. Boston: Harvard University.

Hoffman, Arnold J. 1989. "Funding Levels by Industry: The Relationship between Output, Unemployment, and Funding." In *Trends in Pensions*, edited by John Turner and Daniel Beller, pp. 137–146. Washington, D.C.: Government Printing Office.

Hoopes, Terence, Kevin Maroney, Judith Mayers, and Amy Shannon. 1989. "Summary of Federal Legislation Affecting Private Employee Pension Benefits." In *Trends in Pensions*, edited by John Turner and Daniel Beller, pp. 452–479. Washington, D.C.: Government Printing Office.

Hutchinson, John. 1970. *The Imperfect Union: A History of Corruption in American Trade Unions*. New York: Dutton.

Ilse, Louise Wolters. 1954. *Group Insurance and Employee Retirement Plans*. New York: Prentice Hall.

Industrial Relations Counselors. 1932. *Superannuation and Permanent and Total Disability Benefits in the United States and Canada*. New York: Industrial Relations Counselors.

International Labour Office. 1977. *Pensions and Inflation: an International Discussion*. Geneva: International Labour Office.

Ippolito, Richard A. 1986a. "Issues Surrounding Pension Terminations for Reversion." *American Journal of Tax Policy* 5:83–116.

————. 1986b. *Pensions, Economics and Public Policy*. Homewood Ill: Dow-Jones-Irwin.

————. 1986c. "Termination of Sufficient Defined Benefit Plans" In *Handbook of Pension Statistics, 1985*, edited by Richard A. Ippolito, Richard A. and Walter W. Kolodrubutz, pp. 305–351. Chicago: Commerce Clearing House.

————. 1990. "Pension Plan Choice, 1979–1987: Clarifications and Extensions." Washington, D.C.: Pension Benefit Guaranty Corporation. Dec.

Ippolito, Richard A., and William James. 1990. "Leveraged Buyouts and Pension Reversions. Unpublished paper. Washington, D.C.: Pension Benefit Guaranty Corporation. Mar.

Jacoby, Sanford M. 1985. *Employing Bureaucracy: Managers, Unions and the Transformation of Work in American Industry, 1900–1945.* 1953. New York: Columbia University Press.

————. 1989. "Reckoning with Company Unions: The Case of Thompson Products." *Industrial and Labor Relations Review* 43(1):19–40.

James, Estelle Dinerstein, and Ralph C. James. 1965. *Hoffa and the Teamsters.* Princeton: Van Nostrand.

Jensen, Michael, and Ruback, Richard. 1983. "The Market for Corporate Control: The Scientific Evidence," *Journal of Financial Economics* 5–50.

Jensen, Michael. 1988. "Takeovers, Their Causes and Consequences." *Journal of Economic Perspectives* 2(1):6–32.

Johnsen, Julia Emily. 1935. *Old Age Pensions.* New York: H. W. Wilson.

Keller, Morton. 1977. *Affairs of State: Public Life in the Nineteenth Century.* Cambridge, Mass.: Harvard University Press.

Kerr, Clark. 1954. "Balkanization of Labor Markets." In *Labor Mobility and Economic Opportunity,* edited by Edward Bakke. Cambridge, Mass.: MIT Press.

Kirkland, Lane. 1961. *Pensions and Collective Bargaining: A Reference Guide for Trade Unions.* 1952. Revised by Richard Shoemaker. Washington, D.C.: AFL-CIO.

Kotlikoff, Laurence J., and Daniel Smith. 1983. *Pensions in the American Economy.* Chicago: University of Chicago Press.

Kraw, George M. 1984. "Pension Funds and the Wall Street Crisies: Some Shareholders Become More Equal Than Others." *Employee Benefits Journal* (June):22–25.

Labor Management Services Administration. *The Prudence Rule and Pension Plan Investments under ERISA.* (Washington, D.C.: United States Department of Labor.

La Botz, Dan. 1990. *Rank and File Rebellion.* New York: Verso.

Latimer, Murray Webb. 1932. *Industrial Pensions,* vol. 1. New York: Industrial Relations Counselors.

Latimer, Murray Webb. 1932. *Trade Union Pension Systems.* New York: Industrial Relations Counselors.

Latimer, Murray Webb, and Karl Tufel. 1940. *Trends in Industrial Pensions.* New York: Industrial Relations Counselors.

Lawrence, Helen. 1989. "Trends in Private Pension Plans." In *Trends in Pensions,* edited by John A. Turner and Daniel J. Beller. pp. 69–94. Washington, D.C.: U.S. Government Printing Office.

Lazear, Edward. 1980. "Agency, Earnings Profiles, Productivity and Hours Restrictions." *American Economic Review* 71, 4:606–619.

————. 1983. "Pensions As Severance Pay." In *Financial Aspects of the United States Pension System*, edited by Zvi Bodie and John Shoven, pp. 57–85. Cambridge, Mass.: National Bureau of Economic Research.

Leibeg, Michael. 1980. *Social Investments and the Law*. Washington, D.C.: Conference of State and Local Policies.

Lester, Richard. 1958. *As Unions Mature*. Princeton: Princeton University Press.

Levin, Doron. 1990. "G.M. Seeks Sharp Increase in Top Executives' Pensions." *New York Times*, May 3:c1.

Levine, Jonathan. 1989. "When the Safety Net is Frayed." *Business Week* 6 (Nov.):158.

Lichtenstein, Nelson. 1982. *Labor's War at Home* Cambridge: Cambridge University Press.

Longman, Phillip. 1987. *Born to Pay: The New Politics of Aging in America*. Boston: Houghton Mifflin.

Lubove, Roy. 1986. *The Struggle for Social Security: 1900–1935*. 2d ed. Pittsburg: University of Pittsburgh Press.

Lynn, Robert J. 1983. *The Pension Crisis*. Lexington: Lexington Books.

McCarthy, David. 1986. "Private Pension Benefit Levels." In *The Handbook of Pension Statistics, 1985*, edited by Richard A. Ippolito and Walter Kolodrubetz, pp. 119–176. Chicago, Ill: Commerce Clearing House.

McCarthy, David, and John Turner. 1989. "Pension Rates of Return in Large and Small Plans." In *Trends in Pensions*, edited by Daniel Beller and John Turner, pp. 235–286. Washington, D.C.: U.S. Government Printing Office.

McDonald, Charles. 1987. Internal Memo to Pension Fund Investment Unit of the AFL-CIO, Field Department.

McGill, Dan. 1972. *Preservation of Pension Benefit Rights*. Homewood, Ill.: Irwin.

Marglin, Stephan. 1984. *Growth Distribution and Process*. Cambridge, Mass.: Harvard University Press.

Marshall, Ray. 1987. *Unheard Voices: Labor and Economic Policy in a Competitive World*. New York: Basic Books.

Mennis, Edmund A., and Chester D. Clark. 1983. *Understanding Corporate Pension Plans*. Charlottesville: Financial Analysts Research Foundation.

Miller, Meredith. 1988. "Women and Pensions." National Senior Citizens Law Center, for the Pension Equity Forum, Washington, D.C., Mar. 7.

Mischo, William, Sook-Kuen Chang, and Eugene P. Kaston. 1980. *Corporate Pension Plan Study: A Guide for the 1980s*. New York: Banker's Trust.

Mitchell, Mark, and J. Harold Mulherin. 1989. "Pensions and Mergers." In *Trends in Pensions*, edited by John A. Turner and Daniel Beller, pp. 211–234. U.S. Department of Labor, Pension and Welfare Benefits Administration.

Mitchell, Olivia S. 1982. "Fringe Benefits and Labor Mobility." *Journal of Human Resources* 16(2):286–298.

———. 1988. "Worker Knowledge of Pension Provisions." *Journal of Labor Economics* 6(1): 21–39.

Mitchell, Olivia S., and Alan L. Gustman. 1990. "Pensions and Labor Market Activity: Behavior and Data Requirements." Working Paper no. 3331 Cambridge, Mass.: National Bureau of Economic Research.

Mitchell, Olivia S., and Rebecca A. Luzadis. 1989. "Explaining Pension Dynamics." Working Paper no. 3084 Cambridge, Mass.: National Bureau of Economic Research.

Mittlestaedt, H. Fred. 1989. "Wealth Transfers Associated with Terminations of Acquired Firms Overfunded Defined Benefit Plans." Final Report for the Department of Labor Contract J-9-P-8-0095.

Moldea, Dan E. 1978. *The Hoffa Wars: Teamsters, Rebels, Politicians, and the Mob.* New York: Paddington Press.

Moody, Kim. 1989. *An Injury to All.* London: Verso Press.

Mork, Randall, and Martin Feldstein. 1983. "Pension Funding Decisions, Interest Rate Assumptions and Share Prices." In *Financial Aspects of the United States Pension System*, edited by Zvi Bodie and John Shoven, pp. 177–210. Chicago: University of Chicago Press.

Morrison, Malcolm H., editor. 1982. *Economics of Aging: the Future of Retirement.* New York: Van Nostrand Reinhold.

Munnell, Alicia. 1977. *The Future of Social Security.* Washington, D.C.: Brookings Institution.

———. 1982a. *The Economics of Private Pensions.* Washington, D.C.: Brookings Institution.

———. 1982b. "Guaranteeing Private Pension Benefits: A Potentially Expensive Business." *New England Economic Review* (Mar./Apr.):33–44.

———. 1984. "ERISA—The First Decade Was the Legislation Consistent with Other National Goals?" *New England Economic Review* (Nov./Dec. 1984):44–63.

Munnell, Alicia (with the assistance of Nicole Ernsberger). 1987. "Pension Contributions and the Stock Market," *The New England Economic Review* (November/December) 3–14.

———. 1988. "It's Time to Tax Employee Benefits." Unpublished paper, delivered at the American Economic Association meetings, New York. Dec.

Murray, Roger F. 1968. *Economic Aspects of Pensions: A Summary Report.* New York: Columbia University Press.

National Labor Boycott Shell Committee. 1987. *The Royal Dutch/Shell Group of Companies Alternative, Corporate Report.* Washington, D.C.: United Mine Workers of America.

Nektarios, Miltiadis. 1982. *Public Pensions, Capital Formation, and Economic Growth.* Boulder: Westview Press.

Newsweek. 1990. "How Safe Is Your Job?" November 5:50–58.

Oi, Walter. 1962. "Labor as a Quasi-Fixed Factor." *Journal of Political Economy* 70:6 (December) 538–555.

Olson, Laura Katz. 1982. *The Political Economy of Aging.* New York: Columbia University Press.

Orloff, Ann Shola. 1988. "The Political Origins of America's Belated Welfare State." In *The Politics of Social Policy in the US,* edited by Theda Skocpol, Margaret Weir, and Ann Shola Orloff, pp. 39–80. Princeton: Princeton University Press.

Pensions and Investment Age. 1983a. "Firms Upped Assumptions" and "Higher Assumptions Lower Pension Costs at Companies." Mar. 7:58 and 14.

———. 1983b. "Higher Assumptions Lower Pension Costs at Companies," Mar. 7:14.

———. 1984. "Interest Rate Assumptions Surveyed." Aug. 20:1.

———. 1989. "War of Conscience Tugging at Pension Funds." Nov. 27:3.

Pesando, James. 1984. "Valuing Pensions (Annuities) with Different Types of Inflation Protection in Total Compensation." *Canadian Journal of Economics* 17:569–587.

Piore, Michael, and Suzanne Berger. 1982. *Dualism and Discontinuity in Industrial Society.* New York: Cambridge University Press.

Pitelis, Christos. 1987. *Corporate Capital: Control, Ownership, Saving and Crises.* Cambridge: Cambridge University Press.

Pollin, Robert. 1987. "Structural Change and Increasing Fragility in the U.S. Financial System." In *The Imperiled Economy,* edited by Robert Cherry et al., pp. 145–158. New York: Union for Radical Political Economics.

Pontiff, Jeffery, Andrei Shleifer, and Michael Weisbach. 1989. "Reversions of Excess Pension Assets after Takeovers." Unpublished paper. University of Rochester, Rochester, New York.

President's Commission on Pension Policy. 1981. *The Coming of Age in America: Final Recommendations of the Commission.* Washington, D.C.: U.S. Government Printing Office.

Quinn, Joseph. 1977. "Microeconomic Determinants of Early Retirement: A Cross-Sectional View of White Married Males." *Journal of Human Resources* 12(3):329–346.

Reid, Ed, and Ovid Demaris. 1963. *The Green Felt Jungle.* New York: Trident Press.

Root, Lawrence. 1982. *Fringe Benefits and Social Insurance in the Steel Industry.* Beverly Hills: Sage Publication.

Rosenberg, Samuel. 1987. "From Segmentation to Flexibility." Discussion Paper no. 5, Geneva: Internal Institute for Labor Studies.

Ross, Arthur. 1948. *Trade Union Wage Policy.* Berkeley: University of California Press.

————. 1950. "The New Industrial Pensions." *Review of Economics and Statistics* 32:133–138.

————. 1958. "Do We Have a New Industrial Feudalism?" *American Economic Review* 48:903–920.

Rubery, Jill. 1978. "Structured Labor Markets, Worker Organizations and Low Pay." *Cambridge Journal of Economics* 2:17–36.

Sass, Steven. 1989. "Pension Bargains: The Heyday of U.S. Collectively Bargained Pension Arrangements." In *Workers versus Pensioners: Intergenerational Justice in an Aging World,* edited by Paul Johnson, Christoph Conrad, and David Thompson, pp. 92–112. Manchester: Manchester University Press.

Scherer, F. M. 1988. "Corporate Takeovers: The Efficiency Arguments. *Journal of Economic Perspectives* 2(1):69–82.

Schiller, Barry R., and Randall D. Weiss. 1979. "The Impact of Private Pensions on Firm Attachment." *Review of Economics and Statistics* 61:369–380.

Schuller, Tom. 1986. *Age, Capital and Democracy: Member Participation in Pension Scheme Management.* Aldershot, England: Gower Publishing Limited.

Schulz, James H. 1976. *The Economics of Aging.* Belmont Mass.: Wadsworth.

Schwartz, Eli. 1990. Letter to the editor, *New York Times,* Apr. 13.

Skocpol, Theda, Margaret Weir, and Ann Shola Orloff, editors. 1988. *The Politics of Social Policy in the United States,* Princeton: Princeton University Press.

Scott, Frank A., Mark C. Berger, and Dan Black. 1989. "Effects of the Tax Treatment of Fringe Benefits on Labor Market Segmentation." *Industrial and Labor Relations Review* 42:216–229.

Sharp, William E. 1976. "Corporate Pension Funding Policy." *Journal of Financial Economics* 3:183–194.

Shoven, John, and Michael Hurd. 1982. "Real Income and the Wealth of the Elderly." *American Economic Review* 72:314–318.

Simon, Ruth. 1988. "Look Before You Leave." *Forbes* (Nov. 14), 142(11):88–92.

Slichter, Sumner H., James J. Healy, and E. Robert Livernash. 1960. *The Impact of Collective Bargaining on Management.* Washington, D.C.: Brookings Institution.

Smith, Adam. 1965. *An Inquiry into the Nature and Causes of the Wealth of Nations.* New Rochelle: Arlington House.

Smith, Randall. 1984. "Use of Pension Funds to Create Union Jobs Raises Issue of Legality." *Wall Street Journal*, Jan. 17.

Stein, Norman. 1986. "Raiders of the Corporate Pension Plan: The Reversion of Excess Plan Assets to the Employer." *American Journal of Tax Policy* 5:117–189.

————. c.a. 1988. "The Curious Evolution and the Curiouser Evolution of the Term Erroneous Actuarial Computations in Treasury Regulation Section 1.401.-2(b)" Special Report Tax Analysis.

Stevens, Beth. 1988. *Complementing the Welfare State: The Development of Private Pension, Health Insurance, and Other Employee Benefits in the United States.* Labor-Management Relations Series. Geneva: International Labour Organization.

Tackett, Michael. 1989. "Pension Funds Become a Bonanza for Companies." *Chicago Tribune*, Dec. 4: 1.

Tepper, Irwin. 1981. "Taxation and Corporate Pension Policy." *Journal of Finance* 36(1):1–13.

Tepper, Irwin, and Robert D. Paul. 1978. "How Much Funding for Your Company's Pension Plan?" *Harvard Business Review*, reprinted in *Pension Management*, no. 21470.

Tilove, Robert. 1959. *Pension Funds and Economic Freedom.* New York: The Fund for the Republic.

Treynor, Jack, Bill Priest, and Patrick Regan. 1976. *The Financial Reality of Pension Funding Since ERISA.* Homewood, Ill.: Dow-Jones-Irwin.

Turner, John, and Daniel Beller, editors. 1989. *Trends in Pensions.* Washington, D.C.: U.S. Government Printing Office.

Uchitelle, Louis. 1990. "Company-Financed Pensions Are Failing to Fulfill Promise." *New York Times*, May 29:1.

Uehlein, Joseph. 1985. *Developing New Tactics: Winning with Coordinated Campaigns.* Washington, D.C.: AFL-CIO IUD.

Ulman, Lloyd. 1955. *The Rise of the National Trade Union.* Cambridge, Mass.: Harvard University Press.

————. 1961. "Unionism and Collective Bargaining in the Modern Period." Reprint no. 157, Institute of Industrial Relations, ca. 1979. Berkeley: University of California.

Upp, Melinda. 1983. "Relative Importance of Various Income Sources of the Aged, 1980." *Social Security Bulletin* 46.1:3–10.

U.S. Bureau of the Census. 1987. *Pensions: Worker Coverage and Retirement Income, 1984.* Current Population Reports, Household Economic Studies, Series P–70, no. 12, Washington, D.C.: U.S. Department of Commerce.

————. 1991. *U.S. Statistical Abstract.* Washington, D.C.: U.S. Bureau of the Census.

U.S. Bureau of National Affairs. 1985. "Building Trades Using Pension Funds in Fight with Non-union Sector of Industry." *Pension Reporter* 12(43):1987.

———. 1986a. "Divestment, Social Investment Trends Noted in Report from Johnson and Higgins." *Pension Reporter* 13(17):792.

———. 1986b. "Pension Assets Total Nearly $2 Trillion: High Growth to Continue, EBRI Report Says." *Pension Reporter* 13(46) Nov. 17:1918.

———. 1986c. "Plan Trustees Urged to Invest in Jobs; PWBA Adheres to Previously Stated Policy." *Pension Reporter* 13(47):1969.

———. 1988a. "Actions to Prevent Market Crashes Should Not Be Directed at Pension Funds." *Pension Reporter* 15(16):666.

———. 1988b. "The Employee Benefit Provisions of Omnibus Budget Reconciliation Act of 1987." (PL 100–203) 15(4) Special Supplement (Jan. 25).

———. 1988c. "Sheet Metal Workers Union Participates in Bonding Project through Pension Plan." *Pension Reporter* 15 (May 5, 1988):886.

———. 1989. "Continental Can Cited for Scheme to Forestall Benefits Eligibility." *Pension Reporter* 16(20):844.

———. 1990a. "Labor Secretary Releases Proposals to Strengthen ERISA." *Pension Reporter* 17(13):513.

———. 1990b. "Pension Funds Could Support Some Level of Taxation." *Pension Reporter* 17 (May 7):747.

———. 1991. "Martin Counters Criticism of Administration's Pension Proposals." *Pension Reporter* 18(21):899.

U.S. Chamber of Commerce Research Center. 1951–69, 1980, 1981, 1985, 1986, 1988, 1990. *Employee Benefits.* Washington, D.C.: Chamber of Commerce.

U.S. Department of Commerce. 1989. *Statistical Abstract of the United States: 1988.* 108th ed. Washington, D.C.: U.S. Government Printing Office.

U.S. Department of Labor. 1989. *Inspector General's Report on Oversight of Private Pension Plans.* Washington, D.C.: Government Printing Office.

VanDerhei, Jack L., and Scott Harrington. 1989. "Pension Asset Reversion." In *Trends in Pensions,* edited by John Turner and Daniel Beller, pp. 187–210. Washington, D.C.: U.S. Government Printing Office.

Viscusi, W. Kip. 1985. "The Structure of Uncertainty and the Use of Nontransferable Pensions as a Mobility-Reduction Device." In *Pensions, Labor and Individual Choice,* edited by David Wise, pp. 223–248. Chicago: University of Chicago Press.

Wachter, Susan M., editor. 1988. *Social Security and Private Pensions: Providing for Retirement in the Twenty-first Century.* Lexington, Mass.: Lexington Books.

Wall Street Journal. 1986. "Investors Can Do All Right by Doing Good." *Wall Street Journal,* Aug. 2:31.

Warshawsky, Mark J. 1988. "Pension Plans: Funding, Assets, and Regulatory Environment." *Federal Reserve Bulletin* (Nov.):717–730.

―――. 1989. "The Adequacy of Funding of Private Defined Benefit Pension Plans." Finance and Discussion Series, no. 58. Board of Governors of the Federal Reserve Board.

Webb, Beatrice, and Sidney Webb. 1894. *History of Trade Unionism.* New York: Longmans, Green and Co.

Webman, Nancy. 1983. "LTV Makes Its Second Non-Cash-Contributions." *Pensions and Investment Age* 5 (Sept.):1.

Westerbeck, Mark. 1985. "Foundations Mix Investments, Jobs." *Pensions and Investment Age* 1 (Apr.):1.

William Mercer-Meidinger, Inc. 1985. "What FASB Statements 87 and 88 Will Mean to Employers." New York: Mercer-Meidinger.

Williamson, John B., Judith A. Shindul, and Linda Evans. 1985. *Aging and Public Policy: Social Control or Social Justice?* Springfield: C. C. Thomas.

Wilson, Charles. 1977. "The Nature of Equilibrium in Markets with Adverse Selection." Working Paper No. 7715. Madison: University of Wisconsin.

Wise, David A., editor. 1989. *The Economics of Aging.* Chicago: University of Chicago Press.

Wistert, Francis. 1959. *Fringe Benefits.* New York: Reinhold Management Science Series.

Wyatt Insider. 1991. "California Commissioner Takes over Executive Life: Implications for Plan Sponsors." *Wyatt Insider* 1(5):1.

Yankelovich, Skelley, and White, Inc. 1985. *A Fifty Year Report Card on the Social Security System: The Attitudes of the American Public.* Washington, D.C.: American Association for Retired Persons.

Zorn, Paul. 1985. *Small Business Barriers: Public Pension Investment Restrictions and Small Business Capital: A Report.* Washington, D.C.: Government Finance Research Center.

Index